Mother Carey's Chicken

Her Voyage to the Unknown Isle

by

George Manville Fenn

Double 9
BOOKS

Mother Carey's Chicken
Her Voyage to the Unknown Isle
by George Manville Fenn

ISBN: 978-93-69072-58-3

Published by

DOUBLE 9 BOOKS

2/13-B, Ansari Road
Daryaganj, New Delhi – 110002
info@double9books.com
www.double9books.com
Tel. 011-40042856

ABOUT THE AUTHOR

Edward C. Taylor was an author best known for writing adventure novels set in the American West. His most notable work, Ted Strong in Montana: Or, With Lariat and Spur, exemplifies the action-packed, morally clear stories that defined the Western genre in the late 19th century. Taylor's stories often featured larger-than-life heroes who embodied the virtues of rugged individualism and self-reliance, both of which were central to the idealized image of the cowboy during this era.

Taylor played an important role in the development of Western fiction, crafting narratives filled with the genre's classic elements: heroic cowboys, skilled in riding, roping, and shooting, and set against the backdrop of the untamed frontier. His protagonists faced various challenges, including outlaws, settlers, and the dangers of the wilderness, in straightforward narratives that often drew clear distinctions between good and evil. These tales reflected the public's fascination with the American frontier and captured the mythic qualities of the cowboy, which would go on to shape the Western genre both in literature and film. Taylor's work is marked by moral clarity and dramatic confrontations that became staples of Western literature.

CONTENTS

CHAPTER I
TALKING ABOUT SMART HOGS!

Carl Schwartz burst into the living room of the Moon Valley Ranch house with fire in his eye and pathos in his voice:

"As sheur as I standing here am, dot schwein I'm going to kill!"'

"I'll jest bet yer a million dollars ter a piece o' custard pie yer don't," said Bud Morgan, rising from the lounge where he had been resting after a strenuous day in the big pasture.

"I'll pet you," shouted Carl. "Der pig pelongs mit me der same as you."

"Go ahead, then," said Bud, lying down again. "But I want ter tell yer this, and take it from me, it's ez straight ez an Injun's hair, yer kin kill yer own part o' thet hawg if yer want ter, but if my part dies I'll wallop yer plenty. I've spent too much time teachin' thet pig tricks ter lose it now."

"Vich part der pig you own, anyvay?"

"Ther best part; ther head."

"Den I dake der tail. By Chiminy, I get skvare yet so soon. I cut der tail off, und dot vill make der pig not able to valk straight ven he can't der tail curl in der opposite direction. Den ve see how mooch der tricks he done. Vat?"

"I'll hev ther law on yer if yer interfere with thet pig."

"What's the matter with you two fellows?" asked Ted Strong, the leader of the broncho boys, who was writing some letters at the big oak table in the center of the room.

"Der pig, he moost die," cried Carl tragically.

"Why, what has 'Oof' done now?"

"He has ate all mein gabbages," answered Carl, with almost a sob.

"Well, s'posin' he hez," said Bud. "What in thunder is cabbages fer, if they ain't ter be et by pigs?"

"Yes, you, but not fer dose kind of pig. Maybe you might eat dem und it vould be all right, but not der pig mit four feet."

Carl had a small garden back of the ranch house, in which he had been raising cabbages, devoting all his spare time to them and good-naturedly taking the joshing the boys gave him. They were of the opinion that a cow-puncher was degrading himself by working in a garden.

"Jumpin' sand hills, he'll be takin' up knittin' when winter comes on, an' makin' of his own socks," said Bud, in disgust.

"No, he's going in for tatting," said Ben Tremont. "He's going to make a lot of doilies for the chairs so we won't soil the satin upholstery with our oily hair."

As all the chairs in the living room were very plain, made of solid oak, with bullhide seats and backs, this remark was received with laughter.

"Go aheadt!" said Carl. "Ven you ain'dt drough, let me know. I know your own bizziness. Ven der vinter comes und I haf dot deliciousness sauerkraut, und am eating it, und ven your mouts vater so dot you slobber like a colt off der clover, den—ah, den, I gifs you der ha-ha, ain'dt it? Den you see who der knitting und der tatting do, eh?"

Carl laughed at the thought of how the boys would miss the sauerkraut which he was going to make. But now "Oof," the pet pig of the establishment, had eaten them nearly all, and was standing in his sty too full even for the utterance of his usual lazy grunt. He looked like an animated keg of sauerkraut with four pegs at the corners for him to stand on, so full was he of Carl's cherished and esculent cabbages.

"How in the world did he get into the cabbage patch?" asked Ted. "I thought you had made it pig tight."

"So did I," answered Carl. "No pig but vun mit der teufel inside him vould haf got der fence over."

"Got over ther fence!" snorted Bud. "Why, yer feeble-minded son of a downtrodden race, thet thar pig couldn't hev got over ther fence without a balloon. Thet fence is six feet high. A deer couldn't jump it."

"I didn't saying so. He cannot yump, dot pig. He cannot moof, so full mit gabbages are he. No, he didn't yump, he yoost sving himself over mit dot fence."

"Slush! Yer gittin' plumb dotty. No pig could swing hisself over thet fence."

"But it's der only vay vat he could, und Song, der Chineser cook, saw him did it."

"You don't believe what a Chinyman tells yer, do yer?"

"What did Song say? How did the pig do it?" asked the boys, roused to interest in the squabble by this statement.

"Vell, Song he say dot he vos looking der vinder ouid und he saw der pig take der end of dot long rope vot hangs down mit der roof of der hay house in his teeth, und he svings on it some. Song say he t'ought it vas some of Pud's foolishment he vas teaching dot pig, und didn't no more look at him for a leetle vile. Ven he looked again der pig vas svinging avay oop high by der rope. Den I coom along und see der pig in der gabbages, und I takes me a stick und vallops him goot ofer der hams, und drife him his pen into."

"Shucks! Is that all ther story? That don't prove nothin'. Thet pig, Oof, is a animile of high intelligence. He wuz needin' exercise before dinner. He found a hole in ther fence, er maybe he tunneled one fer hisself, an' he wuz jest kinder doin' some gymnasium work ter git up a good appetite. Yer cain't make me believe a Chinyman, nohow."

"I don't know," said Ben thoughtfully, "pigs are mighty smart. He might have swung himself over by the rope, and, if so, I think he was entitled to his dinner as a reward for his ingenuity."

"I don't pay for no pig's inchenoomity mit my gabbages," said Carl hotly. "Vere I get more gabbages fer der sauerkraut, tell me dot?"

"Yer don't git no sauerkraut, that's all," growled Bud. "But speakin' about pigs bein' smart, I jest reckon they aire."

"There are three animals that people persist in calling stupid, when they are only strong-minded and more intelligent than the other animals," said Kit Summers, quietly breaking into the conversation.

"What aire they?" asked Bud.

"The pig, the mule, and the goose," answered Kit.

"Come ter think o' it, yer right ez a book," said Bud, rising from the lounge and joining the other boys in front of the fireplace. "Why, I remember onct down on the Pecos—"

Ben Tremont rose lazily and stretched himself.

"Well, so long, boys," he said. "If I ain't back for supper don't wait for me."

"Whar yer goin'?" asked Bud, with a black look from under his brows.

"I've got some work to do this evening, and I don't want to be getting drowsy," answered Ben, with a wink at Kit.

"Go then, yer varmint," said Bud savagely. "This yere incerdent what I'm goin' ter relate is fer intelligent persons only."

"In that case I shall have to remain," said Ben, throwing his huge bulk into a chair, that creaked like a house in a high wind.

"How about that Pecos story?" said Ted.

"'Tis erbout pigs."

"I didn't know there were any pigs down in that country," said Ted, with a sly smile.

"Oh, yes, there aire. Some folks calls them peccaries, an' others alludes ter them ez wild hawgs. Yer pays yer money an' chooses what yer likes best."

"Well, what about them?"

"'Tain't noways what ye'd call much o' a story, but it 'lustrates ther intelligence o' ther hawg, which in my 'pinion ez almost ez great ez thet o' some collidge gradooates what I hev mixed with."

Bud stopped and looked hard at Ben, who seemed to be taking a nap in his big chair.

With a snort of disgust Bud turned his back on the big fellow and began:

"Me an' 'Peep-o'-day' Thompson wuz ridin' herd on a bunch o' cattle belongin' ter ole man Bradish. All we hed ter do wuz ter keep 'em from driftin' too fur, which nat'rally left us much time fer meditation an' conversation.

"But it wa'n't long before I'd told all my stories, an' Peep bed plumb fergot I'd tole them ter him, an' wuz tellin' them all over ter me, claimin' they'd happened ter him.

"I stood it fer a spell because I didn't want ter make no friction betwixt him an' me, but it made me sore jest ther same, because ther derned lump allays got ther story balled up so's I hed trouble in reconnizin' it sometimes. An' he inveribly got ther p'int o' ther story hindside fore, which made me jest bile. But when yer on a long watch with a feller, an' got ter see him from sunup ter moonrise, it's better ter overlook a lot o' things.

"Well, 's I wuz sayin', we wuz on this stunt, an' had been out all o' three month, takin' turns cookin' an' watchin' so's one o' us could git erway from ther other fer a spell, an' go off an' sit down an' tell hisself what a awful chump ther other wuz, an' how yer hated him.

"We hed a chuck wagon with us filled with flour, salt sowbelly an' saleratus, with some coffee an' a few pounds o' fine terbaccer fer makin' cigareets. I ain't sayin' nothin' erginst sowbelly ez ther national food o' ther plains an' ther staff o' life in farmin' communities, but ez a steady diet it begins ter pall when taken day in an' day out with nothin' ter wash it down with but weak coffee made outer alkali water.

"I reckon both me an' Peep wuz gittin' tired o' one another's cookin', if ther truth wuz knowed, fer Peep could make ther wust biscuit I ever et.

"My biscuit jest suited me ter a ty-ty, an' I reckon Peep felt ther same way erbout hisn. Every time we set down ter vittles, if it wuz my week ter cook, Peep w'd begin ter talk o' ther fine cookin' his wife uster do before she run erway with er Sant' Fe conductor down ter Raton, Noo Mex. He'd tell me how she'd make beef stoo an' hot biscuit thet would melt in yer mouth. 'I don't like them kind,' sez I, one day. 'I like somethin' I kin chew on. What'd ther Lord give us teeth fer if grub is ter melt in ther mouth? No, sir; give me mine gristle an' hide. Ther tougher they be ther better I like 'em,' sez I.

"'Is thet thar meant ez a reflection on my wife?' sez Peep, bristlin' up.

"'I never met yer wife,' sez I, 'an' we'll let thet part o' it pass, fer ye knows me well enough thet I never make no remarks erbout wimminfolks what ain't smooth an' complimentary. But I stands on ther gristle-an'-hide propersition ontil I'm ready ter fight fer it.'

"Yer see, I wuz gettin' some peevish erbout Peep. Ole man Bradish hed left us alone tergether too long. It ain't right fer two fellers ter camp side by each fer so long without a third party buttin' in ter break ther monotony.

"'All right,' sez he, unlimberin' his six foot three o' len'th from ther ground. 'Thet,' sez he, real dignified, 'is either a challenge or a invitation ter fight.'

"'It be,' sez I. 'Either way yer wanter take it.'

"We both riz up.

"'How d'yer want it?' sez he.

"'Please yerself,' sez I. 'Any ole holt is my fav'rite.'

"'Anythin' goes, then,' sez he, makin' a rush at me.

"Jest then we hear a turrible noise, gruntin', squealin', an' sich. We both stopped an' looked eround, an' thar stood watchin' us a big band o' wild hawgs.

"'Fresh meat!' we both hollers simultaneous. At this ther hawgs ups an' runs.

"It wuz my day off, an' hostilities stopped right thar ez I runs an' gits my rifle an' leaps my cayuse an' takes after ther hawgs, Peep hollerin' after me ez friendly ez yer please.

"I chased them hawgs a couple o' miles ter ther river bank, whar they hid in ther canebrake. I couldn't get ther cayuse ter go in after them, so I gits down an' breaks my way in tryin' ter git a shot at one o' them, my mouth waterin' fer fresh pork so's I wuz almost wadin' in it.

"Purty soon I come in sight o' them. A ole boar wuz in charge o' them, an' he wuz a hard-lookin' citizen, I want ter tell yer. He hed tushes five inches long an' both o' 'em ez sharp ez razors. I took a shot at him, but his hide wuz so tough thet ther ball just glanced off him, an' he made a break fer me. I turned an' fled. Ther river wuz not fur erway, an' I knowed thet if I beat them hawgs ter it I wuz safe.

"I jest did it, an' waded out ez fur ez I could an' started ter swim. 'When I gits ter ther other side I'll take some long shots at yer,' thinks I, 'an' we'll hev hawg meat yit.'

"I gits out inter ther middle o' ther stream when I hears a puffin' an' a gruntin' behind me. I looks over my shoulder an' here comes ther whole herd swimmin' right after me as—"

"That settles it," said Ben, as he rose with a snort of disgust.

"What's ther matter with yer?" asked Bud calmly.

"Yer story is what I thought it would be—wild and woolly and full of cockleburs."

"How is thet ag'in?"

"It's rotten. Don't you know, as long as you have been on earth, that swine cannot swim without committing suicide?"

"Go ahead. Will you kindly tell us fer why, perfessor?"

"Certainly. The hoofs of pigs are so sharp, and their forelegs are set so far under their bodies, that when they attempt to swim their hoofs strike their fat throats, cutting them, and they die from loss of blood."

"Thet's c'rect, my son. Every schoolboy knows thet thar p'int in nat'ral history."

"Then why are you insulting our intelligence by stating that a herd of hogs followed you into the water and swam after you? Now don't spring any such flower of your fancy on us as to say that the hogs all killed themselves crossing and that you and Peep-o'-day had all the fresh meat you wanted during the rest of your stay on the Pecos, for we won't stand for it. I don't believe there is any such thing as a Pecos, anyway."

Bud looked so crestfallen that the other boys felt sorry for him.

"You think you're smart, don't you?" said Kit, taking Bud's finish out of his own mouth. "You big chump, it wasn't your story, anyhow."

"Don't worry, Kit," said Bud, smiling confidently. "Ben's so intellectooal thet it hurts him ter pack his knowledge eround in thet pinhead o' hisn. But he didn't finish ther story none. I knows ez well ez him thet hawgs can't swim fer ther reasons he give. But these yere hawgs I am tellin' erbout wuz different."

"How was that?"

"Yer see, thet thar ole boar wuz ez smart ez a copperation lawyer. He'd fixed them hawgs ter swim. First they got thar hoofs all balled up with gumbo, er sticky clay, then they worked ther dry grass inter ther clay and mixed 'em good an' stiff, lettin' 'em dry in ther sun. This made a hard ball on their toes thet jest slipped off their throats when they struck."

Ben slipped into his chair with a grunt.

"O' course, I didn't know thet when I was swimmin'," continued Bud, 'an' I thinks I've run ercross a new web-footed breed o' hawgs. When we come ter ther other side I waited fer them ter land, then I turns an' swims back, ther hawgs follerin'. Back ercross I goes erg'in, an' ther pork keeps right on my trail.

"Purty soon I see they ain't swimmin' so spry, an' I allow they're gittin' some tired. Ther last time over ter our side o' ther river they come slow, an' I picks out ther kind o' pork I likes best, an' ez they land I nails what I want an' slits thar throats, an' I hev my pork. But when ther rest o' them lands they's full o' fight ez ever, an' I takes ter ther water ag'in, but they won't foller me. This seems strange, an' I looks ter see what ther matter is.

"Ther ole boar wuz mighty smart, but he'd overlooked one p'int. He'd fergot thet ther water would melt his balls o' clay, which it did, an' they couldn't swim no more. I jest stood hip high in the water with my Winchester an' popped erway at them until they got tired an' run off, leavin' me enough fresh pork ter start a packin' house."

A hollow groan escaped from Ben.

"What's the use?" he moaned. "You can't beat him."

CHAPTER II
BUD'S BAD BRONCHOS

It was time for the fall round-up, and Stella had written from her uncle's ranch, in New Mexico, that she and her aunt, Mrs. Graham, were coming North to do their winter shopping in Denver, and would visit the Moon Valley Ranch to take part in the round-up and the festivities which the boys always held at that time.

Her letter did not say when she would be there, but the boys knew her well enough to expect her at any moment following the letter.

Therefore they were not surprised to hear a clear, high imitation of the Moon Valley yell one morning while they were all sitting at the breakfast table.

They did not need to be told that Stella Fosdick had come, and without ado they sprang from the table, overturning chairs in their haste to get out of the house to greet her and her aunt.

"Hello, boys!" she called from the carriage, in which she and Mrs. Graham had driven over from Soldier Butte. "You're a gallant lot of young fellows not to meet us at the station, particularly when I wrote you that I was coming this morning. I'm real mad." But her smiling face belied the statement.

"You didn't say when you were coming," said big Ben, who was the first to reach the carriage step and was helping Mrs. Graham to descend. "If we had taken your general statement that you were coming, to meet you at the station we would have camped right there forever. Never can tell about your movements, young lady."

"But I did write that I was coming this morning, and to meet us and take breakfast with us in the Butte."

"We didn't get that letter. When did you write?"

"Last night."

"That's good. Always take time by the fetlock. We'll get that letter some time to-morrow. Why didn't you wait and write us to meet you after you got here?"

"Saucy as ever, Ben. But we're positively starved. Hello, Song!" she called to the Chinese cook, who was standing on the veranda grinning like a heathen idol, "got anything good to eat?"

"Yes, missee, plenty good glub. Mebbeso you likee some fried ham and eggs?" said Song, shaking hands with himself and bowing low.

"Ham and eggs! No! Positively, no! I'll be turning into a ham and egg if I get any more of it. That's all the cook at the ranch knows how to do. Anything else?"

"Yes, missee. Plenty paltlidge, what Misto Ted shootee lesterday. I cookee you some plenty quick."

"All right, Song, cook us some partridges."

The boys stood around in a group of admiring servitors waiting to carry Stella's hand bag and gun and saddle and other things with which she was burdened.

Suddenly she looked toward the porch.

"Who's that?" she asked breathlessly, pointing to a little girl who stood shyly beside a post looking on.

"Why, that's Lilian," said Ted. "I didn't know you were up yet," he called to the little girl. "Come here, dear, and see Stella. You haven't forgotten Stella, have you?"

"If it isn't Lilian!" cried Stella, rushing toward the child with wide-open arms and folding her within them.

"I wouldn't have known you, honey," said Stella. "What have you boys been doing to her? She's improved so much. Where did you get all these clothes, and who takes care of her?"

"Isn't she a little beauty?" asked Ted Strong proudly, patting the head of the blushing little girl.

"But how did you do it?" persisted Stella.

"Oh, I went over and saw Mrs. Bingham, the major's wife, at the fort, and asked her to come and advise us what to do. She came and was delighted with Lilian, and promised to oversee her wardrobe. She was going down to Omaha, and when she returned she had a trunk full of things for Lil. She also brought a colored woman to look after her, and Mirandy has proved a blessing and a treasure."

"But the clothes didn't make themselves."

"No, and none of us made them, either, although Bud said he could sew, and insisted upon trying. He cut up several yards of cloth, and at the end of the week, when we saw the product of his needle, he narrowly escaped lynching. If Lilian had not interceded for Uncle Bud, of whom she is very fond, I'm afraid we'd have no little Buddy now. No, we sent down to Omaha for a dressmaker and boarded her in town until she had Lil all fixed up, as becomes the heiress of the La Garita Mines."

"Whose idea is this way of making the things?" demanded Stella, who was looking Lilian over with critical eyes.

"Oh, we all had a finger in it. I sent away for a lot of fashion magazines and things of that sort, and we sat up nights as a board of strategy and picked out the sort of thing we wanted, and I reckon there isn't a better-dressed kid in the State."

"I agree with you. Well, Ted Strong, you're a constant wonder to me. Where in the world did you learn to do all the things you do so well?"

"The honeyed flatterer. Quit your joshing, Stella; hand it to Ben. He likes it, and the thicker it is the more he can stand of it."

"Hello! Breakfast!" called Song from the veranda, and they all trooped back to the living room to finish breakfast and talk about the things they had passed through, and to lay plans for the coming round-up festivities.

After breakfast Ted and Stella went out to the corral to look at the saddle stock.

"Why, there's old 'Calamity Jane,'" cried Stella, as a bay pony came trotting across the corral and put its velvet nose in the hand she held out.

"Jane knows you, all right," said Ted.

"Sure. Why shouldn't she? I rode her all one season down here. I believe she wants me to choose her for my own again. Do you, Calamity, old girl?"

Calamity Jane, which had at one time been the wickedest and stubbornest mare on the ranch, nickered and again rubbed Stella's hand with her nose.

"Talk about your smart horses," said Stella. "Calamity can do everything except talk. Who's been riding her?"

"Kit. He's wrangler, and he won't let any one on her. He's light, you know, and he was saving her for you. You'll find that she hasn't been spoiled at all."

"Then, if Kit has been riding her, she's all right, for if there ever was a horseman it's Kit."

"Isn't she getting fierce?" said a quiet voice behind them. "Say, she's getting to be one of these regular society jolliers. She didn't used to be that way."

They wheeled around to see Kit, who had come up to them in his usual quiet manner.

"Yes," said Ted. "She tried to hand me a package this morning."

"You mean things. That's what a girl gets for being civil and confidential, and talking as she would like to fellows she thinks are her friends. I'm going back to the house. I don't like you very much this morning."

The boys winked at one another.

"Say, Kit, I want Sultan after a while. I'm going to ride down to the lower end of the ranch to look at that bunch of new horses," said Ted carelessly.

"Oh, may I go with you?" asked Stella eagerly.

"I thought you were mad at us, or I would have asked you."

"I was only fooling. I'll be ready in ten minutes. Let's take Lilian with us."

"That was what I was going to do. It is time for Lilian's regular riding lesson. I am trying to make her as good a rider and all-around cowgirl as you, Stella, but I doubt if ever she will."

"Who is jollying now, Mister Ted?" cried Stella, with a laugh, but she was blushing with pleasure at the compliment.

That is the difference between a boy and a girl. A healthy, well-conditioned boy becomes embarrassed and cross at a well-meant compliment spoken in the presence of another, believing that the person who is complimenting him is making fun of him in some unknown and covert way. But to a girl a compliment that is sincere is as grateful as dew to a rose, and Stella always felt much elated when Ted complimented her on her prowess in any of the arts of the range.

They rode away with Lilian, who was learning to ride well for her age and experience under the best of riding teachers, Ted Strong.

As they were nearing the lower pasture they observed a great commotion among the horses that were huddled in a fence corner.

"Hello, what's going on there?" exclaimed Ted.

"Looks like the worst sort of a riot," said Stella. "I believe those boys need help."

They could see Bud and Ben and several cowboys circling around the bunch of ponies, evidently trying to get into it, and break it up and scatter it.

"What's the row?" asked Ted, galloping up.

"Thar's a cayuse in thar thet I'd plumb like ter electrocute," said Bud, who was mad clear through. "My, but he's got er bad dispersition."

"Which one?" asked Ted, laughing. "From what I can see there isn't one of them you could call angelic."

"Thar's ther meanest bunch o' horse meat thet ever come ter this man's ranch, bar none, an' ther prize devil o' ther lot is thet black demon in thar. He near broke my pony's leg a minute ago with a stem-windin' kick sech ez I never see before. Thet hoss is shore double-j'inted."

The horses were bunched, heads in, heels out, around a splendid-looking black stallion, which was biting and kicking at everything that came near him.

"Let him kick his foolish head off," said Ted, viewing the squealing, struggling throng.

"I reckon they're just showin' off because Stella got here this mornin'," said Bud disgustedly. "They're tryin' ter knock us, Stella, by showin' yer thet we aire a bum lot o' horsemen fer not makin' them behave first off."

Stella laughed and nodded. She understood.

"Where did you pick up such a mean bunch of horses?" she asked.

"Them hosses is intended fer ther tourneymint what takes place after ther round-up. We're goin' ter hev some roughridin' fer fair here, an' if we all git out with whole bones we shore kin send up a balloon in celebraytion."

"But where did you get them? Were they bred mean on purpose?"

"I reckon not. I bought 'em from ther wild range in Montana. They ain't seen men closer than a mile, except'n' it wuz Injuns, an' they don't count, until we butted in on 'em. They belonged ter ole man Stallings. I reckon you remember him, what we met on our way ter Fort Grant, when yer run erway an' got lost on Red Mesa."

Stella nodded.

"I wuz lookin' fer a bunch o' cow hosses. We sold a big run o' 'em ter a Newbrasky cowman who was short o' saddle stock, an' who said he'd heard we had the best-broke cow ponies in ther West, an' I reckon we had. He was willin' ter pay a good price fer our spare stock, an' we unloaded."

"Then you will have to break in a lot of new ones. Isn't that a waste of time?"

"Young woman, we're ranchmen, not rockin'-chair gents. It's part o' our business ter take somethin' what ain't much good, an' make it better. That's the way we earn our bread an' bacon."

"So I see."

"Ted says ter me ter go up inter Montana an' pick up a lot o' good, gingery hosses, an' I struck John Stallings. He says ter me, when I made my wants known, 'Go out on ther range an' he'p yerself,' says he. 'They're all mine, an' Ted Strong an' his boys kin hev anythin' I've got except my fam'ly. But,' says he, 'you'll find some purty lively stock out there.'"

"Well, you did," said Stella, laughing.

"I reckon I picked out ther orneriest hosses in the whole West, an' I'm savin' them fer some o' these Smart-aleck cowboys who'll be here from ther ranches round, who think they kin ride," and he winked wisely.

"Gracious, look there!" she cried. "What's Ted trying to do. He'll be hurt, Bud."

"No, I reckon not, but I'll git in thar handy ter help him if he needs it. Keep the kid outer ther way if that bunch breaks."

Ted had done what none of the others had succeeded in doing.

He had forced his way into the very center of the bunch of wild horses, wheeling and doubling and riding like a circus performer, to avoid the batteries of flying heels, until he was close to the wicked black stallion, which was all that held the bunch together and prevented it from being broken up and driven to the upper end of the ranch, where it belonged.

There was not a moment when he was not in danger. A chance kick might break his leg, or bring down his horse, in which event he must be kicked to death or badly hurt by being trampled on.

But so far they had not been able to reach him.

"Be careful, Ted," cried Stella.

He waved his hand at her with a smile, and she hurried Lilian beyond the reach of danger.

Ted wheeled his horse to face the black brute, which stood looking at him with wicked eyes, its ears flattened like those of a panther. In spite of its evil temper Ted admired it for its lithe beauty. It was as clean of limb as a thoroughbred, and its black skin shone like polished ebony. While he was looking at it thus it suddenly sprang at him, reared on its hind legs, striking at him like a boxer. Had he not wheeled on the instant it would have killed him. Ted was thoroughly angry, and went to the attack himself, beating the horse about the head with his quirt. When the horse rushed at him through a rain of blows across its nose Ted retreated beyond reach of its hoofs, then attacked it again.

Suddenly the black horse wheeled and presented its heels, and Ted rode around it, lashing it well, everywhere the whip could reach.

Although the horse continued to lash out with his heels he struck nothing, and always his enemy was at his side or in front.

At last Ted resolved to bring the unequal combat to an end, as Sultan was tiring of the exercise, so instead of riding around the enraged horse, he pivoted with it, keeping in front of it all the time and whipping it on the nose.

The "insurgent" stopped kicking at last and stood with drooping head, trying to shield its face from that cruel, relentless, stinging thing which the man creature wielded. He was cowed, but not conquered.

Taking advantage of the moment, Ted drove him backward and clear of his companions. Seeing their leader retreat, the other horses broke their close formation, and allowed themselves to be driven down the valley, not without an occasional rebellious kick, however.

CHAPTER III
STELLA GOES TO THE "RENT RAG"

"Oh, joy, an' pickled pelicans!" said Bud Morgan, skipping onto the veranda one evening, when all the boys were sitting around Stella and Mrs. Graham.

Bud had just returned from Soldier Butte, where he had been spending the afternoon.

"What's devouring you now?" asked Ben Tremont. "Or is it just one of your weekly sillies?"

"Who are yer alludin' at?" asked Bud loftily.

"As you were going to say—" suggested Kit, looking at Bud.

"Boys, thar's goin' ter be a 'rent rag' in the Butte ter-morrer night, an' we all have an urgent bid ter be present."

"A what?" asked Stella.

"A 'rent rag.'"

"Who tore it?" asked Stella innocently.

At this the boys laughed loud and long, then apologized when they saw Stella's embarrassment.

"It ain't tore yet," said Bud, "but it's lierble ter be before ther rosy dawn."

"What are you talking about?" said Stella impatiently. "I never saw such provoking boys. You say such strange things, then cackle over it as though there was a joke in it, which nobody seems to see except yourself."

"A 'rent rag' is a—'rent rag,'" said Kit, trying to explain.

"That sounds as sensible as the conundrum, 'Why is a hen?'" said Stella. "Must I ask the question and get caught? All right, here goes. What is a 'rent rag'? Now, don't tell me, some one, that it is a rag that has been torn, for I exploded that one myself."

"A 'rent rag,'" said Bud slowly and carefully, "is a rag for rent. A—a—er—well, it's a—"

"Tell me, Ted," said the girl, turning to the leader of the outfit, who was leaning back in his chair smiling at the ridiculous conversation.

"Well, as near as I can make out it is a bit of slang that means this: The word 'rag' is the slang for a public dance. When a man in town who is popular enough falls behind in paying his rent, through some misfortune or other, and owes so much he cannot hope to pay it, he hands out a flag that he wants help. In other words, it is an invitation to his friends to organize a public ball for his benefit. It depends upon his honesty and popularity whether or not they do so."

"That's the strangest thing I ever heard of."

"Well, if the thing goes through, a hall is rented and music is engaged, the cost of which is to be deducted from the money taken at the door. Then the man for whose benefit the ball is given and his wife prepare a lot of sandwiches, fried chicken, and other eatables, and a tub or two of lemonade, and help their profits along."

"So that is a 'rent rag,' eh? Who is the man for whom the dance is to be given, Bud?" asked Stella.

"A feller named Martin, whose wife has been sick all summer," answered Bud. "From what they say, I reckon he's all right. Jest ter be a good feller I bought ten tickets, at one bean per ticket."

"Is that all they are?" asked Stella. "Only one bean? Gracious, they'll have to dispose of an awful lot of tickets to get enough beans to sell to pay their rent with! Why don't they make it something else? I'd like to contribute a dollar, at least. A bean a ticket, pshaw! How awfully cheap! I guess he doesn't owe much."

At this remark the boys fairly cackled.

"Now, what are you laughing at?" cried Stella, almost angry. "I seem to be more humorous to-night than I ever thought possible. I can hardly say a word but you all start to laugh at me."

This was too much for the boys. They couldn't restrain themselves and went off into peals of laughter. When they saw the danger signals of two bright spots in Stella's cheeks, they realized that they had gone too far, and all hastily tried to explain. But Ted was before them, and quietly told Stella that in the expressive, if scarcely lucid, language of the day a "bean," in the sense in which Bud had used it, meant a dollar.

"Such silly slang," said Stella, restored to good humor once more. "I don't mind slang if it's clever and reveals or conceals or twists a word in some sensible way, but a bean for a dollar—no, it won't do. The fellow who invented that should try again. The only fun I can see in slang is its aptness."

The boys murmured something to the effect that it wasn't a particularly witty bit of slang, but they continued to grin at one another.

"Suppose we all go to the 'rent rag,'" said Stella suddenly. "I never saw anything of the sort, and I'm crazy to go."

"It's likely to be pretty rough, and break up in a row before its natural time," said Ted.

"We'll only stay a short while," said Stella. "But I should like to do my share toward helping the poor fellow."

"It's done already. I bought ten tickets. Thet's as much ez they expect from ther Moon Valley Ranch, an' it goes inter ther running expenses o' ther ranch, anyhow, in ther charity account."

"I don't care, I want to go."

"I move we go," said Ben. "It will add some tone to the proceedings."

"Ben wants to air his spike-tailed coat and low-neck vest," said Kit.

"Not for me," said Ben, laughing. "I wonder what those cow-punchers and miners and gamblers would do with a chap who sauntered in there in evening dress."

"He shore would come up ter Stella's conception of a rent rag, which is a torn rag," said Kit.

"Ted, won't we go?" pleaded Stella.

"Sure, if you want to; you are our guest, and whatever you want, all you have to do is to ask for it," answered Ted.

It was agreed that they should wear their everyday uniforms, and Stella was for going in her distinctive cowgirl costume, but this Mrs. Graham would not permit, and insisted that she should wear a frock which she had had made in Denver.

When, the next night, Stella walked into the living room, where the boys were waiting to escort her and Mrs. Graham to the ball, there was a general exclamation of wonder and admiration, at which Stella hesitated with a blush, then came forward with smiling assurance.

Instead of the bold and dashing Stella in her bifurcated riding skirt and bolero jacket, the boys saw a beautiful young woman in a pale-blue gown of silk and chiffon, with her pretty hair piled on top of her head, instead of flowing over her shoulders.

For a moment they were awed. They had never seen her so, and perhaps had never thought of her as being a young lady. Most of them were content to regard her just as Stella, their girl pard, and to-night she had given them a surprise.

At her throat was a superb sapphire set in a brooch, which had come out of the broncho boys' sapphire mines on Yogo Creek, and in her hair was an ornament of diamonds and rubies which the boys had made from jewels which had come as their share of the treasures of the Montezumas, which they had discovered beneath the castle of Chepultapec, near the city of Mexico.

Altogether Stella was very stunning, and in their admiration of her in this new rôle of society girl the boys were between two preferences, as she was now, and as they knew her in the saddle, throwing her lariat or handling her revolver.

Most of them, however, came to the conclusion that she was still Stella, no matter what she wore.

"Say, Stella, that's not fair," drawled Ben, "to dress up like that and make us wear our working togs. I've got a good mind to go and get into my spike."

"If you do, I won't go," said Stella. "Unless the other boys wear theirs also. You and I would look fine going in there dressed up, and the other boys as they are now. No, I wouldn't have worn this dress if aunt hadn't insisted upon it, and this time I couldn't shake her determination. I hate it, and would much rather have my working clothes on. But, never mind, it won't be for long. How do you like me in this?" She revolved slowly before them.

"Scrumptious!" said Ben appreciatively.

"Prettier than a basket of peaches," ejaculated Kit.

"Thar ain't nothin' in art er nature what kin show up more gaudy," said Bud. "Except, mebbe, it might be a pink rose in er garden at airly mornin' with ther dew on it."

"Say, hasn't Bud got us all faded?" said Ben. "I didn't know the old sandpiper had so much poetry in his soul."

"So perfectionately lofely a younk lady nefer did I saw," exclaimed Carl, clasping his hands and holding them before him, while he rolled his eyes toward the ceiling.

"She's all thet," said Bud. "But come down ter airth. Stella ain't up among ther rafters."

Ted had said nothing, and Stella looked at him. He was regarding her attentively.

Her look said: "What do *you* think?"

He answered it with a look of admiration that satisfied her that he thought her perfect.

"I think I like you best in the everyday clothes," he said quietly. "But that gown is as if you were made for it and it was made for you."

The thought had come into Ted's mind that some day, in the far future, they would lose their girl pard, and society or duties elsewhere would claim her.

Stella understood him and agreed with him.

Soon they were ready to start for the ball. The carriage was got out and Carl volunteered to drive the horses, while the other boys rode.

Just as they were about to start Stella cried: "Where is Jack Slate? I don't see him. Isn't he coming to the ball?"

"Haven't saw him," said Bud. "I reckon he'll be moseyin' erlong after a while. We won't wait fer him. He knowed when we wuz goin' ter start."

"He came in a little while ago from the lower pasture," said Kit, "and went to his room. He said he had been thrown by his horse, and that the jar had given him a headache."

"Oh, don't let us wait for him," said Ben. "If he gets to feeling better he'll be along. You couldn't keep Jack away from a ball with an injunction."

So they proceeded to town, the boys acting as outriders to the girl, whom they were convinced would be the belle of the ball.

When they arrived at the hall in Soldier Butte they found the people flocking in, as Martin, the beneficiary, was a very popular fellow, and any man in hard luck in the West always gets all the help he needs, if he deserves it.

Ted escorted Stella into the ballroom, while Ben followed with Mrs. Graham, the other boys taking the horses around to the corral.

As Ted and Stella entered the room there was a hum of admiration, and conversation stopped as men and women craned their necks to look at the handsome couple.

Ted was both proud and pleased, but a little bit embarrassed at the attention they received, while Stella held her head up proudly, with a look of indifference on her face, as if she had been used to admiration all her life.

The ball certainly was a mixed affair.

In one corner were a lot of army officers and their ladies.

All down the sides of the ballroom cowboys were sitting with girls from the ranches. Town girls and boys had a corner to themselves. The gamblers flocked together, and miners and others wandered here and there, mixing with cavalrymen from the fort.

When the boys returned from the corral they found that Mrs. Graham and Stella and their escorts had preëmpted a vacant corner.

There was a piano in the room, but no one to play it. Soon, however, a fellow dressed after the cowboy fashion entered and took a seat on a raised platform, producing a fiddle from a green bag.

A round of applause greeted him.

He tuned his instrument, and after a few preliminary scrapes began to play a monotonous tune, repeating over and over again the same few bars.

At the first scrape the cowboys and their girls leaped to the floor and began to dance, but none of the people from the fort cared to dance to such music.

Suddenly the door flew open and a band of a dozen cow-punchers walked into the room, and were greeted by joyous shouts by the other cowboys in the hall.

At their head was a handsome young fellow, slender and dark, with a resolute face and a pair of piercing eyes that flashed around the room for the purpose of seeing and locating his possible enemies.

"Who is that?" asked Stella.

"That's Billy Sudden," answered Ted.

"And who is he?"

"Foreman at 'Cow' Suggs' ranch. That's the Suggs bunch of cow-punchers. There'll be something doing here to-night."

"Why?"

"There are a lot of fellows in this part of the country who don't like Billy, and some of them are liable to tread on his feet."

"Oh, is he quarrelsome?"

"No, Billy is the best sort of a fellow, but he won't let any one hobble him. When he first went to the Dumb-bell Ranch, as the Circle-bar Circle is called, they took him for a kid and tried to run over him. He kicked them, then fired them, and they don't like him."

"Did you see him look around the room?"

"Yes, he has every man who is likely to make trouble for him spotted and located. But we won't wait long enough to see the trouble. I never did like trouble myself."

"Well, for a chap who gets into it as often as you do—"

"What's the trouble now, over there?" interrupted Ted, looking at the door.

Around the entrance to the hall was a crowd of young town fellows led by a youth named Wiley Creviss, the son of the local banker, a dissipated and reckless young man, and a crowd of cow-punchers.

They were shoving some one here and there, making a punching bag of him, at the same time laughing uproariously.

Just then Ted saw the head of Jack Slate in the mix-up.

"Excuse me," said Ted, turning to Stella. "Ben, take care of the ladies until I return."

He strode across the floor toward the door.

As he neared it he heard Billy Sudden say:

"Be careful, there. That is one of Ted Strong's fellows."

"I don't care if it is," said some one. "I'd give it to Strong just as hard if he was here."

"Here I am," said Ted, pushing through the crowd.

CHAPTER IV
THE TROUBLE IS STARTED

The crowd of men and youths opened out in front of Ted, and he strode into the circle.

There he saw Jack Slate in a much disheveled condition, dressed in his evening clothes.

Ted gasped as he stared for an instant at the youth from Boston.

He wanted to tell Jack that "it served him right," but that was not the part of loyalty, and in the presence of the enemy it did not make any difference to a broncho boy if his pard was right or wrong, if he was in need of help.

"Where is the fellow who was going to throw me around?" asked Ted, looking into the faces about him.

No one replied, although Ted waited for a moment or two before looking at Billy Sudden.

Billy winked at him, but said nothing.

"Seems as if somebody's sand has run out," said Ted contemptuously.

"Oh, I don't know," said Wiley Creviss. "There's plenty of sand left if you need any to prevent your wheels from slipping downhill."

"No, my sand box is always full," said Ted quietly. "But there is some sneak in this bunch who hasn't the nerve to back up his brag."

"Are you talking to me?" said Creviss, swelling up as to chest.

"Oh, are you the misguided chump whom I heard make the remark about pushing me about, as I came up?" said Ted, in a tone of surprise.

The cowboys from Suggs' ranch were snickering.

"Well, what if I was?"

"I'm going to make you try it."

"Oh, I can do it, all right."

"Well, why don't you? I'm the easiest proposition you ever saw to be hazed by a bunch of hoodlums, such as you and your pals are!"

"For two cents I'd punch your nose."

"You're too cheap. I'll give you a heap more than that if you will. It's been so long since my nose was punched that it feels sort of lonesome. I'll pay you well for the job, if you succeed in pulling off the stunt."

"You think you're the whole works because you've got a crowd of dudes around you. You're not the only dent in the can."

Ted flushed at this allusion to his pards.

"I'll put a dent in you if you open your face to remark about my friends again," he said, with some heat.

"See here, you town rough, you better take in your slack and clear out for home, or you'll begin to taste the sorrows that come from inexperience and bad judgment," said Billy Sudden to Creviss.

"It's up to you to mind your own business," snarled Creviss. "What are you but a lot of greasy cow-punchers. We haven't much use for your sort in this town, anyway."

"Now, son, keep quiet and behave yourself," said Billy paternally. "If you get me riled I won't be as patient with you as Ted Strong has been. I'll fix you so as to keep two doctors busy the best part of the night."

"What are you fellows butting in for, anyhow?" said Creviss angrily. "Can't this freak that comes here in a dress suit and tries to lord it over us take care of himself?"

"Surest thing you know," drawled Jack Slate. "But there are ladies here, a thing you don't seem to realize. If you'll step outside, I'd be glad to whip you right and propah."

"What's the use, Jack, of fussing with these rowdies?" said Ted. "Let it go until some other time."

"You bet," said Creviss, courage returning when he heard Ted propose peace. "I guess you'd like to let it go forever."

"That settles it," said Ted. "Go to him, Jack, and if you don't give him what's coming to him, I'll finish the job."

"Git!" said Billy Sudden, opening the door and shoving Creviss out into the street. The rest followed.

As Jack stepped into the open air he peeled off his swallow-tailed coat and threw it over Ted's arm.

He had no sooner done so than Wiley Creviss made a rush at him from the front, while one of the crowd ran in on him from the rear.

It seemed an unequal beginning, and Ted was preparing to take on the second fellow.

But Jack had seen him out of the corner of his eye, and as he came on the Boston boy stepped backward and threw his right elbow up.

It was a timely and masterly trick, for the sharp elbow caught Creviss' ally full in the nose, and he dropped like a limp rag to the ground, with a howl of anguish.

At the same moment Jack swung his left. Creviss had struck at him and missed when he back-stepped, and coming on swiftly ran into Jack's fist with a thud that jarred him into a state of collapse.

"Finish him!" shouted the cow-punchers, who stood about the fighters in a circle.

"Go to him," said Ted, in a low voice. "I saw him signal his pal to tackle you from behind."

Creviss had partially recovered from the blow and was getting ready for another rush, when Jack slipped in and to one side and hit like a blacksmith at the anvil.

This time Creviss went down and out.

"Hooray fer ther bantam!" shouted a big cow-puncher, slapping Jack on the back. "Say, I hear them say you're from Bosting. I'm goin' ter buy a hundred-pound sack o' beans myself ter-morrer an' begin trainin'. If beans'll do that fer you, a sack o' them will make me fit ter lick Jess Willard."

But Jack was busy smoothing down his ruffled hair and pulling his white lawn tie around into its proper place, and when he had put on his coat he and Ted walked into the ballroom as calmly as if they had just stepped out to view the stars.

"What was the trouble?" asked Stella, when they reached her side.

"Some town rowdies became noisy, and they were put out," answered Ted carelessly.

But Jack's dress suit was the joy of the cow-punchers, who had never seen anything like it before, although they all knew that it was the way well-groomed men dressed for evening in the big cities.

"Say, pard," said a cowboy to Jack, as he crossed the room, "I axes yer pardon fer buttin' in, but yer lost ther front part o' yer coat tails."

"That's all right," answered Jack. "Can't help it, don't you know. I left the blooming coat hanging on the line at home to air, and a goat came along and ate the front half of the tails off before I could get to it. I was just on my way to apologize to the master of ceremonies for it. You see, it is the only coat I have, and I was bound to come to the ball."

"Ha, ha! that's on you, 'Honk,'" laughed the cowboy's friends, who had overheard the conversation, and Jack passed on, the boys alluding to him as a "game little shrimp," for the news of his summary punishment of Creviss had got abroad.

But Jack was not through yet. He went into the men's dressing room to leave his hat. As he was coming out he was met by a crowd of town youths, friends of Creviss. There was no one else about.

They scowled and sneered at Jack, and one of them bumped into him.

"Heah, fellah, that will do," said Jack, with his Bostonese drawl. "You're solid; you're no sponge."

"I ain't, eh?" answered the bully. "I'll tell yer, Mr. Slate, you're covered with bad marks what I don't like, an' I'm just the sponge to wipe them off."

"Step lively, then," said Jack, "for I've an engagement to dance the next waltz."

"I'll waltz you all you'll need this evenin'."

But before he had finished speaking Ben Tremont stepped around the corner.

"Hello, Jack! What is this I see?" said Ben. "Disgracing yourself by talking with these hoodlums."

"Yas, deah boy," drawled Jack. "This—er, what shall I call him?— stopped me to tell me he was going to rub the marks off me, at the same time wittily making a pun on my name. I was just telling him to hurry, or I'd miss the next waltz."

"Well, I'll take the job off your hands. Stella was asking for you a moment ago."

"Yes, run along to your Stella," said the hoodlum. "I reckon she's pining for the sassiety o' another dude."

That was where he made the mistake of his life.

It didn't really make much difference what these fellows said about themselves, but the boys would not permit Stella's name to be bandied about by the roughs.

So swiftly, that they didn't know what had happened to them, both Ben and Jack sailed into them.

They went sprawling like tenpins before the ball as Ben jumped in among them and mowed them down with his powerful blows, while Jack, hovering like a torpedo boat around a battleship, sent in several of the telling blows Ted had taught him during the boxing lessons at Moon Valley.

The fight was soon over, and Ben and Jack slipped quietly back into the ballroom, leaving a well-thrashed crowd to stanch bloody noses, and patch up swollen lips and black eyes as best they could.

Meanwhile, a diversion had been created in the hall by the joshing that the Suggs' ranch outfit had directed toward the fiddler, who knew only one tune, and sawed that off for a waltz, quadrilles, and two-steps, without fear or favor.

The musician had been engaged because he was a friend of the beneficiary, and had volunteered his services. As the ball grew more and more hilarious the cow-punchers felt the restraint of the folks from the fort and Moon Valley the less, and began to take it out of the fiddler, who paid no attention to them, but kept on scraping.

Suddenly there was a crack from a revolver and the top of the fiddler's bow was knocked off, and the playing and dancing stopped simultaneously.

There was more or less commotion, but the women did not scream or get panic-stricken. They were used to that sort of thing.

Nobody knew who had fired the shot, but the cowboys and soldiers were mad clear through because there was no more music to dance by.

The shot had come from the part of the hall in which the coatroom was situated, and directly afterward two slender young fellows climbed out a rear window, and a few moments later Billy Sudden and Clay Whipple came calmly through the front door and joined the throng about the musician, who said:

"Honest, folks, I don't blame no hombre fer takin' a shot at thet fiddle bow o' mine, fer I never could make it work right. I know it was bum music, but it was the best I could do."

Ted Strong had observed the quiet entrance of Billy and Clay directly after the shooting, and he put this and that together. He knew that both of them were finished musicians. Clay Whipple was an exceptionally good violin player, and Ted had often heard Billy Sudden make a piano fairly sing. Evidently they had got to the point where they could stand the fiddler's music no longer, and had put a stop to it.

But for all the badness of the music the people should not be deprived of their dance.

He hunted up the culprits, who were hovering on the outskirts of the crowd, listening to the threats against and denouncing the vandals who had "shot up" the fiddler.

"See here, you hombres, I'm on to you," said Ted. "Now you've got to do the square thing. You've beaten the dancers out of the music, and you've got to get in and furnish it, or I'll tell these punchers who plugged the fiddler's bow."

"How did you get on to it?" said Clay, with a grin.

"Never mind. Is it a go?"

"I reckon it'll have to be," said Clay, looking suggestively at Billy Sudden.

"All right," said Billy.

The cow-punchers, who had come to dance with the girls from the ranches, were growing angry, and were telling what they would do to the fellow who had spoiled their fun if they caught him, when Ted Strong stepped upon the platform, and, holding up his hand for silence, said:

"Gentlemen, please do not get obstreperous. You shall have all the dancing you want. Ladies, please be patient; the music that is to follow is such as has never been heard at a dance in this part of the country. Mr. Clay Whipple, of the Moon Valley Ranch, and Mr. Billy Sudden, of the Dumb-bell Ranch, will play the violin and piano respectively. Both of them are cow-punchers, so don't take any liberties with them, or some one will get hurt."

There was such cheering that the roof almost went off as Clay hunted up a violin and tuned it.

Then began a waltz such as they had never heard, and in a moment the floor was covered with dancers, the officers in their uniforms, and the ladies in their light dresses, adding beauty to the scene. But the finest-looking couple on the floor was Stella and the leader of the broncho boys.

Just before the dance began Bud approached Stella, and said:

"See that gal over thar? Ther one with ther corn-silk bang? She is mine, an' I'm goin' ter dance this with her; see? She's ther kind o' girl I admire. She's shore corn-fed, an' some woman."

"Don't you know who that is?" asked Stella.

"'Deed an' I don't, but I soon will. Who is she?"

"That's Sophy Cozak, from over on the Bohemian prairie. She's rich, Bud."

"I don't care nothin' erbout thet. She's shaped up jest erbout right. Yaller hair, and soft as feathers. Watch my smoke."

Bud sauntered over to the girl, who was really pretty and fat and pink. Apparently he was talking his usual nonsense to her, for she smiled, then arose from her chair, and went sailing around the room, Bud's partner in the waltz, and every time they passed Ted and Stella in the waltz Bud winked at them.

Later, however, he met the irate escort of the girl, when he took her back to her seat, and they glared at one another for a moment; then the escort walked off, leaving Bud master of the situation.

After this came the "sour-dough" quadrille, in which only old-timers were permitted to dance, and Bud led it with Mrs. "Cow" Suggs to the tune of "Turkey in the Straw."

But finally, as the ball was drawing to a close, Ted heard Stella utter a slight scream, and saw her trying to draw her hand away from a young fellow, whose back was turned to him.

He was across the room in an instant, and had the fellow by the shoulders and swung him around. It was Wiley Creviss, who had been drinking.

"What has this cur been doing?" asked Ted.

"He insisted on dancing with me, and when I told him I would not, he said he'd make me," answered Stella. "Then he caught hold of me, and I suppose I cried out, although I didn't mean to. That is what comes of wearing these clothes. If I'd had on my others, I'd have had my gun with me."

Ted had heard enough. There was a window close by, which was about ten feet above the sidewalk. Ted rushed the struggling and cursing Creviss toward it, and by sheer strength lifted him to the sill and threw him out.

"I guess we've had about enough of this," he said quietly, when he returned to Stella. "No more mixed balls for mine."

As Ted was escorting Stella to the carriage, Billy Sudden ranged up alongside of him.

"Look out for Creviss and his bunch on the way home. They're telling around what they're going to do with you. Want any help?"

"No, I reckon not, Billy. Our bunch can take care of them."

"They are going to try to kill you to-night."

CHAPTER V
SHOTS FROM THE DARK

As the broncho boys swung through the streets of Soldier Butte, after leaving the ball, Ted Strong was in the lead, and Bud, Ben, Kit, and Clay were riding on either side of the carriage, while Jack Slate, with his black coat tails flapping in the breeze, brought up the rear.

They were passing an alley, at the corner of which an electric lamp shed a path of light across the street, when a revolver shot cracked out, and Ted's hat left his head.

The ball had just grazed his scalp, and the merest fraction of an inch lower would have killed him.

Instantly every one pulled up, and Ted, wheeling suddenly, rode at full speed for the mouth of the alley.

As he did so another shot came from the alley.

Ted's revolver was in his hand, and he fired at the spot where he had seen the flash from the muzzle of the assassin's weapon.

He heard Mrs. Graham scream, and turned back to the side of the carriage only to find that one of the horses attached to it had been hit by the bullet, and was down, but that neither Stella nor Mrs. Graham had been injured, and he rode straight into the dark alley, followed by Bud and Kit, leaving Ben and the other boys to guard the carriage, for he did not know from what direction another attack might come.

The alley was as dark as a pocket, and as Ted rode into it he well knew that he was taking his life in his hands.

At the far end of the alley he heard the beat of feet running swiftly, and fired his revolver several times in that direction, and heard a yell of pain.

"Come on, fellows," he called. "I think I got one of them that time."

As he said this they saw two dark figures dart out of the alley into the street at the end opposite that at which the boys had entered, and they spurred in that direction.

But when they came to the street there was no one in sight, but splotches of blood on the sidewalk testified to the fact that a wound had been inflicted upon some one.

They rode up and down the block, but without discovering where their attackers had taken refuge.

It was a low part of the town, and there was scarcely a house on either side of the street into which a criminal would not be taken and concealed.

"We'll have to give it up," said Ted, at last. "We could hunt here all night without being any the wiser."

Disappointed, they rode back, after tracing the bloodstains along the sidewalk to where they were lost in the dusty street.

They found that the carriage horse had been so badly hurt that its recovery was impossible, and Ted mercifully put a bullet into its brain.

The carriage was surrounded by people from the dance hall, who had been brought by the shots.

Among them was Billy Sudden.

"I reckon I called the turn," said he, as Ted came up.

"You sure did," said Ted.

"I ain't presuming to give advice none," said Billy, "but if it was me that got his sky piece knocked off and had a horse shot I believe I'd almost be tempted to round up this yere man's town and capture every hoodlum in it, and sweat them to find out who fired them shots."

"It wouldn't do any good, Billy," said Ted. "The people in this town have got it in for the ranch people. They think the ranches are taking trade away from them. They'd sooner see the ranches split into farms of forty acres each. They'd have so many more farmers to rob that way."

"I reckon so. But what are you going to do? I want to tell you that me and my boys stand with you till the burning pit freezes over, whenever and wherever you need us."

"May have to call on you one of these days, but not now."

"Ain't you going after that young imp, Creviss? Say, he's the meanest boy I ever saw. If I was his father I'd make him behave, or I'd bust him wide open."

"I understand his father thinks Wiley is just smart and spirited, and is ready to back him up in anything he does."

"Ought to make the old man popular."

"Not so you can see it. But that boy is a tough citizen, and getting tougher every day."

"I'm hearing a good deal about that kid these days. He trains with a bunch of bad ones over at Strongburg."

"For instance?"

"Lately he's been running with 'Skip' Riley, a crook who has the reputation of having made more money out of holding up trains than by working."

"I know his record. How long has he been there?"

"Several months. He came there from the Nebraska penitentiary, and he was smooth enough to work the reformed-criminal, first-offense racket on the women there until they finally got him a job in the fire department. He seems to be a hero in the eyes of a lot of tough young fellows here and in Strongburg, and they follow him in anything he suggests."

"That's not a healthy proposition for a boy. Mr. Riley ought to be conducted out of town."

"The worst of it is he has banded them into some sort of secret organization."

"What do they call it?"

"I did know, but I've plumb forgotten. There's a young fellow uptown whom I'm trying to keep straight on account of his folks back East. I know his sister." Ted could see Billy's face get red as he said this. "His name is Jack Farley. Perhaps you know him."

Ted shook his head.

"Well, he's a good kid, but he got into bad company at home and skipped. I corresponded once in a while with his sister, and she wrote me about him, and one day I run across him in a gambling house here. I hadn't seen him since he was a kid, but I knew him straight off because he looks so much like Kate—Miss Farley I mean—and I called him outside and had a talk with him. He was mighty uppy at first, and threw it into me so hard that I had to turn in and whale some sense into him."

"That's one way of doing it," said Ted dryly.

"It was the only way for him. He thought he'd get sympathy by writing home about it, but all he got was that they reckoned he deserved it or he wouldn't have got it. After that he was good. But he'd got in with that Creviss bunch and didn't seem able to get out of it, so I let him stay, only I made him come to me every day or two and tell me what he'd been up to, and that's as far as I've got."

"Send him out to me."

"He won't work on a ranch, or I'd had him out at the Dumb-bell long ago. He likes to work in town, so I got him a job, and so far he has stuck to it. But the gang keeps him from doing any good for himself. He knows the name of this organization of boys under Skip, and the next time I see him I'll find out what it is. Then you keep your eye peeled for it, for Creviss is one of the leaders, and I'm afraid, after to-night, he'll do all he can to make things lively for you. He's a mean, vindictive little cuss."

"I'll keep a weather eye out for him, never fear. Thank you for the tip. This is the first time I've heard of the bunch, I've been away from the ranch so much lately."

The boys had hitched Jack Slate's horse into the carriage, and he got on the seat with Carl, and they were ready to start.

With an "Adios" to Billy Sudden and his boys, they were off, and arrived at the ranch house without further incident.

Mrs. Graham and Stella had retired for the night, and the boys were sitting before the fire in the living room, for the night was chilly and Song had built up a good blaze against their return.

Naturally, the conversation drifted to the shots fired at them from the alley.

"While I wuz ambulatin' eround ter-night I overheard some conversation what wuz interestin'," remarked Bud, who was sprawling on a bearskin in front of the fire.

"What was it?" asked Ted, who had been turning over in his mind what Billy Sudden had told him of the organization of tough boys under the guidance of the ex-convict.

"I wuz standin' clost ter one o' ther winders what opens out onter ther alley when I hears two fellers talkin' below me," said Bud.

"What were they saying?"

"I wuzn't aimin' ter listen ter no one's privut conversation, but I caught your name, an' I tried ter hear what wuz said erbout yer."

"Naturally."

"One feller wuz talkin' pritty loud, ez if he'd been hittin' up ther tangle juice, an' ther other feller wuz tryin' ter make him put on ther soft pedal, what Clay calls talkin' pianissimo. But when the booze is in ther wit is out, an' ther feller would shut it down some fer a while, then he'd get a good lungful o' air an' bust out ergin."

"What was it all about?"

"Erbout runnin' us off'n ther reservation."

"They'd have a fine chance to do that," said Ted, laughing.

"It seems they hev some sort o' a club, ther 'Flyin' somethin' er other' —I couldn't jest catch what. To hear them fellers talk they're holy terrors."

"How do they propose to run us off? Did you hear that?"

"No; they didn't discuss ways an' means, but they said as how ther boss, they mentioned his name, but it's clear got erway from me, hed riz up on his hind legs an' hed give it out straight to ther gang thet ez long ez we wuz in ther country they couldn't do no good fer theirselfs, consequentially we must skidoo, ez they needed this part o' ther country fer their own elbowroom. They wuz real sassy erbout it, too."

"I suppose they thought all they had to do was to serve notice on us, and we'd vacate."

"I reckon thet's ther way they hed it chalked up."

"Well, that bears out what Billy Sudden told me to-night after we were shot at."

Then Ted related what Billy had told him about Skip Riley and his influence on the boys of Soldier Butte and Strongburg.

"Thet thar's ther very feller they wuz talkin' erbout, thet Skip Riley. Now I recolict it, an' ther name o' their sweet-scented aggergation is ther 'Flyin' Demons.'"

"Oh, mercy! Aren't they just awful?" said Ben, with a grin. "But which way are they expected to fly, toward you or from you?"

"If they come monkeyin' eround these broad acres they'll be flyin' fer home," said Bud.

"Or to jail, if we can prove what I believe against them," said Ted thoughtfully.

"What is that?" asked Kit.

"You haven't forgotten the mysterious robbery of the Strongburg Trust Company's office, have you?"

"Nope."

"You remember that a great many people to this day disbelieve that the office was robbed at all, because everything was found locked and barred, and the most careful examination showed that no one could have broken into the room from which a box containing twenty thousand dollars in currency and a package of negotiable bonds was stolen."

"Shore, I remember. That's allays been ther greatest mystery in these parts."

"You haven't forgotten the robbery soon afterward of the Soldier Butte post office and the disappearance of the registered mail pouch that came in on the train at two o'clock in the morning. It was thrown into the inner office by the carrier, and the office securely locked. Yet in the morning it could not be found, and there was nothing to show that the post office had been entered."

"I reckon I haven't. We lost a bunch o' money in it ourselves."

"But we got it back."

"That's so, but the carrier is still in jail, awaitin' trial fer stealin' the sack, an' I don't believe he had any more ter do with it than I had."

"And yet the most careful examination by the post-office inspectors failed to show that the place had been forcibly entered, and, although the carrier, Jim Bliss, had witnesses to show that he went into the post office with the sack, and came right out without it, still he is in jail, accused of stealing it," said Kit.

"There are several other cases of mysterious robberies which I might cite, but those are enough," said Ted. "But the curious thing about it all is that the robbers left not the slightest trace, not a broken lock, not a mark to show that a window was forced or a hole bored. When the place is closed up at night there is the money, when it is opened in the morning the money is gone. And again, these robberies only occur when valuables are accidentally left out of the vaults."

"It is curious. Everything yer say is true, but I never thought erlong it ez much ez you, an' I didn't figger out how near they wuz alike."

"Well, what's your theory?" asked Ben. "You started to tell us."

"Yes, who do you think committed these robberies?" asked Kit.

"Who but a gang of bad boys under the leadership and tutelage of a criminal?" answered Ted. "Who but the gang of Strongburg and Soldier Butte young toughs who go by the silly name of 'The Flying Demons'? If they get gay around this ranch, we'll have to tie a can to them and head them for the reform school or the penitentiary."

CHAPTER VI
THE "FLYING DEMONS'" MESSAGE

When Ted Strong stepped out on the veranda the morning after the ball he found Stella staring curiously at a large, square piece of paper stuck on the wall of the ranch house.

Nobody in the house had risen early, as they had all been up very late, except Song, the cook, who, when he saw that no one was disposed to turn out for an early breakfast, had gone out to work in the garden, in which he had with much skill raised an abundance of vegetables that year.

"Good morning, Stella; what is so interesting?" said Ted.

"It beats me," answered Stella. "I wonder if this is one of Ben's witticisms. If it is, he ought to be spanked."

Ted was standing by her side, reading what had been printed on the paper.

"H'm! this is good," said he, and read aloud, as if to himself, the following warning:

"TED STRONG AND BRONCHO BOYS: You ought to know by this time that you are not wanted in this part of the country. Advise you to sell out and skip. If you stay your lives will be made a hell on earth, and we have the stuff that will do it. This is no bluff, as you will find out if you disregard this word of friendly warning. You will be given a short time to sell your stock, then git. This means business.

"THE FLYING DEMONS."

"That's a pretty good effort for a lot of kids," said Ted. "Wait, here's a watermark in the paper. Let's see what it is?"

Ted took the paper from the wall and held it up to the light.

In the paper was the representation of the fabulous monster, the griffin, and woven into the paper were the words "Griffin Bond."

"That's as easy as shooting fish in a tub," said Ted, as he folded the paper and put it in his pocket.

"The fellow who put that warning up certainly left his footprints behind him," said Stella, with a smile.

"He did, but even without that I should have known the authors of it."

"How?"

Ted then told Stella the substance of the conversation between the boys the night before, and of his suspicions as to the guilt of Creviss and his gang in the mysterious robberies that had occurred in the two towns. "But," he concluded, "it is not up to me to get at the matter. It is work for the sheriff. However, if those boys try any of their foolishness with us, we'll turn in and send them to the reform school, where they belong."

"They're certainly a bad lot. I was talking to a lady at the 'rent rag' last night, and she was telling me what a horrid boy young Creviss is."

"I wish I knew at what time this notice was put up here. It must have been done in daylight, for it was getting light in the east when we turned in."

"Perhaps some one was so quiet as to put it there while you were all inside talking."

"I hardly think so, for we were all sitting near the fireplace, and the room was so warm that Kit opened the door, and it stood open until we separated to go to bed."

"Sure you could have heard them? Some of you were talking pretty loud, for I heard you in my room just before I went to sleep."

"Well, of course, I couldn't be certain about it; but I came out on the veranda to take a look at the sky just before I turned in, and I didn't see it then. Surely, as I turned to come back into the house my eye would have caught that big piece of white paper beside the door."

"What time was it that the most important part of your conversation took place?"

"Just before we broke up. I remember we were going over the mysterious robberies, and I expressed the opinion that they were the work of the gang under Skip Riley and Creviss."

"That was probably the time the fellow who put up that notice was about. You see, if he followed you from Soldier Butte he wouldn't get here much earlier than that, for he wouldn't dare ride a pony the length of the valley at that time of the morning, so he had to walk from the south fence."

"By Jove! I believe you are right."

"If my theory is true, the fellow who brought the warning also carried back your conversation to the gang."

"Then they surely will have something to fight us on."

"Yes, fear that you will get on their trail will compel them to try to make their bluff good, as expressed in that message."

"I'd give something to know when this thing was put up."

"Let's see; it was about four o'clock when you turned in, wasn't it?"

"Just about."

"And just about that time Song gets up to cook for the boys in the bunk house who get out to relieve the night watch in the big pasture. Doesn't he?"

"Those are the orders."

"Then have Song in, and we'll ask him if he saw a strange man around the place when he got up. He might have seen him and thought nothing of it, and would never think of reporting it."

"Good idea. Wait here and I will call him."

In a few minutes the Chinaman came shuffling in from the garden."

"See here, Song," said Ted. "Did you see a strange man here early this morning?"

"Stlange man!" said Song meditatively, with a smile of innocence on his broad, yellow face. "No savvy stlange man."

"Man no b'long here," said Stella,

"Oh, yes, I savvy. No see stlange man."

"What time you get up?"

"Me gettee up fo' clock."

"Did you go outside?"

"Yes, me go out an' call cowbloy. Tell gettee up, P. D. Q. No gettee up, no bleakfast."

"What did you see outside that you don't see every morning?"

"Evely moling? No savvy."

"Yesterday morning, day before that, day before that, all mornings."

"Lesterday moling, evely moling?"

"Oh, the deuce! You try him, Stella."

"Say, Song, you see something makee you flaid this moling?" said Stella, imitating Song's pidgin English.

"Oh, yes, me lookee out, plenty jump in."

"What you see?"

"Plenty wolf. He sneakee lound side house. I lun like devil."

"What wolf look like?"

"Plenty big wolf. When he see me he lise up on hind legee, and lun likee man."

"Ah ha! There's your clew," said Stella, turning to Ted. "The fellow who posted this notice was disguised in a wolfskin so that he could sneak up to the house unnoticed by the Chinaman, or, if seen, he would make a bluff at scaring Song."

"Stella, you're a wonder."

"Say, Song, you no likee wolf?"

"No, me plenty flaid wolf," answered the Chinaman, shaking his head violently.

"All right, Song. I givee you shotgun. Next time you see wolf, plenty shoot. Savvy?"

"All light. You givee me gun, I shootee wolf plenty. Makee go 'ki-yi' and lun belly fast."

Song went away with a grin on his face like a crack in a piece of stale cheese.

"Stella, you've solved it. I believe whoever put that message there heard our conversation, and at least they'll hate us a bit worse than before, if that is possible."

"Let them bark, the wolves. I never was afraid of a wolf, anyhow. If you want to throw me into spasms show me a bobcat. That's the fighting animal."

During breakfast the boys were shown the warning that had been posted beside the door, and it was decided to pay no attention to it, but to watch for the appearance of a messenger from the "Flying Demons," and if one was caught to make it hot for him.

Ted had no doubt but Creviss and his gang would try to injure the broncho boys by every means in their power, but until they committed some overt act the boys could hardly afford to become the aggressors.

For several days nothing happened, and the Moon Valley Ranch went the even tenor of its way.

Preparations were under way for the fall round-up, and Ted had received letters from several heavy stock buyers that they would be present at that time to make their selections of such cattle as they desired to buy.

It had always been the custom at the ranch to have an entertainment of some sort at the ranch afterward. This was started for the purpose of amusing the buyers with cowboy tricks and that sort of thing, but it had developed into something far greater, until now all the world was invited to the barbecue and the "doings" afterward. No one was barred who behaved himself.

This year Ben Tremont had charge of the entertainment, and he was not limited as to expense, for every fellow was on his honor to provide the best entertainment for the least money.

The manager's plans were generally kept secret from every one except Ted and Stella, who were the exceptional ones and were in every one's secrets and confidence.

Ben had declared himself as to the superlative excellence of his show this year.

"It's going to be hard to beat," said he, in boasting about it. "We've had some pretty good shows, but nothing like the one I'm getting up now."

Kit had charge of the cowboy end of it, the races, the bronchobusting, the roping and tying contests; in fact, all the arena acts.

This year Clay Whipple attended to the inner man, and was to provide a genuine old Southern barbecue, with trimmings.

The round-up was to begin in less than a week, and the festivities were to follow immediately.

Invitations had been sent broadcast into Nebraska, Colorado, Wyoming, Idaho, Montana, and the Pacific coast States; everywhere, in fact, where the boys had friends, and from the responses received an enormous crowd would be present.

Three days elapsed after the finding of the warning beside the door before anything more was heard from the Flying Demons.

Then Ted found another message from them near the front door.

It was as follows:

> "TED STRONG AND OTHERS: You think you know who committed the mysterious robberies, but you are on the wrong track. You will never find out, while your secrets are known to us. This is warning number two. The third and last will come soon; then look out.
>
> "THE FLYING DEMONS."

"Now, why in the world do they call themselves the Flying Demons?" asked Ted reflectively, as they were reading the second screed from their enemies. "It seems to me that there is the secret of the whole thing. You never can tell what a pack of boys like that are going to do. They are more to be feared than older criminals, for they have no judgment, and will rush into the most reckless things just to show off before one another."

"Pay no attention to them," advised Stella. "That's what I think they are doing now—showing off. I doubt if they think they can frighten us, but they are afraid of us."

"Oh, by the way," said Ted, suddenly thinking of something. "You remember I looked at the watermark on that first warning we received from these terrible demons. Well, this screed has the same mark—'Griffin Bond.' When I was in town to-day I went into the bank. Old man Creviss was behind the counter, and that precious son of his was beside him. I had a check cashed, and Mr. Creviss asked me why we didn't keep our bank account there. I told him we had thought something about it, but I didn't mention that we had decided not to. Then I asked him for a couple of sheets of paper on which to write a note, and he handed them to me. I took them to the window and held them up to the light to see the watermark."

"And what was it?" asked Stella eagerly.

"The griffin."

"Then the paper on which these things were written came from the bank?"

"They certainly did. After I had looked at the watermark I turned to young Creviss and looked him square in the eye. He turned as white as chalk, and his lip trembled."

"He's a coward," said Stella positively. "Why didn't he bluff it out?"

"He had nothing to stand on; but, as you say, he's a rank coward, and it's my opinion that it's only fear of Skip Riley that keeps him at it, anyway. At all events, I gave him a good scare, for instead of writing the note I folded up the paper and put it into my pocket. He stepped forward as if he would interfere and make me give the paper back, not having used it, but I gave him a glassy glare and walked out."

"Then it was he who wrote the warnings."

"Of course, and he knows that I have him dead to rights. That is another mark against me with the gang."

"Better watch out."

"They can have me if they can get me."

CHAPTER VII
SONG SHOOTS A WOLF

Early one morning the broncho boys were startled out of their beds by the double explosion of a shotgun, followed by excited yells and screams of agony.

"That Chinaman has shot somebody," thought Ted, as he rapidly skipped out of bed and pulled on his trousers.

In the living room he met all the boys, as scantily clad as himself, hurrying out to see what the noise was all about.

They could hear Song behind the house screaming in Chinese at the top of his voice, and in an ear-splitting falsetto, which showed that he was tremendously excited.

Thither they rushed, and for a moment the ludicrous scene far outbalanced the seriousness of what had happened.

On the ground was a young fellow about seventeen years of age. He was writhing with pain, and the blood was oozing through his clothes in fifty places.

"Ha, ha!" shrieked Song. "Me shootee wolf, turnee into man light away. Ha, ha, me allee same plenty smart man, likee magician."

"Yes, you're a hot magician," said Bud; "You've made this feller second cousin ter a porous plaster. That's what you've done."

"Who is he, Song?" asked Ted.

"Me no savvy him. Me comee out chicken house getee eggs fo' bleakfast. I cally gun, shotee plenty wolf all samee Mliss Stella say."

"But this is not a wolf."

"All samee wolf. I open chicken house do'. I see wolf. Plenty glowl at Song. I no likee gun. Shutee my eye. Pull tligger, an' gun goee off. All samee wolf no mo' glowlee, him yellee like thundeh. When smokee blow way wolf gonee, all samee man comee. I plenty magician, I thinkee."

Ted looked in the chicken house, and on the floor lay the dried hide of a big gray wolf.

Now he understood. The message had come the third time from the Flying Demons.

"Kit, run around to the front door and see if there is a message there for us from our friends the Demons."

In a moment Kit was back, holding a piece of paper in his hand.

Ted took it from him, and read it.

It was the third and last warning. It said:

> "TED STRONG: We have warned you twice before to leave this part of the country, but you have made no move to do so. This is the third warning. If you are not away from here in a week the vengeance will fall upon you. Beware!

> "THE FLYING DEMONS."

"Did you bring this?" asked Ted, of the wretched youth, who still lay upon the ground groaning from his numerous wounds.

There was no reply. The fellow could only toss his head from side to side and rub his legs, into which the bulk of the shot had been fired by the excited Chinaman.

"You won't answer, eh? Well, we'll find a way to make you. I'm glad you've given us a week," said Ted, laughing. "That will at least give us time to hold our round-up and festivities."

"Oh, if I live through this I'll never go into anything like it again," moaned the youth upon the ground.

"Here, stand up," said Ted to him. "You're not badly hurt. You're only stung, twice. Get on your feet and we'll see what we can do for you. You're a long way from dead yet. What's your name?"

"Jack Farley. Oh, if I could only be sure that I wasn't going to die!" exclaimed the youth.

He was the young fellow Billy Sudden had spoken about.

"We can't tell how badly you are hurt until you get up," said Ted. "Rise, and we'll go into the house and examine your wounds."

Slowly young Farley got to his feet, but when he tried to walk he uttered a howl of pain, and sank down again.

"Yellow all through," said Ben, in a tone of disgust.

"Ever have about three ounces of duck shot pumped into yer system through yer hide?" asked Bud.

"Never had."

"Then yer don't know all ther joys o' life. I've had one ounce shot inter my leg, an' if ther contents o' two shells gives double ther pain one does, then excuse me. An' mine wuz only snipe shot, at that."

"Pick him up, boys, and lay him on the lounge in my room," said Ted. "I'll take a look at him after a while, meantime some of you watch him to see that he doesn't get away. We need him for evidence."

When Bud and Ben had carried the wounded boy into Ted's room and laid him on the lounge, Bud stood over him regarding him with interest.

"I sorter envy yer, kid," he said at last.

"You can have 'em, but I don't see why you envy me," said Farley.

"I wuz thinkin' how happy you'll be all through these lonesome winter evenings, pickin' ther shot out o' yer legs."

When Farley had been carried into the house, Ted called Kit to him and said:

"Kit, I wish you'd ride over to Suggs' ranch and tell Billy Sudden that his protégé is over here with his hide peppered with bird shot, and ask him to ride over and take a look at him."

During breakfast they related to Stella the story of Song's wolf hunt in the chicken house, and the result.

Song was as proud as a peacock, and wore "the smile that won't come off" as he flitted around the table waiting on every one.

"Say, Missee Stella," he said, "Song all samee one cowbloy now, eh? What you sayee?"

"Yes, Song, you have certainly followed instructions. You got your wolf that time, sure. How you likee shootee?"

"No likee, Missee Stella. Makee too much noisee, all samee too much plenty fiahclackers. Kickee like blazes. Plitty near knockee arm outee Song."

The boys stripped Farley after breakfast, and found his legs in pretty bad condition. They looked as if Song's gun had been loaded with smallpox, and all of it had lodged in the lad's legs.

"Boys, we'll have to take relays in picking the shot from our first victim," said Ted. "There's too much work here for one man."

"He's a turrible-lookin' demon now with a hide full o' shot. Ther punctured demon of Demonville! Say, kid, I'd hate ter laugh at yer, but yer a sight. Why didn't yer fix it so's them two charges o' shot would hev been distributed among ther gang? Then yer could sit down o' evenings an' pick shot out o' one another instid o' plottin' agin' ther whites."

"Let him be, Bud, he's having all he can do to think about these shots, as it is. The things for us to do now is to pick them out of him."

"We'll let him count 'em ez they come out. That'll help take his mind off his troubles, but he'll hev ter hev a great head fer figgers."

They went to work on him with their penknives, as most of the shot were just beneath the skin. But it was painful enough, at that, and every time a shot came out Farley groaned deeper. While they were engaged in this, to them, pleasing occupation, Billy Sudden arrived.

"Hello, kid," he said to Farley. "So you got it at last. I could have told you to keep away from Ted Strong and his bunch. They're bad medicine for a herd o' mavericks like you to graze with. You tackled the wrong outfit. They're too many fer you, and if you'll all take a fool's advice you'll keep away, or else some of you will be looking through a griddle in a door up at the penitentiary."

Farley made no reply, only hid his face and groaned at every extracted shot.

"Say, kid, what about this gang you belong to?"

The boy shook his head.

"D'ye mean to say you're not going to tell me about it?"

The boy nodded.

"What's the reason you won't?"

"The oath."

"Slush with the oath. You had no business to take it. What'll the home folks think when I tell them about this. Shot by a Chinaman in the chicken house at dawn!"

Billy paused to let the ignominy of it sink in. It did sound pretty bad and mean and cheap. There were no heroics in this, such as Farley had at first considered his rôle.

He hid his face on his arm, and his body shook. Billy had probed deep into his pride.

"Well, come on," said Billy. "This is no time for a conspirator to do the baby act. I suppose you thought it was to be a spotlight scene where you stood in the center doing the heavy stunt, and all the rest sat on the bleachers and applauded. By gee! Peppered by a Chinaman, and with snipe shot, at that."

"Oh, quit it!" said Farley. "I know I was a chump for sticking with those fellows, but I needed the money."

"What money?"

"My share of the—"

"What?"

"Oh, nothing."

"Yes, there is something. What robbery was it you shared in?"

"I didn't steal anything."

"I suppose not. You did the dirty work of being lookout, or something like that, and they threw you the bone while they kept the meat and fat, eh?"

"What shall I do with him?" asked Ted.

"Keep him locked up as a hostage. That may bring those young fools to their senses," said Billy. "I'm disgusted with him for not making a clean breast of the whole foolish business, and if it wasn't for his sister, I'd toss him up in the air and forget him."

The rest of the day was spent in picking shot out of Farley, and by evening he was relieved of the last one.

"We'll put him in that empty room at the corner of the house, and take turns watching him through the night," said Ted.

Until bedtime Farley sat in the living room with the rest of them, and they were unusually guarded in their conversation.

When it came time to retire Farley was conducted to the room which was to be his prison, and it fell to Carl to take the first watch, and to call Ben at one o'clock.

In the room there was a lounge and a pair of blankets for Farley, a table and a lamp, and a chair for the watch.

"Whatever you do, don't go to sleep, Carl," said Ted. "The reason I'm putting you on the first watch is because you're such a sleepyhead."

"Don'd vorry aboud me," said Carl, with a yawn. "I pet you I vas der sleepinglessness feller in der whole bunch. If he gets avay on my vatch it vill not be pecause I don'd sleep."

"I guess you mean all right, but I swear I can't understand you. Only keep awake."

"Oh, yah; I avake keeping all der time."

Carl sat in the chair watching his prisoner, and soon saw Farley's chest heaving regularly and heard his deep breathing as he slept. Then things seemed to waver and fade away.

Carl started up at hearing some one beating on the door, and sat rubbing his eyes. It was broad daylight.

"All right, I'll get up pooty soon yet. Is preakfast retty?"

"Here, open the door. This is Ted."

"Vait a minute."

Carl staggered sleepily to the door and unlocked it.

"Where is your prisoner?" asked Ted, stalking into the room, and looking at the open window.

"My vat? Ach, Gott in himmel, vat haf I dided? I am schoost coming avake. He iss gone! I haf slept on vatch. I am foreffer disgraced. Kill me, Ted! I haf no appetite to live any more alretty," cried Carl.

Ted had been angry at discovering the escape of Farley, for he had conceived a plan to use him against Creviss. He had risen early, and when he found that all the boys were in bed except Carl, he immediately suspected the truth.

But Carl's despairing manner turned him from anger.

"Never mind, Carl," he said. "It was my fault for putting you on watch. You were not cut out for a watchman. Or, perhaps, you were, according to the funny papers, but not of prisoners."

During breakfast Carl was compelled to endure the jokes of the boys at his failure to guard the prisoner, which he did with a lugubrious countenance; then, at a signal from Ted, the subject was dropped.

About ten o'clock Billy Sudden rode up to the ranch house.

There was something in his manner that betokened news of importance, and he strode unbidden into the living room, where Ted was sitting at his desk.

"Where's the kid?" he asked abruptly.

"Who, Farley?" asked Ted, looking up from his work.

"Yes."

"Skipped."

"What?"

"I said skipped."

"Great Scott! I'd give a hundred dollars if he hadn't."

"Why?"

"What time did he get away?"

"Don't know, exactly. Carl was watching him, but he fell asleep almost as soon as they were in the room together, and didn't wake up until six o'clock this morning, and Farley was gone. No one knows how he got away or at what time. It might have been any time. He probably woke up in the night and saw that Carl was dead to the world, and opened the window, dropped to the ground, and hit the trail. That's all I know about it. But what makes you so anxious about it?"

"Then you haven't heard the news?"

"Guess not. What is it?"

"The First National Bank was robbed last night."

"Great guns! Creviss' bank! That's the United States depository!"

"The same."

"What are the details?"

"I rode through town this morning on my way over here to see if being confined for the night wouldn't make the kid talk, when I saw a bunch of men standing in front of the bank. I butted in and asked what the excitement was, and they told me that the bank had been robbed."

"But how?"

"That's what nobody knows. When the cashier, Mr. Henson, got to the bank this morning everything apparently was all right. The doors and windows were fastened, and there was no sign anywhere that the bank had been forcibly entered. Of course, he didn't look at these things first. He went to the vault and opened it at the proper time and examined its contents casually. Everything seemed to be as usual. But when, a few minutes later, he went to get out the currency, it was all gone. He hadn't counted up when I left there, so no one knows the exact amount, but it was large."

CHAPTER VIII
THE BATTLE WITH THE BULL

The excitement incident to the mysterious robbery of the Creviss bank was intense.

How had it been done? This was the question that every one was asking his neighbor. But none could answer it.

The evening before the robbery had taken place the bank had been closed by the cashier, and by Mr. Creviss himself.

The money, books, and papers, with which the business of the day had been conducted, had been carried into the vault by the cashier, and Mr. Creviss, who was an unusually cautious man, looked into the vault after the cashier came out, to see that everything was in. Then he closed the vault doors, and turned the handle of the combination, setting the time lock, thus securing the doors from being opened until nine o'clock the next morning.

The only way in which it could be opened, and an almost impossible way, at that, was by blowing it open.

And yet the vault had been robbed, and the vault lock had apparently not been tampered with.

It had the appearance of necromancy.

Ted rode into town with Billy Sudden, arriving about noon.

Billy rode on to the Dumb-bell Ranch, and Ted stopped at the bank. It seemed deserted. But as he entered the door he saw a big man, dressed in the flashy clothes affected by managers of cheap circuses and fake shows, standing at the end of the counter talking to Wiley Creviss.

"I can't do anything with that check," Ted heard Creviss say. "You'll have to come in when the cashier is here. The safe is locked, and I can't get into it, anyway, and all the currency is in it. I'm only staying here until the cashier gets back from dinner."

"When will that be?" asked the stranger.

"In about half an hour."

The stranger picked up his valise, which seemed to be heavy, and walked out grumbling about banks that closed up for dinner.

Ted said nothing to Wiley, but he took a good look about the bank, disregarding the other lad's scowls.

He observed that the vault door stood open, but that there was no money in sight, and the place had an air of desertion, as if business was slack.

When Strong had seen all that he wanted of the apparent entrances to the bank that a criminal might use to force his way in, he left with two distinct impressions on his mind. One was that the vault door had been open when he came in, and that Wiley Creviss had abruptly closed it when he saw Ted staring at it. The other was the remarkable appearance of the showman, for without doubt he was that.

As before, the mysterious robbery of the bank proved to be too hard a nut for the citizens to crack, and when they had thrashed out all the theories advanced and knocked them to pieces again, they forgot it.

Not so Ted Strong. This succession of robberies, none of them leaving behind the slightest clew to the perpetrators, interested him. Its very difficulty of solution, which had made the lesser brains abandon it, compelled his attention and interest.

Had it been his business to tackle the problem, he gladly would have done so. But the only Federal end to it was the robbery of the post office, which the inspectors of that department were working on, unless, perhaps, it might be found that the funds of the government for general purposes at Fort Rincon had been stolen. Then the case would come under the operations of the United States marshal's office.

But other and more pressing things of a personal nature gradually took his attention from crime, and he devoted himself to the coming round-up.

All the spare room in the Moon Valley Ranch house was occupied by visiting cattle buyers, who had come to the round-up. The rooms of the boys had been given up to guests, while they camped on the prairie behind the house.

At last the great day came.

Early in the morning the boys were out, and with them was Stella.

Cow Suggs had loaned Ted his outfit for the day, and Ted was glad to have the boys, for there was no cleverer cowman in the country at a round-up, saving Ted himself, who was king of them all, and so conceded, than the dark, lithe cow-puncher, Billy Sudden, who had been through college and had traveled in Europe before he deserted the East for the toil, freedom, and excitement of the range.

It was now time to round up all the stock on the Moon Valley Range, cut out the marketable stuff, and brand the yearlings.

This is not only a troublesome task, but it is dangerous, and not a moment of the time until the task is accomplished but has its exciting adventures and escapes from death.

The boys did not know exactly how many head of cattle they owned. They had been selling and replenishing their stock from time to time, and the increase of calves had been very large, for Moon Valley, situated in the lee of Dent du Chien, or Dog Tooth Mountain, with its rich grass, the richest in the Black Hills, and its abundance of fresh, clear spring water, was an ideal breeding place.

There were on the ranch at that time several dangerous bulls, and this added to the hard work of the day, because the monarchs of the range did not like to be disturbed and have their following broken up and scattered.

In the big pasture, which lay at the foot of Deni du Chien Mountain, was the largest herd in the valley.

The king of this herd was known as "Gladiator." He was always looking for a fight, and never refused a challenge, whether from another bull or from what he considered his natural enemy, man.

A man on foot in that pasture would have stood no more chance for his life than if he tried to stand in front of the engine that hauls the Empire State Express going at top speed. Gladiator would kill him just as quickly and as surely.

So it was that strangers were kept out of the big pasture, whether they were mounted or not, unless they were escorted by some member of the broncho boys, or one of the older cowboys about the place. Stella, with her red bolero, nearly caused a tragedy one day by coming within the vision of Gladiator, who took the bolero for a challenge.

Stella turned in time and fled, and had it not been for the fleetness of her pony and her own superb riding, there had been no more to relate of the adventures of the girl pard of the Moon Valley boys.

The morning of the round-up Ted undertook personally to turn the herd to the rendezvous.

Stella insisted upon accompanying him, and at last he was persuaded to give his consent, but only on the condition that she wear subdued colors, which she did, with skirt and jacket of a light-dun color.

The herd was grazing in the noble range that stretched for miles along and across the valley in the shadow of the splendid mountain.

It was widely scattered, and as the band of horsemen rode out toward it the cattle lifted their heads for a moment and took a quiet survey, then returned to their feeding.

Not so Gladiator.

The great white-and-black bull raised his head proudly, and his fierce, steady eyes regarded them without fear.

Indeed, Gladiator knew no fear, whether of man or beast, wolf pack or mountain lion, serpent or bird of prey.

He was monarch of that herd, and no one said him nay except Ted Strong, who ruled the ranch and all that was on it, by the general consent of his comrades and his own fitness for his rulership.

Ted and Gladiator had had numerous differences, and it was the bull that had backed down every time.

Yet he did not fear Ted. Rather he hated him because he could not conquer this quick, brave, and resourceful fellow.

"That bull will be the death of you some of these days," said Stella to Ted once when Gladiator, resenting Ted's intrusion into the herd for the purpose of cutting out some calves, charged him. But Ted in the end threw the bull with his rope, humiliating him before all the herd. From that time forth Gladiator's eyes always became red with anger when he saw Ted, but he did not misbehave, because he respected Ted's lariat and quirt, and the strong arm that wielded them.

When they got to the herd the boys circled it from behind, riding in slowly.

Ted and Stella were on the left point, with Bud and Kit opposite.

Bill Sudden was in the rear to drive, while the other Moon Valley cowboys and Billy Sudden's boys came in from the sides.

At the first interruption of their grazing the cattle moved along sluggishly, but Gladiator did not move.

The big bull stood his ground, with eyes gazing steadily at Ted and Stella, who were approaching him slowly and persistently.

Suddenly Gladiator threw up his head and gave a low, menacing bellow.

"The old chap is waking up," said Ted.

"Be careful, Ted," said Stella. "He's not in very good humor."

"I see he isn't. But if we go at him easily he'll be all right."

"Don't take any chances with him alone, Ted."

"Still, I'm not going to let him boss this job. He's got to lead this herd out, and that's all there is to it, for it's a cinch that they won't go without him."

Stella knew that it was useless to say anything more, as when Ted made up his mind to do a thing, it would be done if everything broke.

Billy Sudden had got the herd moving up from the rear, but the forward end of the herd was stagnant.

Gladiator refused to budge, and stood with his stubborn forefeet planted on the sod, his head raised insolently.

But it could be seen that his anger was working within him, and would soon break forth.

Bud was working the cattle nearest him gently on the move, but when they saw that their leader was standing still they ceased their progress and began to crowd and mill, and the steers were getting reckless and beginning to throw their tails in the air and utter low, growling bellows.

It was a critical moment. Who was to be the master must be decided quickly. If the bull conquered then the cattle would get to milling generally, and the mischief would be to pay.

It would not take long for them to stampede, if the bull started the panic, or made a charge. Ted saw the danger, and knew that the condition must be treated diplomatically, which was the easier way, or with force, of which the outcome was most uncertain.

It depended, in a measure, on the temper of the bull himself.

The cattle were crowding up from the rear, and those nearest the bull were beginning to feel the pressure and were pushing toward Gladiator, who was fifteen feet in advance of the herd.

When he noticed that the herd was moving, his anger increased, and he lowered his head and began to paw the ground.

Ted held up his hand to Billy Sudden as a signal to cease pushing the animals, but they had got the impetus and would not stop.

In a moment they had begun to crowd upon the bull, who, with legs planted stubbornly, would not be crowded, and began to gore aside those who were being pushed upon him.

Ted saw instantly that this was going to result in disaster if not stopped, as the frightened steers, feeling Gladiator's sharp horns, turned back on the herd, and were pushing their way frantically into the center of it, while others, coming up, were forced upon the bull's horns.

"Darn a stubborn bull, anyhow!" exclaimed Ted. "I've got to get in and put a stop to that, or Gladiator will have the herd to milling or running in less than ten minutes."

"Be careful," was all Stella said, but there was a world of anxiety in her voice.

"You better get out of the way, Stella," said Ted "Ride to the rear. You will see it all, and have just as much fun, and will be out of danger."

"What are you going to do?"

"I'm going to make that bull move along or bust a string."

Ted's jaw was set with determination, and when Stella saw that she knew that it would be useless for her to say anything more.

Ted loosened his rope, grasped his quirt firmly, and rode slowly toward the bull, while Stella signaled to Billy Sudden to ride up to the head of the herd.

The boys, observing Ted's actions, knew what he was about to do, and ceased moving the cattle and sat on their horses to watch for the outcome of the contest.

Most of them felt like spectators at a performance of a specially hazardous feat, and held their breath. But each was on the alert to rush to Ted's assistance the moment he seemed to need it.

As the bull looked up, and saw Ted approaching him, he ceased pawing, and stood with watchful eyes. Occasionally he sent forth a challenging bellow. His tail was switching from side to side, like that of an angry cat.

Ted was coming alertly. No one knew the danger of openly attacking the bull better than himself, and yet it must be done.

It was rule or kill, so far as the bull was concerned, for if the boys could not manage him they would be compelled to kill him so that they might be able to handle the herd, substituting a more amiable bull in his place.

A cowman cannot always tell what a bull is going to do when it is faced on the range. It may dodge the issue or it may attack, and Ted was wary enough to be on the watch for the latter contingency.

Therefore, when Gladiator, without so much warning as the lowering of his head, sprang at Ted when he was not more than ten feet away, he covered the distance in two or three lumbering bounds, and Ted had just sufficient time to wheel his pony to one side to avoid being bowled over. But the horns of the bull struck the gaiter on his left leg, as it rushed past, and tore it off, almost unseating him. Stella, breathlessly watching the encounter, gasped as she saw Ted reel in his saddle. But she breathed easier as she saw him straighten up and turn his horse rapidly to face the bull again.

With almost incredible agility, the bull turned and came rushing at Ted again, but the leader of the broncho boys rode swiftly away from him, tolling him away from the herd.

Finally the bull stopped and began to paw the earth. Ted, to tempt him to another attack, directed Sultan toward him at full speed, intending to swerve when he got close to his bullship, and dodge him and infuriate him further, so that he would follow. He knew that Sultan could outrun Gladiator.

But, as he got close to the bull, in spite of the warning cries from Stella and Bud, Gladiator swerved to meet the attack, and before the fleet-footed pony could escape he was struck, and went rolling over the ground.

A cry of horror went up from the boys as they all dashed to the scene. Ted Strong was on the ground. The pony had scrambled to his feet, and stood trembling a few feet distant. The bull, with lowered head, was charging upon Ted.

CHAPTER IX
TED GETS AN ASSIGNMENT

To the horror-stricken onlookers it appeared that Ted's end had come. He lay prone upon the sod with his face turned to the sky, evidently stunned.

The bull, with all the ferocity of his kind when goaded to anger, was charging upon him, his needle-like horns a few inches from the ground, and the foam flecking from his lips.

Stella, her face white and drawn, was galloping toward him as fast as her pony could go, while Bud was lashing his pony to the height of its speed as he crossed the face of the herd. Billy Sudden was neck and neck with Stella, calling to her to hold back.

Suddenly Ted Strong came to life, and looked over his shoulder.

He saw his danger, and quick as thought he rolled over, away from the bull.

But that was all. Every one could see that it would do no good. He could not expect to escape from the infuriated beast in that manner, and a hollow groan escaped the lips of more than one.

Ted surely was doomed.

The bull's horns caught Ted in the side as he continued to roll away from it, and it stopped for an instant, settling itself to toss him. Stella turned her head away with a muttered prayer, and even the cowboys, used to accidents in the round-up, gasped.

But suddenly they saw a cloud of dust fly upward, and thought at first that Ted had fired his revolver into the face of the infuriated beast, and it seemed strange that they had not heard the report of the weapon.

Then, miracle of miracles, the bull, with a snort of pain, threw up its head, and Ted was not impaled upon its horns.

There was another cloud of dust, and the bull began backing away, slowly but surely, shaking its head, as if in pain.

"Screamin' catamounts, did yer see thet, Stella?" cried Bud Morgan, as he rode alongside the girl,

"What did he do?" asked Stella.

"He's saved hisself by blindin' ther bull. He throwed dust inter its eyes. I'm dinged if I see how thet feller kin think o' things like thet when he's down an' out. Look at him!"

As the bull rubbed its face in the grass Ted rolled over twice, then leaped to his feet and ran to where Sultan was awaiting him.

A mighty cheer went up from the boys, and the color came back into Stella's face with a rush, but she could not have uttered a sound to save her life.

In the meantime, the bull had recovered, having rubbed the dust from its eyes in the short grass, and looked about for its enemy.

It caught sight of Ted in the act of mounting, and sprang toward him with the swiftness of a deer.

Then Stella recovered her voice.

"Run, Ted! Run!" she cried.

But Ted had seen the necessity of that himself, and, wheeled Sultan and dashed off, looking over his shoulder at the enraged monster that was following him, while he rapidly uncoiled his lariat.

Having run several hundred yards and outdistanced the bull, he turned and stopped with his rope in his hand, closely calculating the animal's distance and speed.

Bud and Stella were following the bull closely, both of them preparing their lariats for the throw.

As the bull charged, Ted's rope was seen to leave his hand and go sailing through the air in graceful loops and curves that lengthened out one after the other.

One of the most difficult throws a cow-puncher can make with a lariat was that which Ted attempted. He had to calculate to a degree the speed with which the bull was advancing toward him, and that at which the rope was leaving him. To calculate the point where the two would come together would seem an almost impossible task.

But so nicely had Ted estimated it, that the open noose fell over the bull's head and settled down, and, turning swiftly, Ted spurred Sultan to one side, and the bull, shaking his head and emitting short, angry bellows, rushed past.

The intelligent pony had suddenly come to a stop, bracing himself for the shock, and when Gladiator came to the end of the rope he turned completely over, and landed on his back with a thud that shook the earth.

Bud had galloped forward, and was about to throw himself from the saddle to tie the brute, when, with the agility of a cat, the bull was on its feet, shaking its head and stamping the earth in a perfect fury of anger and desperation. But it was by no means beaten, and ran at Bud, who took to his heels. When again it arrived at the end of the rope, it went head over heels, much to its loss of wind and dignity.

This time it did not rise so briskly, and Ted gave it all the time it wanted.

Suddenly Stella dashed out and rode toward the bull, and when a few feet from it curved off, with the angry brute in full pursuit. Had her pony stumbled it would have been all up with her, for Gladiator was wild with rage, and when it was again thrown its fury knew no bounds.

"A few more throws like that will settle him, I think," shouted Ted. "Bait him again, Bud."

Again Bud rode out, and the bull took after him as before, and, when he was jerked onto his back by the rope, he lay there.

Ted rode rapidly up to him, and, detaching a rope which had been knotted around his waist, tied the bull's legs fore and aft, and the exhausted brute did not make an objection.

For several minutes the bull lay panting, then it recovered.

When it came to its normal condition at last, it struggled furiously to get to its feet, but each time it got up Ted jerked it to its side, standing close to it so that it could see him.

Time and again it thus fruitlessly struggled.

It seemed to realize suddenly that it had been a very foolish bull, and that it had met its master, who now stood over him ready to tumble him over at any moment.

So he lay quite still, following Ted's movements with its great, dark eyes, out of which all the ferocity had vanished.

Ted stepped up to it and patted its head, and it made no objection to these attentions. Then he began to untie the bonds that held its legs together.

"Look out fer him, he's treacherous," called Bud.

"He's all right," answered Ted. "I'll bet he'll eat out of my hand."

When it felt that it was free again, the bull got slowly to his feet and walked sedately in the direction of the herd.

"You've broken the spirit of that bull," said Stella.

"You bet I have," said Ted. "That's just what he needed. He'll be a good bull now. If he isn't, I'll give him some more."

Ted now rode to the head of the herd with Stella, and the other boys took their places.

"All right, Billy. Send them forward," shouted Ted to the rear of the herd.

Skillfully Ted set the herd to moving toward the south, where the other herds were gathering under the management of the boys.

At first Gladiator threw up his head arrogantly, and did not stir.

Ted again rode toward him, swinging his lariat. The bull saw him as well as the rope, and, recognizing the agents of his defeat, moved off briskly at the head of the herd.

"Say," said Bud, across the head of the herd, "yer could slap that old duffer across the face with your hat, and he'd apologize."

They were almost at the rendezvous, where thousands of cattle had been gathered into a huge herd, and in every direction could be seen dust clouds announcing that others were on the way.

"Here comes Carl hotfoot," said Stella. "He looks as if something had happened, and he was an extra edition with 'a full account of the terrible disaster.'"

"Hello, Carl! What is it?" asked Ted.

"Der United States marshal vaiting for you on der veranda iss," answered Carl solemnly.

"Well, what do I care?" asked Ted. "He's come at a mighty busy time if he just wants to swap a little conversation. Did he say what he wanted?"

"No, but he say it is very important vork, an' for you to hurry."

"My compliments to the marshal, and tell him I'm busy, and will see him as soon as I get through. You entertain him for a while."

"But he der boss iss."

"Not on this ranch. This is a free and unadulterated republic, where there are no bosses. Tell him to make himself at home, and I'll be there as soon as I can."

Now the cattle were all rounded up, and the cutting out of the two and three-year olds began.

This was intensely exciting work, in which Stella joined, as she was as skilled at it as any of the boys. Outside of the big herd, the cowboys were picking up the cut-outs and driving them to the branding pens, for many of them were acquired stock, and even many of the home yearlings had never been branded.

Then the cows with calves were cut out, so that the youngsters might get a touch of life by feeling the sting of the hot iron with the Crescent V brand on it.

The buyers were circulating in the herds, looking over the stock.

Several of the buyers had brought their own cow-punchers with them, and these went to work cutting out the selections of their employers.

The sky was thick with dust, and the air rang with the shouts of the cowboys and the lowing and bellowing of the cattle.

The rattle of countless hoofs on the hard soil added to the din, and the cattle weaving in and out ceaselessly, and the dashing riding of the cowboys as they swooped out of the mass occasionally to drive back an escaping steer, made a scene of excitement, movement, and noise never seen anywhere, except at a Western cattle round-up and cut-out.

Soon the work was pretty well in hand, and, leaving Bud Morgan as segundo, Ted went to the house to see the marshal.

He found that officer sitting on the veranda, quietly smoking a cigar, an interested witness of the proceedings.

"How are you, Mr. Easton?" said Ted, shaking hands with the marshal. "I must apologize for not coming sooner, but my hands were full."

"So I see," said the marshal cordially. "I was watching you work out there. Say, I believe I'd like to be a cow-puncher if I wasn't so old."

"It's a young man's job," said Ted, laughing; "and even at that it is about all a young fellow can stand at times. But this to-day is a mere picnic to what we are up against sometimes."

"Well, you seem to be right in it."

"Yes, I love my business. I wouldn't be anything in the world except a cow-puncher."

"But, remember, you are also a government officer."

"I never forget that. But, if it came to being compelled to quit one or the other of the occupations, I'd still be a cow-puncher, and let the marshalship go."

"That's the very thing I came to see about."

"You want my resignation?" asked Ted, his spirits falling to zero.

"By no means," laughed the marshal. "Not that, but to ask you to undertake a somewhat difficult job. It transpires that when the Soldier Butte bank was robbed the other night, a large amount of money belonging to the government was taken. I didn't know this until early this afternoon, when I received a telegram from Washington to go after the robbers and land them."

"That'll be somewhat of a job," said Ted, drawing his chair closer to the marshal, so that he couldn't be overheard by passing people.

"I'm well aware of that, and that's the reason I come to you. You and your boys must undertake the duty of clearing up the mystery of the robbery, and, if possible, recovering the money."

"I have a very probable theory as to who the robbers are, but it will be entirely another matter to fasten it on them."

"I leave it all to you. I don't want to have anything to do with it. All I want are results."

"But I shall not have time to tackle it for a day or two. Unfortunately our fall round-up is in progress, and, as this is the time we sell the product of our business, we can't leave it until everything is cleared up."

"That's all right, Mr. Strong. But when you do get busy, don't come back home until you land the thieves."

CHAPTER X
A VISITOR IN THE NIGHT

A great deal of money changed hands that day. The stock buyers had their wallets loaded with cash when they came a-buying, for, when they had cut out the cattle they wanted, and the price was struck, they were prepared to drive them off at once.

The sales at the round-up had been large, and Ted and the boys sat up late that night, after those guests who had elected to remain over for the festivities of the next day were safely in bed, counting the money and going over the books.

"It has been a mighty good year for us, boys," said Ted, as he contemplated the total of their sales.

"Yes, and, best of all, it leaves us with all the old stock disposed of, and nothing but young and vigorous animals with which to begin building up again," said Kit, who had a great head for the cattle business and a faculty for seeing into the future.

"What aire we goin' ter do with all this yere mazuma?" asked Bud, looking over the stacks of fifties, twenties, tens, and fives that lay on the table around which they were sitting in the living room, and which was flanked by piles of gold and a few hundred-dollar bills.

"Can't get it into the bank until day after to-morrow," said Ted. "We'll be too busy to-morrow looking after our guests, and I don't suppose we'll be free until after the dance to-morrow night. Still, I'm not worrying about it. We know everybody here to-night, and I'll take care of it till we can ride over to Strongburg and bank it."

Just then the door blew open with a bang, and big Ben scurried in, bringing with him a blast of prairie wind, crisp and chill from the mountain, that scattered the greenbacks all over the room, and two or three of the fives were blown into the fire and incinerated before any one could rescue them.

"Close that door!" shouted Bud, grasping frantically at the money that was capering over the top of the table.

Ben closed the door with a slam that shook the house.

"'A fool and his money is soon parted,'" quoted Ben, when he saw the havoc wrought by the wind.

"You bet," said Kit "Three fives blew into the fireplace, and are no more. We'll just charge them to your account."

"Like dolly, you will!" said Ben.

"If it hadn't been for you they wouldn't be there. What's the reason we won't?"

"Because you won't. I didn't make the wind."

"No, but consarn ye, ye let it in, an' ye're an accessory before er after ther fact. I reckon both," said Bud.

"Let it go, boys," said Ted. "Pick up the bills, and we'll count and stack them again."

"Where have you been, anyway?" asked Kit, addressing Ben.

"Down beddin' my show for the night. They're about all in now. All except the music, which will be here in the morning," replied Ben. "I'm not at all stuck on myself, but—"

"Oh, no, you've got a very poor opinion of yourself, I guess," said Kit.

"But I want to say that I think I got the bunkie-doodelest show that ever paced the glimmering, gleaming, gloaming grass of Moon Valley."

"Listen to the hombre explode," said Bud. "He's tryin' ter be a feeble imitation o' a real showman. I'll bet he shows up ter-morrer like a ringmaster in a sucuss, with high, shiny boots an' a long whip an a tall, slick hat, an' crack his whip an' say: 'What will ther leetle lady hev next?'"

Ben blushed, for his ambitions in the show line, now that he had had a taste of it, had really been in that direction, only he wouldn't have had the boys know it for the world.

"How about the show, anyhow, Ben?" asked Ted.

"What have you got? You might as well let us know now."

"Not on your autobiography," answered Ben haughtily. "I want to say, though, that your eyes will bulge like the knobs on a washstand drawer when you see what I've got, and then come to look at the bill for such a stupendous, striking, and singularly successful aggregation of freaks, acts, and divertisements embodied in this colossal and cataclysmic congregation of—"

"Oh, cheese it," said Kit. "You give me the pip."

"All right, have it your own way," sighed Ben. "This is what a fellow gets for serving his country, from Thomas Jefferson to John D. Rockefeller."

"Come on," said Ted persuasively. "Loosen up and tell us what we are to have to-morrow. This is an executive session of the whole."

"You're like a lot of kids the day before Christmas. You've just got to see what mamma's hidden in the closet," said Ben. "Well, I'll let you in on a little of it."

"Shoot when you're ready," said Kit.

"I was over at Strongburg about a month ago, and, knowing that I'd have to rustle up a show soon, I wrote to a theatrical agent in Chicago to let me know if he could furnish me with a good amusement company at small cost. He wrote me that he had the very thing, and offered me one of these bum 'wild west' shows, with a bunch of spavined ponies, a lot of imitation cowboys, fake Indians, and Coney Island target shooters."

"An' yer didn't take 'em?" asked Bud, in surprise.

"Tush! Well, I was up against it, when Morrison, the hotel man, told me that there was a showman in town, and perhaps I might get something out of him.

"I hunted him up. He was a typical showman. Big fellow, large as a Noah's ark, dressed like a sunset, and loud as an eighteen-inch gun."

"I saw the fellow in Soldier Butte the other day. He was talking to Wiley Creviss in the bank," said Ted. "You've described him more picturesquely than I should, but I'm convinced he's the same man."

"I asked him what he had, and he told me he could furnish me on short notice anything from a three-ring circus to a hand organ and monkey," continued Ben. "I told him how much money I wanted to spend, and he said he'd fix me up a show that would make everybody delighted, and I told him to go ahead. The show blew in to-night, and ran up their tents down near the corral."

"How many have you got in it?"

"I've got a balloon ascension for the afternoon, a giant and a midget, a magician, an Egyptian fortune teller, a trick mule, a Circassian beauty, and a strong man." Ben looked around proudly, and the boys burst into peals of laughter.

"Have you scraped the mold off of them yet?" asked Kit.

"How's that?" asked Ben haughtily.

"Have you pulled the burs off the chestnuts?"

"See here, what do you mean? Are you casting aspersions on my show?"

"Not exactly, but I think you've been stung by some old stranded side show that was taking the tie route back home. Circassian beaut! Ho-ho, likewise ha-ha! and some more."

"Ter say nothin' o' a Egyptian fortune teller from Popodunk, Ioway, an' a wild man from ther Quaker village. Oh! give me ther smellin' salts. I'm goin' ter hev ther histrikes," laughed Bud.

"Haf you not got a echukated vooly pig und a feller vot 'eats 'em alife'?" asked Carl.

"That's right, Dutchy. It's a bum show what ain't got them," laughed Bud.

The boys were laughing until the house rang with it, and Stella poked her pretty head out of the door to ask to be told the joke. Bud complied, with many humorous embellishments.

"Don't pay any attention to them, Ben," said Stella sympathetically, "I'll take in the show from start to finish."

"Could friendship go any farther than that?" asked Kit pathetically.

"Oh, you fellows give me a pain," said Ben, rising and stalking off to bed.

He was soon followed by the others, Ted and Kit remaining behind to gather up the money and slip rubber bands around each of the packages of currency.

"We ought to have a safe in the house, Ted," said Kit, looking over the pile of money. "We often have large sums of money in the house, and some time we might get robbed."

"There's not much danger of that, Kit," answered Ted. "There are not many fellows who would have the nerve to come into this house. Too many guns, and too many fellows who are not afraid to shoot them. I'm not afraid."

"What was that?"

Kit was staring at the rear window.

"What?"

"I just looked up and thought I saw a face at the window."

"You're getting imaginative."

Just then the clock struck twelve.

"No, I don't think so. I heard a slight cracking noise and looked up. Something white appeared at the window for an instant. It looked like the face of a child."

"Nonsense. A child couldn't look through that window. It's seven feet from the ground."

"Well, I suppose I was mistaken. Let's hide that money and go to bed."

"Where shall we put it?"

Kit looked around the room, then smiled.

"Why, in the cubby-hole, of course. There's a safe for you. We haven't used it for so long that I'd almost forgotten it."

"The very thing. Nobody'd find it there in a blue moon."

They crossed over to a corner of the room and threw back the corner of a rug. Where the baseboard was mortised at the corner there appeared to have been a patch put in. Ted placed his hand against this, near the top, and it tipped back. It was hung on a pivot, and, as its top went in and the bottom came out, there was revealed a boxlike receptacle about two feet long and six inches deep.

"This is a bully place," said Ted, placing the packages of money within it. "It is known to only five of us, and I'll bet that most of us have forgotten its very existence."

The board was turned back into place and the rug spread out again.

"Safe as in the Strongburg Bank," said Kit. "Well, me for the feathers. We're going to be kept humping to-morrow. *Buenas noches.*"

In a few minutes the big ranch house was dark and quiet; every person in it was sound asleep.

Ted Strong had sunk into a deep and untroubled sleep, for his day had been very active, and he was tired when he lay down.

But he had not been sleeping more than a half hour when he found himself sitting straight up in bed, very wide-awake, and wondering why.

"Something wrong in the house," he muttered to himself.

He sniffed the air to discover the smell of smoke. But it was not that.

Had he locked up? He went over his actions just before retiring, and was sure that he had attended faithfully to everything.

The money! The thought came to him like a blow.

Something had happened to the money.

He was out of bed in a jiffy and slipped into his trousers, and, grabbing his revolver from beneath his pillow, he opened the door and walked softly along the hall in his bare feet.

The hall opened into the living room through an arch in which a portière, made of small pieces of bamboo strung together, was hung.

As he looked cautiously into the living room his elbow struck this, and it rattled sharply in the stillness.

He had heard a faint creak, and, as he peeped around the corner of the arch, he saw dimly the figure of a man near the door, evidently just in the act of opening it.

With a succession of noiseless leaps Ted was across the room, and arrived at the door just as it swung open and the man was about to depart.

But Ted was upon his back with the swiftness of a bobcat, and they came together to the floor with? a crash.

The burglar was beneath, but this did not prevent him from fighting with a desperation that lent strength to his already strong and lithe body.

He was slenderer and younger than Ted, who could feel it in the fellow's build as they struggled.

"Let me out, or I'll kill you," said the burglar, and Ted saw the flash of a knife.

At the same moment something rushed past them in the dark, and out of the door.

As Ted saw it dimly it was small, and its motions were awkward and lumbering. He thought it was a dog, and was about to raise his revolver to fire at it when he thought better of it, as he did not want to arouse the household if he could conquer his man without making a noise.

"Don't shoot," said the man, who had observed Ted's motion with the gun.

At this extraordinary request Ted paused.

He had twisted the man's wrist until he dropped the knife, and then shoved it beyond reach with the muzzle of his revolver.

His strong left hand was in the nape of the fellow's neck, and Ted had his nose ground into the rug. He had found a gun in the fellow's hip pocket, and relieved him of it.

Then Ted rose, and told his captive to get up

Slowly he did so, and Ted made him move to the center of the room.

Bud's golden head appeared around the corner of the doorway.

Ted could just distinguish it.

"Who's that?" asked Bud.

"It's Ted. Come in and strike a light. I've caught something."

In a moment a light flared up.

"Jack Farley!" exclaimed Ted, in astonishment.

"Yes, blast you, Jack Farley," replied the youth.

"Couldn't keep away, eh?"

"A feller'd think thet once was enough," said Bud.

"I couldn't help myself. I had to come," growled Farley.

"Well, this time you'll stay. You shan't abuse our hospitality again. Bud, get a rope and tie our friend. He's skittish, and is likely to run away if he's turned loose."

Farley was soon tied securely.

"Keep an eye on him, Bud," said Ted. "I want to look over the premises."

Ted went directly to the corner and pushed back the pivot door, struck a match, and looked into the box.

It was empty.

Then, turning back to Farley, he searched him thoroughly.

There was no money in his pockets.

Ted called up Kit, and the three of them ransacked the living room thoroughly, but not a dollar could be found. "What did you do with the money you stole from that hole?" said Ted, gazing fiercely into Farley's eyes.

"I haven't seen a dollar of it," was the reply.

CHAPTER XI
TED STRONG HAS A THEORY

After Farley had been securely locked up in a storeroom without windows, they went to bed, feeling secure that there would be no further attempt to enter the house that night.

At breakfast they discussed the robbery after their guests had left the house.

"I don't understand what became of the money," said Ted. "It looks to me like one of those mysterious robberies, and the capture of Farley puts it up to the Riley and Creviss gang. Now that we've been touched personally we will take some interest in the gang, and I have a large crayon picture of about a dozen hitherto respectable young fellows learning useful trades in a reformatory institution."

"But that doesn't bring back our money, neither does it tell us how it was stolen or what became of it," said Ben.

"I can't get a thing out of Farley," said Ted. "I tackled him this morning as soon as I got up, but he wouldn't open his mouth. My belief is that he is in deadly fear of some one, probably Skip Riley."

"Well, we've got him where the hair is short, anyway," said Kit. "He was caught in the act, and will come out of prison an older and a wiser man."

"What else besides Farley did you see in the room, Ted?" asked Stella.

"I really couldn't say what it was," said Ted. "It was dark, and there was only the faintest kind of light outside from the stars. The room was perfectly dark. I was sitting on Farley's back holding him down. He had thrown the door open, and we were in the doorway, but there was a space between us and the door-jamb.

"Suddenly I heard a faint noise beside me and could just see something scud past me onto the veranda."

"What did it look like?"

"It was about as high as a small dog, only shorter and thicker than a dog, and ran with a clumsy, heavy, sideways motion."

"Are you sure it was a dog?"

"No, I'm not sure, for I didn't see it plainly. All I could see was that it looked like some kind of an animal, but just what kind I couldn't determine."

"Your description would lead me to believe that it was a coon."

"No, I don't think it was a coon, or I would have been able to distinguish it by its smell."

"I didn't know but that it might be a coon trained to steal and sneak out. I've heard of such things, and it is by no means impossible, for you know that coons, like crows, are natural-born thieves."

"By Jove, that gives me an idea. I think it was a dog, and that its strange gait was due to the fact that the money had been tied upon him so that he would get away with it in case Farley was caught."

"No, the dog theory is wrong. What about a trained monkey?" Stella looked around the table to see how this was taken.

"C'rect!" shouted Bud. "Stella, yer struck ther problem a solar plexus thet time."

"That does seem reasonable, and if it is true it solves the mysterious robberies of the Strongburg Trust Company's office, the post office, and Creviss' bank," said Ted.

"It's worth looking into, anyway," said Ben. "Now I wonder if there is such a thing as a trained monkey in my marvelous and magnificent gathering of the splendors of the Orient out there. By Jove, I'm going through that camp with a fine-tooth comb, and if I find a monk, I'll habeas-corpus him, and we'll hang him to the rafters."

"Well, mum's the word about the money," warned Ted. "We don't want this thing to leak out. If it does, there's a chance against us."

Although they all felt pretty blue about the loss of the money, they had nothing but hearty welcomes and smiles for their guests, who began to arrive from all parts of the county, and from far-distant States and Territories, to help rejoice with the boys for a prosperous year, not knowing that all the prosperity had fallen into the hands of thieves.

The grounds about the ranch house had been gayly decorated for the occasion. An enormous American flag flapped and snapped in the fresh breeze from the top of a tall staff in front of the house, and the Belle Fourche band was playing in a gayly decorated stand. The showmen had erected their tents, and already the boys and girls from the ranches and towns were going in and out, witnessing the wonders to be beheld in them.

Stella was receiving her girl guests on the veranda, for she was a great favorite among the cowgirls in the country on account of her friendliness and unaffected ways.

Mrs. Graham was welcoming the older women, while Ted and Jack Slate were shaking hands with the ranchmen and cowboys.

Clay's fires were going well, and the steer and sheep were being roasted for the noontime feast.

Ben had gone on a still-hunt among the tents belonging to the showman, and, while he found three small dogs, there was no sign of a monkey, and by adroit questioning he learned that they had had a monkey, but that it had died at Leadville, because the air in that altitude was too cold and rare for it.

These facts he communicated to Ted, and seemed to explode the monkey-thief theory.

During the morning there was a baseball game between the cowboys and the clerks from the stores in Soldier Butte and Strongburg, in which the score was forty-one to three in favor of the clerks. The cowboys couldn't play ball any more than a rabbit, encumbered as they were by their chaps, high-heeled boots, and spurs. It took a home-run hit to get one of them to first base.

After dinner the cowboy sports were to come off.

When Ted could get away from his duties as host for a few minutes he sauntered through the crowd, extending greetings to all whom he knew, but at the same time keeping a close watch over everything.

The theft of the money from the cubby-hole had aroused in him all his detective instincts.

He saw two or three of the young fellows who had been with Wiley Creviss the night of the ball, but he paid no attention to them. They were welcome to come to the festivities, and to remain so long as they behaved themselves.

But he determined to have them watched.

Soon he came upon some more of the Creviss gang and saw them mingle with several boys, whom he knew to be tough characters, from Strongburg.

"The clan is gathering," he said to himself. "We're likely to have trouble with those fellows before the day is over. I'll put Bud next to them, and have the boys watch them."

"Whom do you suppose I saw just now?"

It was Stella's voice, and she was standing at his elbow.

"Who?" he asked.

"Wiley Creviss."

"Is that so? I have been watching for him to come along. A lot of his fellows are here, and they are sticking pretty well together. Where did you see him?"

"I told Ben I'd take in his show even if no one else did, and I've kept my promise. When I was in that biggest tent I suddenly came upon Creviss in close conversation with the boss showman. When they saw me looking at them they separated in a hurry, and Creviss left the tent."

"H'm! I wonder if Ben knows this fellow who owns the show."

"Don't know, I'm sure. It wouldn't be a bad scheme to find out something about him in view of the robbery last night."

"You're right, Stella. Another thing I've been thinking about: I've been looking for Skip Riley, the Strongburg fireman, the supposed leader of the Flying Demons. If they are going to try any of their monkey business to-day he ought to be here."

"Haven't you heard the news? I intended to tell you, but must have forgotten. The last time I was in Strongburg I heard that Riley had resigned, and left the town for the East."

"I hadn't heard it. Then that puts it up to Creviss."

"But who is the fellow who runs the show? Ben says his name is Colonel Ben Robinson, and that he is an old circusman down on his luck temporarily."

"Look around and find out what you can. They will not suspect you if you ask questions as they would me. If you find out anything, let me know."

"All right, Ted, I'll circulate, and report."

Ted wandered over to the show tents, and entered them all, with kindly greetings to the performers, who all knew him as the leader of the broncho boys, and asked him if they could be excused from performing while the riding and other cowboy stunts were going forward, and Ted told them to lay off if they wanted to, as most of the guests would be out in the grand stand, anyhow.

In the last tent he entered he found the strong man lifting weights against a lot of husky cow-punchers, and the giant and midget.

But it was the midget that struck him most forcibly. He had a sly, cunning face and a bad eye, and when Ted came in he tried to hide behind the giant, who picked him up as one would a baby in arms. But the little fellow wriggled free and climbed down the big man like a monkey down a tree. Then he slipped across to the middle of the tent and shinned up the pole to the top, and hung there, looking down at Ted.

"What's the matter with the little fellow?" Ted asked the giant.

"Oh, he ain't got real good sense," rumbled the giant. "His brain stopped growing with his body, I reckon. But you can teach him tricks the same as you can a dog or a monkey, and he'll do them all right. I reckon he's afraid of you. He is of some people, the boss in particular."

"How long have you been with the boss?"

"Not very long. He just took the show over from the old boss a month ago. We were going to pieces over to Cheyenne, and he come along and bought us. He's been a showman in his time, but says he hasn't been in the biz for several years. He knows the biz, though, and has scads of money. We are well fed and get our salaries regular. Him and Prince Carl, that's the midget, are great pals. The midget sleeps in his tent, and the boss seldom lets him out of his sight."

"Say, Bellows, how many times have I got to tell you not to stand there gassing with patrons of the show? Every one don't want to bother with your theories and troubles." Ted turned, to face the boss showman.

"Oh, it's you, Mr. Strong?" he went on. "I didn't recognize your back. It's all right to talk to you. But I've got to call the giant down once in so often for taking up people's time, for he's an awful gabber."

He walked away, but when Ted tried to get the giant to tell him some more about the midget and the boss, he would not say a word.

But the giant had planted the seed of a theory in Ted's mind.

Presently Ted saw Stella beckoning to him in the crowd, and forced his way to her side.

She took his arm, and they got out of the crowd. Ted saw that she had something to communicate.

"Well?" he said, smiling down on her.

"There's going to be something doing here," said she. "The boss showman has been talking with several of the gang."

"All right. Did you hear anything about Skip Riley?"

"Yes. He's been gone from Strongburg about a month."

"Learn anything else about him?"

"Skip Riley is not his name at all."

"That so? What is it? Did you learn?"

"I was talking to a lady from Strongburg, one of those who got him a job on the fire department."

"What did she know about him?"

"She said that she was appointed a committee of one by the Ladies' Aid Society over there to look up the new fireman's career."

"And I suppose she ran onto some hot stuff?"

"It seems that the ex-convict, Skip Riley, had been a circus performer once upon a time, before he took to being a burglar."

"Was burglary the crime for which he was put in prison?"

"Yes, so she says. He was an aëronaut and acrobat."

"Good! And what was his stage name? Did she say?"

"Robinson—Ben Robinson. She says that she was told that he was quite famous in his day as a circus performer, but that he couldn't resist the temptation to steal, and so had to quit the business, as none of the circus proprietors would have him around."

"Did she say where she got this information?"

"Yes. It was sent to her by the warden of the penitentiary in which Riley was confined before he came to Strongburg."

"Then her information is probably correct. Stella, thanks to you, we've got them dead to rights. We've solved the mystery hanging around all these recent robberies."

"Nearly, but not quite. How were they accomplished?"

"That I don't know positively, but I have a theory which I believe will turn out to be correct."

"But about Riley?"

"Ben Robinson, the proprietor of this show, and Skip Riley, burglar and ex-convict, are one and the same man."

CHAPTER XII
ALOFT AFTER A PRISONER

"All ready for the big show," cried Kit, riding up to Ted. "When will we begin the sports?"

Ted looked over the grand stand, which was built around an arena in which the cowboy sports were to come off.

This was the most important event of the day, for while bronchobusting and cattle roping are a cowboy's business, yet he finds unending amusement in doing these same things if his girl and friends are there to witness his skill.

After some ordinary feats of trick riding by the visiting cowboys, several really dangerous steers were turned loose in the arena, and for several minutes a very fair imitation of a Spanish bullfight, minus the killing of the animals, took place.

After several of the steers had been roped, thrown, and tied, there still remained in the arena a sullen and difficult brute, which was as tricky as a rat, and the boys gave him up one at a time.

"Why don't you give the girls a chance at him?" shouted a cowgirl derisively, from the seats.

"Any girl who wants to tackle him is at liberty to do so," Ted shouted back through his megaphone.

Instantly three girls leaped into the arena, and borrowed ponies from their cowboy acquaintances.

Ted motioned to Sophy Cozak, the pretty and buxom girl from the Bohemian prairie, whom Bud had admired at the dance; she rode forward on Bud's own particular horse, Ranger.

Sophy had several brothers who had taught her the cow business, and she had few equals on the range.

As she rode out she was greeted with a round of applause from her admirers. She gathered up her rope and sent the horse forward at an easy lope toward the steer, which looked at her a moment and trotted off.

Sophy followed him, and made three casts of the rope, and every time the brute dodged it, and the rope fell to the ground.

That settled it with Sophy, and she rode in, and another girl took her place. She, too, was unsuccessful, as was the third, and the audience was distinctly disappointed.

"Ladies and gentlemen," cried Ted, through the megaphone. "It was not the intention of any one living on the Moon Valley Ranch to take part in these contests, but if there are no other young ladies in the grand stand who would like to try their ropes on the steer, we can produce one whom we think can rope and tie it at the first trial. I refer to Miss Stella Fosdick. I have not consulted her wishes in the matter, but will ask her if she will undertake it."

At this a wild cheer went up, and Ted dashed out of the arena to find Stella. In a moment he was back, and announced that Miss Fosdick would try it.

Presently Stella rode in on Custer at a hard gallop, gathering up her rope as she rode. There was a sort of gay self-confidence in her manner that captivated the throng, and the cheers split the air.

Stella rode straight at the steer, which, seeing her approach; galloped down the arena with her in pursuit.

Swinging her rope above her head, she chased it back until it was about in the middle of the field, and suddenly the rope left her hand unerringly and shot through the air, seemed to hesitate for an instant, then fell over the steer's head.

Custer came to a stop the moment the rope left her hand, with his body well braced. The steer went to the end of the rope as fast as it could go, then was flung in the air, and lay upon his back sprawling like some ridiculous four-legged crab, while the girl leaped from her saddle, ran swiftly across the intervening space, tied his legs together, and held up her hand.

The crowd fairly went wild with enthusiasm at her feat, as she mounted again, leaving the steer to the tender mercies of the cow-punchers, who flocked about her. Then she dashed out of the arena, waving her hat in recognition of the applause.

Then the bunch of wild Montana horses, which never had felt the saddle, were driven in, and Ted offered a twenty-dollar gold piece to any puncher who could rope, saddle, and bridle, and ride one of the bronchos ten minutes without being thrown.

"Easy money!" shouted the cowboys, flocking into the arena.

The black, which had caused Ted so much trouble when the bunch first came to the ranch, was not with them. He was considered too dangerous an animal to be handled at an entertainment where there were so many women and children.

Only two cow-punchers succeeded in even getting their saddles on the bronchos without throwing them and hog-tying them, and only one, Billy Sudden, stayed the required ten minutes, and he said afterward that it wasn't his fault, because the broncho wouldn't let him get off.

Ted then announced that there was another animal in the herd that he would ask no man to ride, but that he would try to do so himself.

Another great cheer went up as Ted rode away after the black demon, to whom the boys had given the name Lucifer, for his supposed resemblance to his satanic majesty.

But it was found impossible to drive Lucifer into the arena.

"Never mind," said Ted, "we'll throw the saddle on him here, and I'll ride him in."

A crowd of men and boys was standing around, and Ted removed his saddle and handed it to a young fellow in the crowd to hold until he had thrown Lucifer. The animal was standing in the center of the circle, his wary eyes taking in the crowd, and letting fly with his heels at the approach of any one.

"Now, Bud," called Ted, "ride in on him and rope him. You, Kit, get him by the leg and throw him, and I'll slip a bridle on him."

It was not much of a trick to rope and hold him so that he couldn't kick. But when Ted tried to slip the bit between his teeth, he fought like the demon that he was, biting and kicking, so that he had to be thrown to his side and his head held down before the bridle could be put on him.

Then he was allowed to rise. There was no doubt but that the horse was insane with rage and fear, and several cowmen came forward and tried to persuade Ted from attempting to ride him, but Ted was as obstinate as the horse, and said that he would conquer the black, or die in the attempt.

He finally found the fellow who had been holding his saddle, although he had left his stand and was found back behind the crowd talking to a gang of young fellows, among whom Ted recognized several of Creviss' companions. This delayed and angered him, and he called the saddle bearer down for deserting his post, and was answered with sneers and laughter.

After many trials, and the exertion of a great deal of patience, Ted got the saddle on Lucifer and hastily cinched, and as he sprang to the brute's back the ropes were loosed. With a bound and a snort of terror the black dashed forward, and it was with the greatest difficulty that Ted swung it so it went through the gates and into the arena without dashing him against the posts.

Once inside the arena, the brute began to exhibit terrible ferocity.

Stella and Bud had followed in his wake, and when the girl saw how the brute was behaving, she whispered to Bud:

"That demon will kill him yet."

"If he don't kill it," answered Bud.

"Why did you let him ride it? I got there a moment too late, and he was already in the saddle, or I should have stopped it."

"What could I do? He had told the people he would ride it, and that settled it with him."

Lucifer was exercising all the tricks known to wild and terrified bronchos when they first feel saddle and bridle, and which seem to be inbred in them. He bucked, but there was never a horse that could buck Ted off. He reared, he kicked, rolled, and fell backward. But every time he stopped for a moment to note the result, there the unshakable enemy was on his back again. Clearly he was puzzled.

Then a new paroxysm of rage would shake him, and he would go through the same performances again, but with no better success.

Suddenly Ted brought his quirt down on the brute's flanks, and it leaped high into the air in an agony of fear and pain. It had felt that stinging thing before, and hated it.

Then it started to run away from this terrible thing that bestrode its back.

"By Heaven! it's running away," muttered Bud. "It'll be an act o' Providence if Ted isn't killed."

Down the arena they dashed, Ted sitting in the saddle as if he and it and the stallion were all of a piece.

When the brute came to the arena's end, and saw before him the shouting multitude, it suddenly swerved to come back, and Ted realized that something had happened to the saddle. It was slipping, and yet he was sure he had cinched it tight. Back they came tearing again, and passed Stella and Bud like a rocket.

"Great guns!" cried Bud, "his saddle's loose. He's a goner now, shore."

Every one saw Ted's danger, for Ted was leaning well over, and the saddle was on the horse's side. A hollow groan went up.

At Bud's first words Stella was off after Ted like a shot.

The horse, as every one could now see, was trying its best to kill Ted, and many of the spectators were positive that it would do so.

Now the cinch had parted.

"The cinch has broken," the shout went up. "It will kill him, sure!" Ted was now leaning far over on the horse's side, his left leg well under the horse's belly and his foot in the stirrup, while the heel of his left, boot was clinging to the edge of the tipped saddle. It was a most precarious position, for if the saddle slipped farther he would go under and be trampled and kicked to death before any one could reach him.

The powerful brute was bent on Ted's destruction, and seemed about to accomplish it, when Stella galloped to his side, and, grasping his hand, held him safe.

"The cinch is off," she called to him. "I'll help you up, then kick the saddle loose."

Slowly but surely Ted worked himself up until he could release his foot from the stirrup. Then, with a sudden wrench that almost pulled Stella to the ground, he was again on top. With a kick he sent the saddle to the ground, and was riding bareback, while the brute stumbled and almost went to his knees as the saddle fell between his legs.

But now Ted took charge of the situation. With quirt and spur he drove the beast here and there, punishing it, giving it no rest, allowing it to do nothing in its own way until it staggered and heaved and swayed with fatigue and lack of breath, and yet he urged it.

"He'll kill that horse yet," said Billy Sudden.

"No, he knows what that horse will stand, and he's going to make him stand it," said Bud.

The people had never seen such riding as this, and when they realized that Ted had conquered the stallion and was now rubbing it in, they shouted until their throats cracked.

At last the horse could go no farther, and Ted let it stop, as he slipped to the ground and gave the brute a slap with his hand.

"I reckon you'll know better next time, old fellow," was all he said, and walked to where his saddle was lying.

As he picked it up, he was seen to stop and look at the cinch carefully, then hurry to where the boys were awaiting him.

"Fellows," he said solemnly, throwing the saddle on the ground, "that cinch did not break, it was cut."

A dozen of the boys leaped to the ground and examined the cinch.

It was true. The cinch had been cut almost through with a sharp knife, and the strain upon it had parted it. There could be no doubt as to what had been intended.

As Stella came riding up, she shouted:

"The cinch was cut. I saw it. Wiley Creviss did it. I didn't realize at the time what he was doing or know that it was Ted's saddle, and when I did find out, he was mounted and away."

A howl of indignation went up at this.

"Scatter out, boys, and round up Creviss," shouted Billy Sudden. "We know what to do with him when he's caught."

Ted's adventure with Lucifer ended the performances in the arena, and, as the balloon was inflated and ready to ascend, the people flocked to where it was straining at the ropes.

Ted had mounted Sultan again, and left the arena surrounded by Stella and the boys.

"Who's going up in her?" asked Ted.

"Ben Robinson, the boss," answered Ben.

"Do you know who he is?" asked Ted.

Ben stared at him without replying.

"I'll tell you," said Ted. "He's Skip Riley, thief and ex-convict, the leader of the Flying Demons. He is the man who caused us to lose our money last night, and who engineered all the mysterious robberies hereabouts. Do you reckon he intends to come back?"

Ben's eyes started from their sockets in surprise.

"I—I don't know," he stammered. "By Jove! we must stop him. Maybe he's going to skip."

The boys had crowded about Ted as he spoke.

"We'll have to hurry if we get him," shouted Ben. "He's in the basket now."

With shouts of warning Ted and the boys pushed their horses through the crowd, which rushed aside to let them through.

They could see Skip Riley lift a large tin box into the basket from the ground. As he was getting ready to start there was a shrill cry, and the midget came waddling through the crowd and climbed over the side of the car and up Riley's body until it clung to his shoulder like a monkey. A great many of the thoughtless laughed at this. They did not understand the significance of the move.

"Get ready to cut her loose," shouted Riley.

Two or three men stood by with sharp knives in their hands.

Riley saw Ted and the boys pushing rapidly through the crowd.

"Cut her loose!" shouted Riley, and the balloon shot upward, amid the shouts of the people.

"Too late,'" said Ben.

"Not yet," cried Ted, spurring through the crowd.

A long guide rope was dragging from the car of the balloon.

"Follow me, Bud. The balance of you catch Creviss and the rest of them. I'm going with Riley."

Before they knew exactly what he meant, Ted grasped the guide rope as it passed over his head, and was swung out of the saddle and dangled in the air, to the horror of the people, who expected to see him fall and be dashed to pieces at any minute, for the balloon had shot up rapidly and was now several hundred feet above the ground.

But Riley, looking over the country and taking account of the direction in which the balloon was traveling, was unaware that he had taken on another passenger.

Hand over hand Ted climbed steadily, until at last he reached the car and looked over the edge of it.

Riley's back was toward him, and noiselessly Ted slipped over the side and into the basket.

Then the midget happened to turn his head, and saw Ted and uttered a frightened cry, which brought Riley around so that he found himself looking into the cold, dark bore of Ted's forty-four.

"Got you!" said Ted coolly.

"How did you get here?" said Riley, trying to smile. "If I'd known that you wanted to come I'd have waited for you."

"I don't think," said Ted. "But now we'll go down."

"No, I've got to give the people a run for their money. We must go a little farther."

"I said we'd go down."

"But we can't until the gas gets cool and exhausts. I have no escape valve."

"Then I'll shoot a hole in the bag. I guess we'll go down then."

"For Heaven's sake, don't do that! You'd blow us all to pieces."

"Then down with her. I mean what I say."

Riley looked at Ted for a moment, then pulled a string. There followed a hissing noise, and the balloon began to sink, slowly at first, then more rapidly.

Ted did not dare take his eyes off Riley to see how close they were to the ground. But he heard the Moon Valley long yell, and knew that they were near the earth, and that Bud Morgan was not far away.

Suddenly the car bumped on the ground, bounced and struck again, then stopped, and Ted heard Bud's cheerful voice right behind him.

"Jumpin' sand hills, so yer got him, eh? Come, climb out," said Bud to Riley, "we need yer on terry firmy."

"Cover him, Bud, while I search him. If he makes a break, kill him. He's an ex-convict, so don't take any chances with him," said Ted.

Riley yielded up a gun and a knife and then he was hustled out of the car, with the midget still clinging to him, and Ted took charge of the tin box.

Billy Sudden and some of his men had come up, and so had Ben and Kit, and Riley was conducted back to the ranch house strongly guarded.

Once inside with their prisoners and the boys, Ted closed the doors on the curious crowd. The first thing he did was to open the tin box. On top were the packages of bills stolen from the cubby-hole, and beneath it a large amount of money and the bonds taken from the Strongburg Trust Company, as well as registered letters from which the money had not yet been extracted, and a large amount of brand-new treasury notes which answered the description of the government funds stolen from Creviss' bank.

"It's all here," said Ted, "and the evidence is complete."

"But how did he manage to do it without leaving a mark or a broken lock behind him?" asked Ben.

"How? By means of this," and Ted placed his hand on the head of the midget, who shrank from him with a snarling cry.

"Still I don't understand it."

"The day I saw him in the Creviss bank he marched out with the plunder under my very eyes. The day before the robbery this fellow went into the bank with the dwarf in his valise. Wiley Creviss was alone. The valise was opened, and the dwarf slipped out of the valise and into the vault, and concealed himself.

"During the night the dwarf collected all the money and bonds he could, and made himself comfortable. When it came time for the bank to open in the morning he again concealed himself, and remained in hiding until noon, when Wiley Creviss again came on watch while the cashier went to dinner. Then Riley, here, entered with his valise, and the dwarf crept into it, and was carried out of the bank with the money."

"But what had the midget to do with the theft of our money?"

"That's simple. Farley and the dwarf were to do the job. The dwarf was sent up to the roof, for he can climb like a monkey, and came down the chimney and opened the door for Farley. That was a mistake, for they would not have been caught, except for Farley."

"How did they know where you hid the money?"

"The dwarf saw us through the window, and Kit saw him, but I thought it was all imagination. That was how they robbed the post office. The dwarf was lowered down the chimney. That is about the size of it. Am I correct, Riley?"

"Correct enough, so far as I'm concerned. I guess it's back to 'the stir' for me. But this midget didn't know what he was doing, and ought to be sent to an asylum instead of the prison," said Riley.

At that moment there was a great commotion without, and a crowd of cowboys rode up. In the center of the circle made by them was Wiley Creviss and several of his gang. In all, with Riley and the dwarf, there were eight of them in custody, and without ado they were hurried to the Strongburg jail.

The United States marshal was in Strongburg when Ted came in with his prisoners.

"What is all this, Strong?" asked the marshal.

"That bank-robbing gang you ordered me to bring in," answered Ted.

"You made quick work of it. Get any of the money?"

"All of it. It is in the Strongburg bank. You see, they made the mistake of robbing us last night. But for that they would have got away, and we would have had a hard time catching them. As it was, they walked right in to us."

Skip Riley went back to the penitentiary for a long term of years, and the midget was sent to an asylum for the feeble-minded.

Jack Farley turned State's evidence, and Creviss and ten other young reprobates were sent to a reformatory.

As for Lucifer, he turned out, next to Sultan and Custer, the best horse on the ranch.

CHAPTER XIII
THE ANONYMOUS LETTER

A very short time after the capture of Skip Riley, Ted Strong was standing in the waiting room of the Union Station at St. Louis, the metropolis of Missouri, whither he had been summoned by a letter from the chief of the United States secret service.

He was waiting for Bud Morgan, who had gone to the baggage room to inquire about a trunk which had become lost on the way from Moon Valley, and which contained a number of valuable papers, including both their commissions as deputy United States marshals.

The enormous waiting room was crowded with passengers from the incoming trains, with which the numerous tracks were full from end to end.

As Ted Strong leaned over the iron railing, looking down into the lower waiting room, he was conscious that a woman had stepped to his side. Glancing up sideways, he saw that close to him was a very beautiful young girl, who wore a traveling cloak of pearl gray, and a long feather boa, which the draft had blown across his sleeve.

His glance intercepted one from her, and not wishing her to think that he was idly staring at her, he directed his gaze once more to the surging crowd below. As his eyes wandered over the throng, he saw a man look up, and make the most imperceptible gesture with his head.

He did not know the man. Turning swiftly to the young lady at his side, he caught sight of a smile and a slight uplifting of her eyebrows.

Undoubtedly a signal had passed between the two, and Ted, not wishing to be an eavesdropper, looked away again. But in the swift glance he had given the young girl—for now he saw that she was little else—he made a mental note of her. The gray eyes with the long, dark lashes, the oval face, beautiful in shape and of an ivory tint; the scarlet, curving lips, the slender, trim figure, and the strange, subtle perfume which she exhaled, one would never forget.

He also noted the appearance of the man who had signaled the girl.

The man was five feet seven inches in height; his face was well rounded, but not too fat. He had a brown, pointed beard; the eyes were pale, almost colorless; the forehead, broad and high, a fact which Ted noted when the man lifted his hat to wipe his brow. He had the air of a well-bred man of the world, and was probably a resident of New York. There was something familiar about the man that made Ted think that he had seen him before.

Ted saw Bud come through the door into the waiting room from the midway of the station, look up and wave his hand, with a frown and a shake of the head that told him his pard's quest for the missing baggage had been fruitless.

At the same time, the girl at his side seemed to bump into him, and as he turned to her she muttered an apology and hurried away. Although he followed her with his eyes a few moments, she was soon lost in the crowd.

He slipped his hands into the pockets of his jacket, and, with his back to the railing, prepared to wait until Bud reached him.

As his left hand sank into his pocket, his fingers came in contact with a piece of paper.

He knew that he had not placed the paper in his pocket, and glanced around with his usual caution to see if any one was watching him. He saw that wonderful pair of gray eyes with the dark lashes—Irish eyes, he called them—watching him over the shoulders of a man a dozen feet away in the crowd. But the moment the woman realized that she was being observed, she disappeared.

"Deuced strange," he muttered to himself, fumbling with the paper, which he had not withdrawn from his pocket. "That girl placed this paper in my pocket. I wonder why. There is something out of the way here, for the paper was not there before she stood beside me."

One less wise than Ted, and not so modest, might have thought that the girl was trying to flirt with him. But to Ted there was something more important and mysterious than that in her actions.

If he read them aright, she had placed the paper in his pocket when she apparently accidentally bumped into him, and had gone away only to come back to see if he had discovered it.

Although he searched the crowd with eager eyes, he did not see her again, and was confident that she had disappeared as soon as she had accomplished her mission, which was to convey some message to him.

Although he was somewhat curious to know what, if anything, was written on the paper, he restrained himself until he could be alone, for he did not know who might be in that crowd looking for just such a move on his part.

Just then Bud brushed his way through the crowd and came up to Ted.

"Them things ain't come yit," he said, in a tone of discontent, "an' me stranded in St. Looey with no more clean shirt than a rabbit."

"You can easily get a clean shirt," said Ted, "but it's not so easy to get a new commission. That's what's worrying me, for there is no telling how soon we may need one."

"Well, let's git out o' this mob, er I'll begin ter beller an' mill, an' if they don't git out o' my way I'll cause sech a stampede thet it'll take ther police all day ter round 'em up ag'in."

Ted said nothing to Bud about the paper he had discovered in his pocket, but picked up his valise. They then made their way to the street and rode uptown in a car, where they registered at a quiet hotel.

Ted went immediately to the room assigned to him, locked the door, and drew out the paper.

He could not conceive what it would contain, for he was far above the vanity of thinking that the young woman who had stood by his side would interest herself in him enough to write him a silly note.

"The man with the pointed beard!" thought Ted.

Of course, it was he who had caused the note to be slipped into his pocket.

But why?

Taking a chair by the window, he slowly opened the note, observing at the time that the same fragrance came from it as had filled the air while the girl stood beside him in the station.

It was a sheet of pale-blue letter paper folded three times.

In the upper left-hand corner was an embossed crest, the head of a lion rampant, and beneath it a dainty monogram, which he made out to be "O. B. N.," or any one of the combinations of those letters. He could not tell which combination was the correct one.

The writing was in a fashionable feminine hand, and written with a pencil.

It was as follows:

"T. S.: This is a friendly warning from one who dare not communicate with you personally, for reasons which you will discover and understand later on, if things turn out as we" — the word "we" had been scratched out and "I" written above it — "anticipate. Be very careful while you are in St. Louis. Do not go on the streets alone, and go armed. Your mission is known, and you will be watched by persons who will seek to get you out of the way. We — that is, I, also know of your mission, and take this means of warning you of your danger, as you have done me services in the past without knowing it. Now, the sting of this note lies in this, and don't forget it, don't get into any fights, no matter what the provocation, for I have it straight that that, is the lay to do you. If you do so, not being able to avoid it, shoot straight, and you will come out all right in the end. I will see to that part of it at the right time.

"A FRIEND."

Ted read the letter through three times, trying to clarify it, but each time his mind became more confused over it.

What did it mean, and how could any stranger know his business when he had not told a soul about it?

Even Bud did not know why they were in St. Louis; that is, he did not know the real reason. Ostensibly, they were there to inspect the local horse market.

There was a loud rap on the door, and Ted went to it and unlocked it. Throwing the door open, he saw a stranger standing on the threshold, just about to step in.

He looked at Ted in apparent surprise, then up at the number on the door, but his eyes fell to the letter which Ted still held in his hand, and he stared at it like one fascinated.

Ted noticed this, and put the letter behind his back.

As the stranger did not speak, Ted broke the spell by saying, in a sarcastic tone:

"Well?"

"Oh, I beg your pardon," said the stranger hastily, "but isn't Mr. Fowle in? I expected him to come to the door, and was surprised to see you, don't you know."

"I don't know any Mr. Fowle," said Ted, with a smile that must have told the stranger that he was not taken in by the question.

The fellow threw a quick glance around the room, but did not retreat from his place in the doorway.

Ted was starting to shut the door, considering the incident closed, when the stranger, who was a large, powerful man, well dressed and with the air of a prosperous business man, started to enter.

"This is not Mr. Fowle's room; it is mine," said Ted, blocking the way,

"I'll just step in and wait for him," said the man. "The clerk downstairs said it was his room."

"Wait a minute," said Ted sternly. "I don't know you, and I don't know Fowle. If you have any business with me, state it from the hall."

The warning in the letter flashed through his mind.

Suddenly the man sprang upon Ted, and they fell to the floor together.

"Give me that letter, curse you!" hissed the man, "I saw you get it, and I saw it just now. Give it to me, I tell you."

Ted had managed to put the letter back into his pocket. His right arm was twisted under his body, and he could not release it.

He looked up into the face of the man, who was straddling his body, and saw a gleam of malignant hatred in his eyes.

"Let me up, you cur," said Ted.

"After I get the letter," was the reply.

"It's a private letter, and not for you. Let me up!"

Now Ted saw that the man had a knife in his hand—a long, keen knife, with a pearl hilt and a silver guard.

"If you don't give me that letter at once, you'll not get another chance, but I'll have it," snarled the man.

Ted began to struggle, but he soon saw that he could do nothing with one arm out of commission. The man was not only powerful, but heavy, and it was all Ted could do to more than wriggle his body.

"I tell you you shan't have it," said Ted.

The knife went above the man's head, and in the wielder's face was a look of the most diabolical hatred Ted had ever seen in a human countenance.

"For the last time," said the man hoarsely.

There was something about the fellow's actions that told Ted he was desperate, yet at the same time afraid of the act he was about to commit.

The knife was about to descend when Ted cried out an alarm, the first he had sounded.

He heard some one running in the hall. His assailant heard it, also, and hesitated, looking around with frightened eyes.

"Yi-yipee!" It was Bud's voice, and Ted breathed a prayer of thankfulness.

"I'll give it to you, anyhow," muttered the man, and again the knife went up in the air.

But it did not make a strike, for at that moment Bud bounded into the room, and, taking in the situation with a lightning glance, his foot flew out, and the toe of his heavy boot struck the man on top of Ted fairly in the ribs. There was a cracking sound, and with a groan the fellow dropped the knife and struggled to his feet.

Rushing at Bud, he bowled that doughty individual over like a tenpin, and dashed into the hall, along which he ran swiftly and lightly, for so large a man.

When Bud had picked himself up and run to the stairway, he could hear the fellow clattering down the stairs three flights below.

"Well, dash my hopes," said Bud, "if he didn't get clear away. He shore treated me like a leetle boy. But I reckon he's in sech a hurry because he's on his way ter a drug store fer a porious plaster fer them ribs o' hisn."

Ted had picked himself up and was rubbing his arm, which had been strained by his falling on it.

"What's this yere all erbout?" asked Bud. "I'm comin' up ter call on yer when I hears yer blat, an' I come runnin', an' what do I see? A large, pale stranger erbout ter explore yer system with er bowie. Yer mixin' in sassiety quicker'n usual, seems ter me."

Ted had picked up the knife, which had fallen beneath the bed, and was looking at it.

"I wonder where this came from," he said, turning it over in his hand.

"Wherever it came from, it's a wicked-lookin' cuss," said Bud. "But what wuz ther feller goin' ter explore yer with it fer?"

"This letter," said Ted, taking the crumpled paper from his pocket and handing it to Bud.

"Jumpin' sand hills, ther plot thickens," said Bud, when he had finished reading it. "I don't seem ter be in it at all. What's it all erbout? Ye've got my coco whirlin' shore."

CHAPTER XIV
THE ABANDONED MOTOR CAR

"I'll tell you," said Ted, "if you'll take a seat and keep quiet until I get the thing straightened out in my own mind, for the incidents of the past hour certainly have got me going."

Bud sat down and waited patiently for Ted, who was thinking deeply.

"I didn't tell you the precise object of our visit to St. Louis," began Ted, "not because I didn't trust your ability to keep a secret, but in order to keep every one else in the dark."

"D'yer mean ter say that ye hev stalled me along ter this town ter give me a leetle airin', an' not ter sell hosses?" asked Bud indignantly.

"Not exactly. I want to sell the horses for the top price, but there was something else behind it."

"A large man astraddle o' ye with a keen an' bitin' bowie at yer throat. Yer must be hard up fer amoosement."

"Not that, either," said Ted, laughing. "I manage to get all the amusement that's coming to me."

"I'm still gropin' fer enlightenment."

"Here goes, then. For a couple of months the trains on the Union Pacific, in Nebraska and Wyoming, have been running the gantlet between bands of train robbers. If a train missed being robbed at one place, it was almost sure to get it at another, especially if it carried wealth of any description."

"But ther railroads is erbout ther biggest chumps ter stand fer all this monkeydoodle business o' train robbin' ez long ez they hev. Why don't they get inter ther exterminatin' business, an' clean up ther last o' them?"

"Too busy making money, I guess. But this time it is not the railroads who are going after them."

"Who is it, me an' you?"

"Almost. By orders of the government."

"That's more like it. I don't hev no love fer a train robber, fer all I ever come in contact with wuz a bunch o' cowardly murderers, who fight like rats when they're cornered, an' kill innercent express messengers fer amoosement er devilment. But if Uncle Sammy sez so, an' needs my help, he's got it right swift an' willin'.'"

"Well, he seems to need it, for just before we left Moon Valley I received a letter from the United States secret service, telling me about the robberies, of which I had heard something, but not much, as they have been kept away from the newspapers as much as possible."

"Hev there been so many of them?"

"As I tell you, they have been so numerous as to lead one to believe that there was a chain of train robbers clear across the continent, and strong and capable robbers they have proved themselves to be."

"Did they git much?"

"They have got away with a vast amount of money belonging to individuals. They seem to have had information in advance of all the big shipments of treasure leaving San Francisco and Carson City, Nevada, as well as of private shipments."

"Wise Injuns, eh?"

"I should say so. They have even been able to spot shipments of United States gold en route from the mints in Frisco and Carson to Washington, and in two instances have got away with it."

"Wow! There's where your Uncle Samuel reaches out his long arms and takes a hand in the game. How much did they get away with?"

"The chief did not say. That is not for us to know, I guess, or he doesn't think it will make any difference with us in our enthusiasm for our work of running down and capturing that gang, or gangs, as the ease may be."

"But it wouldn't do a feller no harm ter know. I'd feel a heap more skittish if I wuz runnin' after a million than if it wuz thirty cents."

"There's something in that, but we won't let it interfere with the performance of our duty."

"How does the chief put it up to us?"

"He tells the facts briefly, and says: 'Go and get the robbers.'"

"That's short an' ter ther p'int. Anything else?"

"He says that the worst bunch of train robbers in ten years has been organized, with men operating on various railroads, and that from past performances it would seem that they had inside and powerful friends who were keeping them informed as to what trains to rob. In other words, the thing seems to be a syndicate of robbers operated and directed from a central point by men of brains and resource."

"An' whar's ther central p'int?"

"St. Louis."

"Ah, I begins ter smell a mice. So yer gradooly led up ter this place, pretendin' ter sell hosses, eh?"

"No; we'll kill two birds with one stone. We'll sell the horses if we can get our price for them, and it will be an excellent cloak to hide our real purpose, which is to try to get next to the headquarters of the train robbers."

"Good idee. But how aire yer goin' ter go erbout it?"

"To tell you the truth, I haven't an idea. We will have to do our own scouting. If the chief knew, it is not likely that he would employ us to find out."

"Thet's so. Well, let's be on ther scout."

"We'll still pose as ranchers with pony stock to sell, and let folks know it. We'll go over to the stockyards right now."

"All right, but the stunt is ter keep our eyes peeled fer ther train-robber syndicate's office."

"That's it. One never can tell when he will run onto just the thing he's looking for when he least expects it."

"We're being shadowed," said Ted, a short time after they had left their hotel and were walking through the streets toward the bridge that spans the Mississippi River to East St. Louis.

"How d'yer know?" asked Bud, sending a cautious eye around.

"See that fellow with the checked suit, on the opposite side of the street?"

"Uh-huh!"

"He's on our trail. Don't give him a hint that we're on to him, and if he chases us all day he'll see that we are what we represent ourselves to be, just plain cow-punchers."

"I'm on."

The man in the checked suit got on the same trolley car with them at the bridge, and while they were walking through the stockyards they saw him frequently, not always in evidence, but always somewhere in their vicinity.

They visited the offices of the commission merchants who dealt in horseflesh, and got their prices for the sort of stock the boys had to sell, and before the day was over they had disposed of six carloads of horses for immediate delivery.

While they were talking the deal over with the purchaser, they noticed that the man in the checked suit hovered around, and Ted purposely permitted him to overhear part of the conversation about the delivery of the ponies.

Ted then sent a telegram to Kit Summers, informing him of the sale, and telling him to select the sort of horses from the herds that were wanted, and to come through with them, bringing a sufficient number of the boys with him to protect the stock and deliver it.

When the operator took the message and began to send it, Ted noticed that the man with the checked suit was leaning against the wall, apparently not paying any attention to what was going on. But Ted knew by the way he was holding his head that he was a telegraph operator also, and that he was reading the message as it went onto the wire.

"Say, Bud, we've had enough of that gentleman for one day, haven't we?"

"I shore hev."

"Then let's give him the slip."

"Easier said than done. Thet thar feller sticks like a leech ter a black eye."

"I think we can do it."

"And how?"

"See that automobile over there? In front of that office."

"I see a long, low, rakish craft painted like an Eyetalian sunset. If thet is yer means o' communication with ther other side o' ther river, oxcuse me."

"Why, what's the matter with that? That's a mighty fine car."

"I reckon it is, but walkin's good ernuf fer me."

"But you'll never walk away from that shadow."

"I'll bet I kin run erway from 'his checkers' before we're halfway ter St. Looey, even if I am a cow-puncher, an' muscle bound from straddlin' a saddle fer so many years."

"What's the use, when we can run away from him in a gasoline wagon. That machine is standing in front of the office of Truax & Wells, and they have sold a lot of cattle for us in times past. It wouldn't surprise me if the car belonged to one or the other of them, and that if we asked for a lift to the other side they would be glad to let us have it."

"All right, if you're so keen on it, tackle 'em. You'll find me game ter ride ther ole thing. I've rid everything from a goat ter a huffier, an' yer kin bet yer gold-plugged tooth I ain't goin' ter welsh fer no ole piece o' machinery."

They entered the office, and were at once greeted by an elderly man, Mr. Truax, in a warm manner. After talking over things in general, Ted said:

"That's a fine car of yours out there, Mr. Truax."

"Funny thing about that car," said the commission merchant. "That's not my car, and nobody seems to know whose car it is."

"That certainly is strange," said Ted. "How does it come to be standing out there?"

"It was this way, and it's a good story, but none of the newspaper boys have been in to-day, and so I couldn't give it out: Right back of us here is a railroad station. There's an eastbound train through here at seven-thirty every morning. She was just pulling into the station this morning as I was unlocking the office door, and I heard a chugging behind me. I looked up, and here came the car with only one man in it. He pulls up short, picks up a bag, which was very heavy, for it was all he could do to stagger along with it.

"The bell on the engine was ringing for the start when he runs through the arcade there as fast as he could with the heavy bag, and just catches the rear of the train as it comes along. He manages to hoist the bag onto the rear platform steps, and is running along trying to get on, and the train picking up speed with every revolution of the wheels. I thought sure he would be left, or killed, for he wouldn't let go, when the conductor came out on the rear platform, saw him, and jerked him aboard by the collar."

"Didn't he say anything about his machine?" asked Ted.

"Not a word. That's what I thought so strange about it. But, thinks I, some one will come for it after a while. Perhaps, thinks I, he was in such a hurry to make the train that he left home without a chauffeur, who will be along when he wakes up."

"And no one has appeared?"

"There she lays, just as he left her. When my partner came down, I spoke to him about it. He's a fan on motoring. That's his car over there; that white one. When I spoke to him about it, he went out and looked it over.

"'That car don't belong here,' says he. 'There's no number of the maker on it, and everything that would serve to identify it has been taken off. Besides, I don't think the license number is on the square.'

"That excited my curiosity, and I called up the license collector's office and asked him whose motor car No. 118 was. In a few minutes he calls me and says it belongs to Mr. Henry Inchcliffe, the banker. I gets Mr. Inchcliffe on the phone and asks him if his car is missing, and he says he can look out of the window as he is talking and see it beside the curb with his wife sitting in it. 'What is the color of your car?' says I. 'Dark green, picked in crimson. Why do you ask?' says he. I tells him that an abandoned car is standing in front of our place with his number on it. But he says he guesses not, for his number looms up like a sore thumb, hanging on the axle of his car in front of the bank, and I rings off. That's the story of the car."

"Since it belongs to no one in particular, I've a mind to borrow it, and put it in a garage over on the other side. It'll be ruined if it stays out here in the weather," said Ted.

"I don't care," said Mr. Truax. "It wasn't left in my care, and I haven't got much use for the blamed thing, anyhow. Take it along. If the owner comes and proves property, I suppose you'll give it up?"

"Sure thing. I'll telephone you the name and address of the garage where I leave it, so that if there is any inquiry for it you may direct inquirers there. But I've got a hunch that this car was thrown away, having served its purpose."

"Great Scott! that's a valuable thing to throw away."

"Yes, but the man who abandoned it probably thought it a good sacrifice."

"How is that?"

"What do you suppose was in that bag he carried?"

"Couldn't say, but it was pretty heavy."

"It would hold a good deal of paper money, wouldn't it?"

"If the bills were of big enough denomination, I should say you could pack away a million in it, for it was a powerful big sack."

"Well, suppose the man whom you saw jump out of the car and get aboard the train had stolen the car, or even if he had owned it, and had made a big haul, and it was contingent upon his getting away with the money that he abandon the car."

"That's possible. But there has been no big robbery to cover that part of the theory."

"You don't know. There may have been a big robbery, and it has not been made public. Not all robberies are reported to the public. If they were, there would be slim chance for the authorities to catch the thieves."

"Perhaps so. Say, Mr. Strong, you're a deputy United States marshal, ain't you?"

"Yes. Both Mr. Morgan and I are in the government service."

"I've been thinking over what you said about a possible robbery, and perhaps you've got it right. I believe you'd better take that car along. You might need it as evidence some day."

"That occurred to me."

"Can you run the pesky thing."

"Yes; I learned to run a motor car long ago. It is, like everything else a fellow can know, mighty useful to me in my business."

"All right, take her along."

The man in the checked suit was nowhere in sight, but as Ted started up the abandoned motor car he came running out of a doorway.

"Hi, there! Come back with that car!" he yelled, running after them in the middle of the road. But Ted let her out a couple of links, and in a moment the man in checks was out of sight.

CHAPTER XV
THE LODGING-HOUSE BATTLE

"What aire ye goin' ter do with ther blamed thing, now yer got it?" asked Bud, as they sped across the Eads Bridge into St. Louis.

"I haven't made up my mind yet. It certainly doesn't belong in this town, and if we use it here we will have to get a local license."

"Jumpin' sand hills, yer not goin' ter run it yere?"

"Why not?"

"Whoever owns it is li'ble ter come erlong some day, an—"

"Then I'll give it to him, if he can prove it is his, but I don't think it will ever be claimed."

"How's that?"

"Because the owner is a thief, and if he finds it is in the hands of an officer he will let it go rather than face an investigation. Besides, I need it."

"Ted Strong, aire yer goin' dotty over them derned smell wagons, too?"

"No, I can't say that I am, but if I lived in a town like this, and could afford it, you bet I'd have one."

"But where aire yer goin' ter keep it? We shore can't take it up ter our room."

"Not exactly," laughed Ted. "You forget that we have friends in this man's town."

"Not a whole heap."

"What's the matter with Don Dorrington?"

"By ginger, that's so. Ther young feller what was with us down in Mexico when we found ther jewels and things under ther president's palace."

"Yes, and we're heading right for his house now."

"What fer? Goin' ter try ter git him inter trouble, too?"

Ted piloted the machine through the thronged downtown streets, and coming at last to Pine Street Boulevard, he let her out, and went skimming over the smooth pavement until he came to Newstead Avenue, and was ringing the bell of Don Dorrington's flat before the astonished Bud could recover his breath from the swift ride.

Dorrington himself came to the door, having looked through the window and seen Ted arrive.

"Well, by all that's glorious," exclaimed Don, as he grasped Ted by the hand. "Where are you from, and why? Hello, Bud, you old rascal! Get out of that car and come in. Where did you get the bubble?"

Ted and Bud entered the house and were taken into Don's workroom, where he was soon put in possession of the facts concerning the motor car, although Ted said nothing about the real object of his visit lo St. Louis.

"Well, what can I do for you?" asked Don.

"Have you a place where I can store this car for a while?" asked Ted.

"I sure have," said Don. "You can run it right into the basement from the back yard. When these flats were built it was intended that the basement be used as a garage, but so far none of the tenants have shown a disposition to get rich enough to buy one. No one will be able to get the machine out of there,"

"That's the only thing I fear," said Ted. "It's a cinch that the owner, if he is a thief who has escaped with a pot of money, as I strongly suspect, will have his pals try to get it back. And I don't want them to get it until I have used it to try to trace them."

"I'll bet a cooky ther feller with ther checked suit wuz after ther machine himself," said Bud. "When we eloped with it he came holler in' after us ter bring it back, but we gave him the glazed look an' left him fannin' ther air in our wake."

The boys rolled the motor car into the basement, which was securely locked. Then Ted and Bud returned to town on a street car.

As they got closer to the downtown section, they could hear the shouts of the newsboys announcing an "extra" newspaper in all the varieties of pronunciation of that word as it issues from the mouths of city "newsies."

"Wonder what the 'extra' is all about?" said Ted.

"Oh, same old thing, I reckon," said Bud. "'All erbout ther turribul disaster.' An' when yer buys a paper yer see in big letters at ther top, 'Man

Kills,' and down below it, 'Mother-in-law!' But in little type between them yer read ther follerin', to wit, 'Cat to spite.' I've been stung by them things before."

"I'm going to buy one, anyway," laughed Ted. "I don't mind being stung for a cent."

He beckoned to a newsboy, bought a paper, and opened it.

"What's this?" he almost shouted.

Great black letters sprawled across the top of the page.

"Express Messenger Found Dead," was the first line, and below it was the confirmation of Ted's belief that a great robbery had taken place. It was "Forty Thousand Dollars Taken from the Safe."

"There's the owner of the abandoned automobile, the fellow who boarded the train with the heavy grip," said Ted to Bud, who was staring over his shoulder.

The article following the startling headlines told the circumstances of the robbery.

The train that entered the Union Station at six o'clock that morning had been robbed in some mysterious manner between a junction a short distance out of St. Louis, where the express messenger had been seen alive by a fellow messenger in another car. When the car was opened in the station, after being switched to the express track, the messenger was found lying on the floor of the car with a bullet through his head. The safe had been blown open and its contents rifled.

The express company had kept silent about the murder and robbery until late in the day, when the body of the messenger was found by a reporter in an undertaker's establishment.

As for the other details, a policeman at the Union Station said that he had noticed a man come out of the waiting room carrying a grip that seemed more than ordinarily heavy. A red motor car was waiting outside the station, and the man got into it and drove away at a fast pace. The policeman had not noticed the number on the car.

How the robber and murderer got into the express car was a mystery, as the car was locked when it was switched into the express track, and there were no marks of a violent entry on the outside of the car.

"What aire yer goin' ter do erbout it?" asked Bud. "Aire yer goin' ter turn over ther motor car an' give yer infermation ter ther police?"

"Not on your life," answered Ted. "At least, not yet. I'm going to work on it a bit myself first."

"But won't Mr. Truax tip it off?"

"I'll warn him not to."

"But how erbout ther feller in ther check suit what wuz so kind an' attentive ter us?"

"He's hiding out, now that the robbery has become public. I'm not afraid of him."

"What's ther first move?"

"Locate and identify the car."

Ted called Mr. Truax up on the telephone. The commission merchant had read about the express robbery, and had connected the man in the red car with it, but promised to say nothing about it until Ted had had an opportunity to unravel the mystery.

Ted lay awake a long time that night thinking the matter over, and in the morning awoke with a plan in his mind.

"Well, hev yer determined what ter do erbout ther red car?" asked Bud at the breakfast table. "I'm shore gittin' sore at myself fer a loafer, sittin' eround here doin' nothin' but eat an' look at ther things in ther stores what I can't buy."

"I've got a scheme that I'm going to try," answered Ted.

"What is it?"

"I'm going to run that car all over this town until I get some of the train-robbing syndicate anxious about it and to following it. Then I'm going to get on to their place of doing business and their methods."

"Wish yer luck," was Bud's cheerless comment.

Bud had been out wandering restlessly around the streets all morning, and Ted was writing letters. When he got through he thought about the missing trunk, and concluded that he would go to the Union Station to see if it had been received.

The words of warning in the note not to go on the street alone were clear in his memory; but this he took to mean at night, for in a crowded street in the daytime he could see no danger.

After he had waited an hour or more for Bud, and the yellow-haired cow-puncher had not returned, Ted decided to delay no longer, and started off at a brisk walk for the station, which was six or seven blocks distant.

His hotel being on Pine Street, he chose that for his route.

He had walked three blocks when he stopped to watch a man who was slightly in advance of him.

It was the fellow he had seen in the checked suit.

He had just come out of a saloon.

In the middle of the block he stopped to talk with another man, who looked as if he worked on the railroad, and Ted loitered in a doorway until the two separated, and the man in the checked suit continued on his way.

A block farther on Ted observed two men standing on the corner talking. A policeman stood on the opposite corner.

The two men on the corner Ted knew instantly for "plain-clothes men," as the headquarters detectives are called.

He was well aware that the police by this time were on the alert to find the express robber and murderer, and knew that every available man on the city detective force was on the watch, like a cat at a rat hole.

To capture the train robber meant a reward and promotion.

Ted stood on the corner opposite the detectives and watched proceedings.

When the man in the checked suit had gone about ten paces beyond the detectives, one of them started after him, and the other signaled the policeman in uniform to cross over.

The detective called to the man in the check suit to halt, but instead of obeying he started to run.

But he had not gone more than ten feet when he was seized by the detective, and was dragged back to the corner.

"Take him to the box, Casey," said the detective, turning his prisoner over to the policeman.

At that moment the two detectives were joined by a third, and they entered into an earnest conversation, drawn closely together and looking over their shoulders occasionally in the direction of the house into which the man in the checked suit was about to enter when arrested.

"I have stumbled right into it," said Ted to himself. "The check-suit man is the spy for the train robbers, and their headquarters are in that house. The detectives are going to raid it, and I'm in on it. This certainly is lucky."

He was glad now that he had not waited for Bud.

The three detectives moved slowly down the street, The policeman stood on the corner holding his man, waiting for the patrol wagon.

The scene was vividly impressed on Ted's mind, for it had happened so quickly, so easily, so quietly, and not at all like his own strenuous times when he had gone after desperadoes in his capacity of deputy marshal.

The detectives did not notice that they were being followed by a youth, and it is doubtful if they would have paid any attention to him if they had.

The foot of the first detective was on the lower step of the stairway leading to the door of the suspected house when suddenly a shrill whistle cut the air from the direction of the corner, and Ted turned to see the policeman strike the man in the check suit a blow with his club.

"Curse him, he's tipped us off," said the detective. "Come on, we've got to rush them now."

Quickly the three sprang up the steps, threw the door open, and entered a long hall.

"Back room," said one.

Ted was following them as closely as he could without being noticed and warned away.

He saw a big, fine-looking policeman entering by a back door.

"That's it," said one of the detectives, motioning to a door.

The policeman walked boldly to the door and threw it open.

As he did so a shot rang out, and the policeman staggered back and fell, a crimson stain covering his face.

He was dead before he struck the floor.

Without a word, the three detectives ran to the door, and within a moment or two at least fifteen shots were fired within the room.

They were so many and so close together that it sounded like a single crash. Then there was silence for a few moments, followed by a few desultory shots which seemed to pop viciously after the crash that had gone before.

It all happened so suddenly that Ted had hardly time to think, and stood rooted to the spot until he was aroused by the cry of "Help!" in a feeble voice, and, drawing his revolver, he sprang into the room.

As he did so, a shot rang out, and a ball sped close to his head.

The room was so dense with suffocating powder smoke that he could not see across it, but he had seen the dull-red flash from the muzzle of a revolver and shot in that direction.

"I'm done," he heard, followed by a deep groan.

"Get me out of here," said a man, trying to struggle to his feet, and Ted hurried to his side. It was one of the detectives, and Ted helped him to his feet and supported him to the hall.

"Let me down. I've got mine. Go in and help Dunnigan," said the wounded man. There was a spot, red and ever widening, on his breast.

Ted laid him on the floor and reëntered the room. Another shot came in his direction, and missed, although he could feel the wind of it as it passed close to his head, and he returned it with two shots, and there was silence.

The smoke had by this time cleared away somewhat, and Ted saw five men lying prone in the room.

One of the detectives lay on his face across the bed, and Ted tried to raise him up, but he was a dead weight. Ted finally got him turned over on his back, and then he saw that the detective was dead.

Kneeling on the floor with his head in his arms, which were thrown across a chair, was the third detective. He was breathing hard, and every time he moved the blood gushed from his mouth. He had been shot through the stomach.

But on the other side of the bed lay three men, apparently all of them dead.

While he was observing this there was a commotion in the hall, and a policeman rushed in, followed by a large man who wore an authoritative air.

"Oh, this is too bad; this is too bad," he kept repeating, as he went from man to man. It was Chief of Detectives Desmond. Turning to the policeman, he said:

"They've killed the boys, but the boys got the whole gang except two, 'Checkers' out there, and a man in the red automobile."

CHAPTER XVI
THE MAN IN THE YELLOW CAR

A patrol wagon full of policemen had dashed up in front of the house, and they came running down the hall, followed by a horde of eager reporters, who stood aghast at the slaughter of a few minutes.

The only participant in the fight who could talk was the detective whom Ted had carried to the hall, and he was telling the chief of detectives in whispers what had occurred.

"That young fellow followed us in," he said, pointing to Ted. "He took me out, and then went in and finished the gang. He's a game one, he is. I don't know who he is, but, by Jove! he's a game un."

"Who were the gang?" asked the chief.

"'Big Bill' Minnis, 'Bull' Dorgan, and 'Feathers' Lavin," was the reply. "Checkers we caught on the corner, and the other member of the gang, Dude Wilcox, got away. I guess it was him that rode off with the swag in the automobile, but where he went we couldn't get."

"I can tell you about that," said Ted quietly to the chief.

Desmond looked up at him curiously.

"Not now," he said. "Don't go. I want to talk to you after a while. Now, brace up, Tom; you're going to come out all right. The ambulance is out here, and we'll get you to the hospital."

"It ain't no use to jolly me, chief," said the man on the floor. "I'm all in. I'm bleedin' inside. I've seen too many fellows with a shot like this ever to have any hopes. Send for my wife and a priest. I ain't afraid to go, chief, but I hate to leave Maggie like this."

"We'll take care of her, Tom. Get that off your mind."

"All right, chief. If you say so, I know it'll be all right. Poor girl, it's hard luck for her."

"That's right, Tom, but brace up and don't let her see that you're worried."

A woman's scream sounded through the hall, and a slender, girlish figure pushed its way toward the prostrate man.

"Tom," she cried, and knelt beside him. "Are you hit? Did they get you at last?"

"Oh, I ain't bad, Maggie," said the dying detective bravely. "The chief's going to have me sent to the hospital, and I'll be all right in a week."

But before midnight he died.

An hour later Ted met the chief of detectives.

"Get into my car," said the chief, "and come down to my office, and we'll have a talk."

In a short time they were at the Four Courts, the big central police station of St. Louis, and when they were in the chief's private office and the door barred to intruders the great detective turned inquiringly to Ted.

"Now, who are you, and how did you happen to be mixed up in that mess?" asked Desmond.

"My name is Ted Strong," began Ted.

Suddenly Chief Desmond sat up straight and looked at Ted sharply.

"Not the leader of the broncho boys, are you?" he asked.

"The same," said Ted.

"I know about you. What were you doing near those detectives, that you should have got in so handily?"

"I'm a deputy United States marshal, as perhaps you know."

Desmond nodded. "Yes, I know," he said.

"I was working on this very case," said Ted, "and I had got hold of one end of it, and was about to follow it to a conclusion, when I saw the man Checkers on the street, and was following him. He led me to the detectives. The minute I saw them and him, I knew there would be something doing."

"What did you know of Checkers?"

"Nothing at all, except that he knew somehow that I was working on the express-robbery cases, and yesterday he shadowed my partner and me to East St. Louis, where we left him behind in an automobile."

Ted then told the chief how he had come about taking possession of the red car, to which Desmond listened carefully. When Ted had finished, Desmond rose and paced the room for a minute.

"Young man, you've got the big end of the chase," he said. "Dude Wilcox is the man who we are positive killed the messenger and got away with the swag. If it were you who found out how he got away with it, you will have got the last of the gang."

"Is that all there is to it?" asked Ted.

"Lord bless you, no. That's only the bunch that has been working in St. Louis. The big end of it is operating from some town farther west. There's where Dude Wilcox came from. I don't know where they make their headquarters, and it is out of my territory. I have all I can do to take care of St. Louis."

"The government officers were of the opinion that St. Louis was headquarters."

"That was true up to a few weeks ago, but we made it so hot for them here that they emigrated."

"Well, there's no use in my staying here any longer. I might as well hike out west. I'm not much good in a big town, anyway. I suppose you'll have no trouble in handling Checkers without any word from me."

"Oh, yes. But let's have Checkers up and hear what he has to say for himself."

The chief pushed a button and presently an officer entered.

"Go down to the hold-over and bring Checkers to me," ordered the chief.

In less than ten minutes the officer was back again.

"The jailer says he has no such man, chief," was the report.

"Where is he?"

"I'll inquire."

Back he came in a few minutes.

"Casey had him on the corner waiting for the wagon, sir, but in the excitement during the fight Casey let go of Checkers for a moment, and he got away."

Ted could see that the chief was very angry, but he controlled his temper admirably.

"Very well," was all he said.

He turned and gave Ted a sharp look.

"If you stay around here much longer, you'll have to look out for Checkers. He's a dangerous man, as well with a knife as with a gun."

"I guess I can take care of him," answered Ted.

"You look as if you could, lad," said the chief.

After a few more minutes of conversation regarding the red motor car, during which the chief advised Ted to keep the car until he was through with it, Ted took his leave, and returned to the hotel.

There he found Bud pacing the floor.

"Peevish porcupines," grunted the old cow-puncher, "but you've got yourself in up to ther neck in printer's ink."

"How's that?" asked Ted.

"Haven't you seen the evening papers?"

"I've been too busy to look at them."

"I reckon you be. Busier than a cranberry merchant. Look at this."

Bud handed Ted a bundle of evening papers.

Of course, the fight between the detectives and the bandits was given an immense amount of space in the extras which followed one another rapidly from the presses. In all of them were accounts of Ted's going to the rescue of the detectives, and the statement that balls from Ted's revolver had killed two of the gang.

"Rubbish!" said Ted. "I didn't kill any bandits. I took a couple of shots at them after they had fired on me, that's all."

"Well, yer won't be able to get away from these newspaper stories. If any of ther gang run across yer, they'll shore go after yer with a hard plank. Ye've placed ther black mark on yerself with ther gang."

"All right. I can stand it if they can. I've got a few up my sleeve for them."

Then Ted related exactly how the thing happened, and of his talk with Desmond.

"And they let that fellow Checkers get away," sighed Ted. "The chief says he's the most dangerous of them all, and warned me to look out for him. Bud, I've got a hunch."

"Let her flicker. I'm kinder stuck on yer hunches; they pay dividends right erlong."

"The fellow in the check suit was the man who tried to stab me because I wouldn't let him see the anonymous letter. I don't know which was the real man, Checkers or the other. But there were many points of similarity between them, and when Checkers called for us to stop the automobile, it was the voice of the man who commanded me to give him the letter. Keep Checkers in your mind."

The next morning they went out to Don Dorrington's house and got out the automobile.

"We'll circulate around pretty well in this," said Ted, "and if Checkers is in town he'll spot us, and we may get a chance at him yet."

"What do you want with him?"

"I'm depending on him to lead us to headquarters."

For an hour or more they rode about the town, making the machine as conspicuous as possible.

"Bud, we're being followed," said Ted, nodding toward a yellow car that had been in evidence oftener than mere chance made possible.

"Yep. I've had him spotted fer some time," answered Bud.

"Why didn't you say something about it?" Ted laughed at Bud's silence.

"Oh, I knew that you were on to it, too," was the characteristic reply.

"What do you suppose he's chasing us for? He must know that he can't harm us."

"He don't want us. He wants that red car. It's a beautiful piece of red evidence against him an' his gang. Yer see, it's ther best kinder a clew."

"Right again. But he needn't think he can steal it, for he can't."

They put the car up during the middle of the day.

"We'll let it rest for a while," said Ted, as they ran it into a public garage. "This evening we'll take it out again, and if we're followed then we'll be sure that it is Checkers, and that he is on our trail."

It was seven o'clock when they trundled forth again.

A bright moonlight night made motoring highly enjoyable, and after they had run about for a couple of hours Bud got out, saying that he was tired of the sport, and would return to the hotel, and leave Ted to take the machine back to Don Dorrington's basement.

They had been followed by the yellow car again, but in going through Forest Park they had managed to give their trailer the slip among the intricate roads and bypaths, and had seen nothing of him for half an hour.

As soon as Ted had let Bud out, he hit up the speed, for the boulevard was comparatively free of traffic, and he fairly spun along to the western part of the city.

Cutting off the boulevard, he entered upon a side street to make a short cut to Dorrington's house.

He noticed, as he turned into the side street, a light-colored car standing close to the curb as he passed, but so many cars were standing in front of houses here and there that he paid no attention to it.

But he had no sooner passed than the light-colored car glided after him noiselessly. Ted's own machine was making so much noise that he was not aware of the presence of another car until it was abreast of him, and so close that he could reach out his hand and touch it.

He thought the car was trying to pass him close to the curb, and started to turn out to give it more steerage room.

"Sheer off, there," he called, "until I can get out of here."

Suddenly something wet struck him in the face. He gave a gasp, as a fearful suffocating pain filled his head and lungs, and he sank down into the bottom of the car, insensible.

At the same instant the man in the other car reached over and throttled the red car, then stopped his own.

Leaving his own car in the middle of the road, he leaped into the red car and gave her her full head.

In half an hour the red car had left the city and was speeding along a smooth country road in the moonlight.

Ted still lay in a stupor in the bottom of the car, and the only sound that came from him was an occasional gasp as his lungs, trying to recover from a shock, took in short gulps of air.

It was midnight before the red car slowed down.

Ahead in the moonlight rose the black bulk of a building.

It presented the appearance of a country house of some pretensions.

The house was dark. Not a light appeared at any of the windows.

The red car approached it cautiously, running into the deep shadow cast by a high brick wall. A dog on the other side of the wall barked a warning.

The man in the red car whistled softly in a peculiar way.

A window was raised somewhere, and the whistle was answered by another.

In a few minutes there was the sound of a man walking on a graveled path, then the creak of rusty iron and a gate swung open.

"All right?" asked a voice at the gate.

"You bet. Got them both," answered the man in the red machine.

"Bully for you. Run her in."

The red machine, with Ted still lying in the bottom, ran into a large yard, and the gate was closed again, and the car was stopped in front of the house.

"Come, help me carry him in," said the man in the car. "He'll be coming around all right in a few minutes, then we may have some trouble with him, for he's the very devil to fight."

Ted was dragged out of the car in no gentle manner, and carried into the house, which was unlighted save where the moonlight shone through the windows.

"Into the strong room with him," said the man of the house.

Ted was carried into a room and dumped upon a lounge. Then a light was struck, and both men bent over the prostrate form of the leader of the broncho boys.

Both of them started back.

"Whew! You must have given him an awful dose, Checkers," said the man of the house.

"Had to do it, Dude. If I hadn't, I'd never got him here, that's a cinch."

"Well, get his gun off before he comes to."

Ted was stripped of his weapons, a glass of water was thrown into his face, and he began to regain consciousness.

He had been shot down with an ammonia gun, and the powerful alkaloid gas had almost killed him. For a long time he breathed in gasps, but his splendid constitution pulled him through.

When they saw that he was recovering, the two men left the room, after examining the iron-barred windows, and as they went out they locked and barred the door behind them.

CHAPTER XVII
MURDER IN THE HAUNTED HOUSE

Ted lay for a long time only half conscious.

But gradually his senses returned, and he opened his eyes to find himself in darkness, trying hard to think what had happened to him.

He knew that he had been felled by something powerful and terrible, that had knocked him in a heap so suddenly that he hardly knew what had happened to him.

Slowly the consciousness of it all came to him. Some one in an automobile had ridden alongside him and thrown ammonia in his face.

His eyes were still smarting with it, and he wondered, seeing no light, if it had blinded him, and he was now lying in the dark when there was light all around him.

He struggled with this thought for a moment, because the idea of going blind was terrible to him.

He wondered where he was, and felt around and learned that he was lying on a couch.

Then he swung his feet to the floor and sat up. The ammonia had left him still weak, but gradually he became stronger, and got to his feet and began to explore the room with his fingers.

He found a chair and a table, and presently came to the door, which he tried to open, but could not.

Passing around the room, he arrived at the window, and, looking through the glass, saw a star, and thanked Heaven that he could see.

He tried the fastenings of the window, unlocked it, and threw it up, stretching out his hand. The window was closed with iron bars.

He had made the circuit of the room, and had discovered that he was securely shut in.

He went back to the lounge and lay down to think matters over.

He felt quite sure that the man Checkers had been his assailant. The warning had not been without reason, after all.

As he lay quietly he heard footsteps in the next room. Two men evidently had entered it. They were talking, and occasionally, when their voices rose higher than usual, he could catch a word or two.

From the tones of their voices he learned that the conversation was not of the most pleasant nature. They were quarreling about something.

By degrees their voices grew higher, and occasionally Ted caught such words as "money," "half," "thousand," enough to tell him that they were dividing something.

"They're quarreling over the swag," said Ted to himself. "Good! 'When thieves fall out, honest men get their dues,'" he quoted. "Keep it up, and I'll get you yet."

They did keep it up.

It was the voice of Checkers that rose high.

"I tell you I'll have half or I'll split on you, if I go to the 'stir' for the rest of my life."

"If you do split, you won't go to the 'stir.' The boys will kill you before you get the chance."

"Well, what's your proposition?"

"I'll give you five thousand. That's enough for putting me next to the train. What do you want? The earth? Didn't I do the dirty work? If I'd been caught, who'd have been soaked? You? I guess not. It would have been me who would have been killed, for I'm like the other fellows—I'd have fought until they killed me. You're not entitled to more than five thousand, and that's all you'll get."

"I won't take it. Half or I squeal."

"Squeal, then."

There was a sudden trampling of feet in the other room, the crash of an overturning table, followed by a yell of death agony, and the thud of a falling body.

"Great Scott, one of them is dead," said Ted, with a shudder.

He was listening intently, and heard a scuffle of feet, then hurried footsteps died away and a door slammed somewhere.

Deep silence followed.

Then the horror of the situation burst upon Ted, The house had been deserted by the only living creature, except himself, who was left to starve to death in this prison, with a dead man in the next room.

One or the other of the two men who had held him captive had done murder and escaped with the stolen money.

Ted lay speculating which was dead and which had escaped, but he could make nothing of it.

The night dragged wearily on for Ted could not sleep, for thinking of the dead man in the next room, and his own precarious position.

He reviewed the chances of his being rescued. They were very slim, indeed.

Bud and Chief Desmond would start a hunt for him about the city, but would not find him, and no one would think of looking for him in this deserted house.

But at last the night passed, and Ted watched with a grateful heart the gradual dawning of the day.

At last it was light enough to see, and he looked around the room.

It was old-fashioned and high. Through the window he could see a bit of the high brick fence, and a few trees and long, tangled, dead grass. That was the extent of his view from the window.

He examined the door, which was the only other means of exit from the room.

It was very heavy, and made of oak. The lock on it was massive and old-fashioned, and set into the oak frame so that an examination of it dispelled all hope of getting it off.

If he was to escape there was only one way, to cut a hole in the door. He felt for his knife. It was gone, and Ted wandered disconsolately to the couch and sat down to ponder. But the more he racked his brains the further he got from a plan of escape.

The day dragged slowly on, but he would not sleep for fear that he might miss some one passing to whom he could call and bring assistance.

Late in the afternoon he stepped to the window and looked at an apple tree in the grounds beyond. It was full of red apples, and he was very hungry, but they were not for him.

He wondered that he had not heard any one pass along the road on the other side of the brick wall.

Suddenly he noticed that the leaves in an apple tree were being violently agitated, although there was not a breath of wind stirring.

Some one was in the tree, and his first impulse was to yell for help, then he reflected that if it was a boy pilfering apples the cry would scare him, and his only chance for rescue would be ruined by the boy running away.

He would wait for the boy to come to the ground, and would then speak to him.

But as he was watching the tree intently the movement of the leaves ceased, and soon he perceived a peering face and two dark, roguish eyes. They reminded him of a bird, so bright and inquiring were they.

Ted smiled at the eyes, and thought he saw an answering twinkle in them.

They disappeared after a few moments. The leaves shook again, and a boy of about ten years, incredibly ragged, with a dirty face, hands, and bare feet and legs, dropped to the ground. His head was covered with a tangled mop of brown hair in lieu of a hat.

The boy stared at the window, all the while munching an apple, while from the bulges in his scant trousers it was evident that he had others for future consumption.

"Hello, boy!" said Ted, with a friendly way.

"Hello! Who are you?" said the boy, coming a few steps nearer, to get a better view.

"Do you mean what's my name?"

"Uh-huh!"

"My name is Ted Strong. What's yours?"

"Napoleon Bonaparte."

Ted laughed at the solemnity of the boy when he gave this answer.

"Well," said the boy, "it's just as much Napoleon as yours is Ted Strong."

"But my name is Ted Strong."

"Aw, come off."

"All right, if you don't believe me, ask me any questions you like to prove it."

"Where do you come from?"

"Moon Valley, South Dakota."

"That's right. What's the names of some of Ted Strong's fellers?"

Ted named them all, the boy giving a nod after every name.

"Now, what's the name of your horse? The one you ride most?"

"Sultan. You seem to know something about me."

"You bet. Well, maybe you're all right, but what are you doing here? I always thought you stayed out West—away out West."

"Usually I do."

"Then what are you doing in the haunted house?"

"Is this a haunted house?"

"You bet. There was a feller killed there once, and nobody will live in it no more."

"Honest, now, what *is* your name?"

"My name's— Say, are you sure enough Ted Strong?"

"Certainly I am."

The boy came closer, looking at Ted fixedly.

"Gee, I wouldn't go inter that house fer a hundred million dollars."

"I've been here all night, and it didn't scare me any."

"That settles it. I reckon you must be Ted Strong. He's the only feller I ever heard of that wouldn't be scared to stay in a haunted house. How did you get there?"

Without hesitation, Ted told the boy how he had been held up by a man in an automobile, and knocked out by ammonia fumes, and then locked up in the house. But he said nothing about the murdered man in the next room.

"Now I've told you all about myself, it's only fair that you should tell me about yourself."

"Oh, I ain't nothin'. I'm just 'Scrub.'"

"Haven't you got any other name?"

"Nary one that I know of that's fastened to me all the time."

"How's that?"

"When I'm living with old man Jones, I'm Scrub Jones, and when I'm with Mr. Foster, I'm Scrub Foster, and that way. I don't belong to nobody, an' I just live around doing chores for my keep. Just now I ain't got no place to stop, and I'm sleeping in hay-stacks and living on apples and turnips and potatoes, when I make a fire and bake 'em, and once in a while I trap a rabbit. But, gee, what a good time you must have!"

"How would you like to go with me out to Moon Valley?"

"Aw, quit your kiddin'."

"I mean it I'd just like to take you out there and give you a good time for once in your life."

"Would you? By golly, you can."

"Then I'll tell you what to do. Go around to the front door and come in, and back to this room, and unlock the door and let me out, and we'll go together."

"Gee, I wouldn't go into that house for four thousand barrels of hoarhound candy. Say, are you a prisoner?"

"I am, and if you don't come in and let me out I can't take you with me to Moon Valley."

"That's so. But I'm scared of the ghost."

"Oh, so you're afraid, are you?"

At this the boy flushed and fiddled with his toes in the grass.

"No kid that's afraid could live in Moon Valley. He'd be scared to death in a week."

"Are there ghosts there?"

"There are no such things as ghosts. Bet you never saw one yourself."

"No, I never did. But all the folks around here say there is ghosts in that house."

"Well, say there are, they wouldn't come out in the daytime, would they?"

"I reckon not. Gee, I'll come in."

The boy disappeared like a flash, and in a few moments Ted heard the front door open, then a scream.

"I'll bet he's found the dead man," said Ted, aloud, in a tone of annoyance. "That's just my luck."

The door slammed, and all was silent. The boy evidently had run away, and Ted was left alone in the house with the dead man.

Once more darkness descended upon the earth, and Ted took up another hole in his belt, and tried to believe that he was not hungry.

About nine o'clock Ted, who was lying on the couch looking at the ceiling, saw a faint flicker of light pass across it, and sprang to his feet. It was the light cast by a lantern somewhere outside.

He sprang to the window and looked out.

Behind the brick wall he could see the reflection of a bobbing lantern, and hear the shuffle of many feet.

"Ho, there!" he cried.

The shuffle stopped, and a voice that was trembling with fear answered him.

"Come in here, and let me out," called Ted.

"We'll be thar in a minute," was the answer, and presently the front door was thrown open, followed by exclamations, as whoever had come in viewed the body in the next room.

Then the voices were outside his door.

"You open it an' go in," said a voice. "You're the constable."

"Well, supposin' he's got a gun?" asked the constable tremulously.

"Don't be afraid," said Ted. "I have no gun. They took everything away from me."

"There! Ain't that enough? Open the door."

Ted heard the bar being taken down, then the key grate in the lock, and the door was thrown open with a bang. He found himself looking into the barrels of a shotgun.

"If yer makes a motion, I'll blow yer head plumb off, blame yer," shouted the man with the gun.

"Honest," said Ted, "I'm not armed."

"How come yuh here?"

"I was made insensible by ammonia fumes and brought here last night."

"How come yuh ter kill that man in ther next room?"

"I didn't kill him."

"That's a likely story. I find yuh alone in ther house with him. Yuh'll hev ter answer ter ther magistrate fer this."

"See here, my friend, how could I have killed that man, then come in here, and locked and barred the door on the outside?"

"He's got yuh there, Si," said one of the men.

"Look here," said Ted, showing his star. "I'm an officer of the law. The fellows who captured and brought me here were robbers, and I was on their trail. That's all there is to it. Now, let me pass. I want to see what is in the next room."

CHAPTER XVIII
STELLA ADOPTS A BROTHER

Taking up a lantern, Ted entered the room. Beside the overturned table lay the body of a man. It was not Checkers. There was nothing in the room except the table, two chairs, a broken lamp, which lay in a pool of kerosene on the floor, and the body of the murdered man.

Wait, what was this?

Beneath the table was a scrap of green.

It was a bank bill, and, drawing it forth, Ted found it to be a fifty-dollar note issue'd by the First National Bank of Green River, Nebraska. A valuable clew, this.

When he had searched the body of the dead man, and found several letters and a small memorandum book, he left the room and locked it.

"Notify the coroner," said he to the constable, "and give him this key. If he wants me as a witness in his inquest, he will find me at the Stratford Hotel, in St. Louis."

The constable promised to carry out Ted's instructions.

"Where is that boy Scrub?" asked Ted.

"Here I am," said the boy, emerging from the crowd.

"Who knows anything about this boy?" Ted asked.

"He's just a loose kid," said the constable. "His father died when he was young, and his mother left him a few years ago. Since then no one has claimed him."

"Then I will. Do you want to come with me?" Ted asked the boy. "I will give you a good home and clothes, teach you something, and make a useful man of you. Is he a good boy?"

Ted turned to the men about him.

"Yes, Scrub is a good boy, only he never ain't had no chance," seemed to be the universal verdict.

"Say the word, Scrub. Do you want to come with me?"

"You bet," said Scrub fervently.

"Good! Come along! We'll be getting back to St. Louis."

"But yuh can't get back to-night. The last train has gone."

"Never mind. I'll get there somehow. Some one lend me a lantern for a few minutes."

Ted was given one, and he went out into the yard and outhouses to search for the red motor car. He could not find it anywhere.

"Did any of you folks see a red automobile going down the road any time to-day?" he asked.

"Yes, there's a red machine down in the lane running over to the Rock Road," said one of the men. "But I reckon it's bust."

"Come on, Scrub, we'll take a look at it," said Ted, Leading off with the man who had seen the car, and followed by the whole crowd, Ted made his way to the lane.

Standing in the middle of it was the red car with its No. 118 swaying from the rear axle in the wind.

Evidently Checkers had started away in it, using it as a swift means of escape, but it had stopped, and, as he could go no farther in it, he had abandoned it in the road.

Ted examined the machinery carefully, but could find nothing wrong with it until he discovered that it had exhausted its supply of gasoline.

But he learned that the grocer at the village, half a mile away, had gasoline for sale, and two young fellows volunteered to go after some while Ted overhauled the car.

In half an hour he was ready to start. He made Scrub get into the seat, and, shaking hands with the constable and shouting a merry good-by to the others, he started for St. Louis.

It was past midnight when he drew up in front of the Stratford Hotel, hungry and tired. Scrub was fast asleep, and, taking him in his arms, Ted entered the hotel.

As he stepped inside, the clerk stared at him as if he had seen a ghost.

"How's everything?" asked Ted of the clerk.

"Great Scott, where did you come from?" asked, the clerk, and added hastily: "Better hurry upstairs to your room. Everybody is crazy about your disappearance."

Ted went up in the elevator with the boy still sleeping in his arms. There was a light in his room and a confused murmur of voices.

Without the formality of a knock he opened the door and entered. As he appeared in the doorway there was silence for a moment, then such a bedlam of shouts and laughter burst forth that every one on the floor was aroused.

"It's Ted! It's Ted!" they shouted, and crowded around him.

The place was full of them. Across the room he saw the shining face of Stella, smiling a welcome at him. Ben and Kit, Carl, Clay, and all of them were there, and sitting at the table was the chief of detectives.

"Hello! Holding a post-mortem over me?" asked Ted.

"It comes pretty near that," said Bud. "Dog-gone you, what do you mean by goin' erway an' hidin' out on us that way? What in ther name o' Sam Hill an' Billy Patterson hev yer picked up now?" Bud was looking curiously at the bundle of rags in Ted's arms, for the boy still slept.

"This is a new pard," said Ted. "If it hadn't been for this kid you'd probably never seen me again."

"Erlucerdate," demanded Bud.

"Not until some one goes out to the nearest restaurant and orders up a stack of grub for Scrub and me. I haven't had anything to eat or drink for thirty-six hours, and I'm almost all in, and this kid has been living on apples and water for a couple of weeks. Now, hustle somebody and let me put this kid on the bed—my back's nearly broke—or maybe it's my stomach, they're so close together now I can't tell which it is that hurts."

While Ted was laying the boy on the bed he woke up, and, finding himself in a strange place, and a finer room than he had ever been in before, surrounded by a lot of rather boisterous young men, he leaped to the floor and started to the door. But Ted caught him by the arm and drew him back.

"What's the matter with you, you young savage?" said Ted.

"Oh, I'm all right now," said the boy. "When I woke up I got rattled, I guess, but as long as you're here it's all right."

The food came up now borne by two waiters and piloted by Kit. There were oysters and steak and potatoes and biscuit and a lot of what Missouri folk call "fixin's," and a big pot of coffee.

Scrub's eyes stood out like doorknobs as he viewed this wonderful array of things to eat. The table was cleared, the waiters set out the food, and the boys stood back to give Ted and the boy "room to swell," as Bud expressed it. The way they tucked into the good things was a caution.

After their hunger was satisfied and the waiters had restored order to the table, Ted began the story of his adventures since he had let Bud out of the automobile. As he talked, Stella wooed the small boy to her side, and listened to the story with her arm around his shoulder, and long before it was done Scrub was her worshiper forever.

Chief Desmond listened with close attention, and when Ted finished and exhibited the bill of the Green River Bank, which he examined carefully, he said:

"Mr. Strong, you've beaten us all to it. I will go out to-morrow—I mean to-day, for it's one o'clock now—and view the body myself. If it is, as seems almost certain to be, Dude Wilcox, one of the most dangerous men in the West is gone, but he has left behind for us to fight, and you to find, the man Checkers. This bill is your clew to the gang, but it is a counterfeit. As I have the thing figured out, the gang knew that forty thousand dollars was going to be shipped, but for some reason or other they dared not hold up the train out there, and telegraphed the gang in St. Louis to get it. Dude was at the head of the bunch here, and as it was a one-man game so near to St. Louis, Dude was elected to pull it off, which he did to the queen's taste. Perhaps the bill you have is the only counterfeit in the lot. Perhaps not. That is for you to work out."

"But how he managed to get away with the swag I haven't managed to figure out yet," said Ted.

"Of course, I don't know either, but deducing facts from what I know of the gang's methods, and from long experience with gentlemen of the road, I would say that the members of the gang who were killed in their rendezvous in Pine Street by my unfortunate men were awaiting the arrival of Dude with the swag. Checkers had secret knowledge that you had been put on their trail, and when he saw you pick up that red car in East St. Louis he was sure that you knew about the robbery and that you were on to Dude."

"That's likely," said Ted. "I hadn't thought of that."

"Well, he got into communication with Dude, and warned him against coming to the Pine Street place. You see, they had another rendezvous out in the country, a haunted house, the reputation of which would keep prying country boys away from it."

"Best sort of a place for a criminal hangout," said Ted.

"You're right, and now that you have discovered it, I'll take pains to see that it's never used for such again. But, as I was going to say, Dude's intention was to get out of town, return, go to the Pine Street room, divide the swag, and skip. He probably left the train at Somerset, or some other little town down the line, hid in the cornfields until dusk, stole a horse and buggy, and drove across the country to the haunted house, and later was joined by Checkers, who had been trailing you, and later succeeded in getting you. Had it not been for the quarrel between Dude and Checkers, it is more than likely that you would have been murdered by Checkers. But one murder was enough for his nerve, and, forgetting you, he vamosed."

The detective arose to take his departure, again congratulating Ted on the outcome of his adventure.

"Keep your eye peeled for Checkers, and if you do run across him, have your gun at half cock," he said, and, bidding good night to all, went away.

"And now, good fellows, all to bed," said Ted. "To-morrow we start for the West, and the capture of the head men of the train-robber syndicate, and the extermination of the business."

In the morning, before the others were up, Ted made Scrub take a bath, and then they sallied forth to a clothing store. When they came out, instead of the ragged and dirty little boy, there walked proudly by Ted's side a fine, clean, fresh-looking lad in a well-fitting serge suit, and other appointments that transformed him completely.

When they arrived at the hotel the boys professed not to know Scrub.

"Hello, picked up another kid?" asked Bud. "I swow, yer allers goin' round pickin' up mavericks. I reckon yer aim ter brand this one as well ez ther one yer brought in last night."

"Why, here's another kid," said Ben, looking over Scrub's new outfit with interest. "He don't look much like the one you brought in last night. I reckon that one has run away, I don't see him anywhere."

Poor Scrub was standing first on one foot and then on the other, fairly squirming with embarrassment.

Ted gave the boys the nod to cease teasing the boy.

"Don't mind those fellows, they're only joshing," said Ted.

"Oh, I don't mind it if they can get any fun out of it," said Scrub, with a smile. "Maybe, some day I can get back at them, when I know them better."

Stella came down in the elevator at that moment, and, catching sight of Scrub, gave a little scream of astonishment at his altered appearance.

"Goodness, what a fine-looking addition to the family!" she said, shaking hands with the boy, who blushed and looked pleased. "I don't like the name Scrub a bit. I'm going to change his name."

"This isn't leap year, Stella," said Ben.

"You hush! What name would you rather have than Scrub? That's no name for a broncho boy," she said to the boy.

"I don't know," answered the boy. "What name do you like?"

"I think she likes Ben better than any," said Ben, posing in a very handsome manner.

"Don't listen to him, he's always teasing. You want something short and easy to say."

"What's the matter with 'Say'?" said Ben. "That's always easy to remember. I notice that when a man wants to call another on the street he just hollers 'Say,' and half a dozen fellows turn around."

"Then that makes it too common," decided Stella. "What name would you suggest, Ted? He's got to have two names."

"Let us get one of the newspapers to start a voting contest on it."

"Ben, if you don't stop your foolishness, I won't play," said Stella.

"You name him, Stella," said Ted. "Anything you say goes."

"Then we'll call him Dick, after my father," said Stella. "He never had a boy, and always wanted one. I'm going to adopt this boy as a brother. His name shall be Dick Fosdick. That sounds funny, doesn't it, but I didn't do it on purpose."

There was a tear in her eye at the thought of her father, and the boys looked rather solemn, for while they hoped for the best, they didn't as yet know the lad, and perhaps they had saddled themselves with a future regret, but Stella trusted and believed in the little chap, who was very proud that at last he had thrown off and buried forever the name of Scrub.

That evening they took the train for the West, their destination being Green River.

The automobile Ted sent on by express that he might have it not only for use, for he was becoming attached to it, but as a clew to the detection of the express robbers.

CHAPTER XIX
EZRA, THE LIFE-SAVING GOAT

Ted had engaged several sections on the through sleeping car to North Platte, Nebraska, the old home of Colonel William Cody, known all over the world as "Buffalo Bill."

But they were to leave the train at Green River, ostensibly to buy cattle for their ranch. This, of course, was to avert suspicion from their real purpose of hunting down the express robbers.

For Mrs. Graham and Stella the stateroom of the car *Orizaba* had been engaged, and the boys made it a sort of ceremonial chamber.

The car was well filled with other passengers, many of them tourists on the way to Colorado or the Pacific coast, and they were much amused at the free-and-easy spirit with which the boys conducted themselves, and when it became generally known that they were the broncho boys, with Ted Strong at their head, they received a great deal of attention, which was not particularly to Ted's liking.

As usual, wherever they were, Bud Morgan, Ben Tremont, and Carl Schwartz provided a fund of amusement for everybody.

Little Dick Fosdick had never known such happiness as he was now experiencing. He worshiped Stella, admired Ted, and looked upon Bud as the greatest pal a boy ever had.

He and Bud were inseparable, and Bud never tired of telling him yarns about cow-punching and Indian fighting, while the boy proved a breathless listener, hanging upon every word that fell from the yellow-haired cowboy's lips.

He knew by heart many of the adventures through which Ted Strong had passed, and often surprised Ted by correcting some inaccuracy which, through a lapse of memory, Ted had made.

They were sailing across Missouri toward the West, and the boy kept his face glued to the window, watching for the first glimpse of the golden West of his fancy. Just at present he saw only farms and little towns, through which the fast train whizzed without stopping.

The boy knew this sort of country well, and was rather disappointed that the boundless prairie did not roll before him from horizon to horizon.

Then he turned his attention to the luxury of the car, but being a healthy boy, this did not impress him long, and he turned to his heroes for relief.

Bud was sitting comfortably sprawled out on two seats, singing softly to himself. Bud could not sing a little bit, but he thought he could, which served his purpose personally quite as well as if he could.

Ben was in the seat behind him, reading. After a while Bud's music, or the lack of it, got on Ben's nerves, and he reached over and poked Bud on top of his golden head with the corner of his book.

"Say," said he, "put on the soft pedal, won't you? Perhaps you can sing, and maybe some one told you you could, but take it from me you have no more voice or musical ability than a he-goat."

"Oh, mercy!" retorted Bud. "Does my music annoy you?"

"It certainly does," snapped Ben.

"Then why don't yer move away?"

"Bah! You're an old goat."

"Thanks fer ther compliment, although yer don't mean it thet away. But when yer likens me ter a goat yer do me proud. If yer were more goatlike yerself ye'd be a heap more wiser."

"I'm glad you like it. The pleasure's all yours. But if a fellow called me a goat, I know what I'd do."

"Maybe, perhaps. But yer needn't be afraid that any one will liken yer ter a goat. Any self-respectin' goat would get sore at it. If I wuz ter pick out yer counterpart in ther animile world, I'd say yer most resembled the phillaloo?"

"What's a phillaloo?"

"A phillaloo is a cross between a penguin and a jassack."

"Say, you long-haired lobster!" cried Ben, leaping to his feet, apparently in great anger, "don't you call me anything like that."

"Well, didn't yer jest call me a goat?"

"Yes, but—"

"Then sit down an' git back ter yer love story; we're square. Nothin' is lost on both sides. But callin' me a goat don't make me sore none. I jest dote on goats. If I wasn't jest what I am, I'd sooner be a goat than a collidge gradooate."

"I've heard about enough, if you're alluding to me."

"Take it er leave it. But, ez I wuz goin' ter say before my conversation was cut inter by a loud an' empty noise, speakin' o' goats reminds me o' a time down on ther Pecos—"

"By Jove! I'm going to ask the conductor to move me into another car. This is too much. I might, perhaps, stand for being called a phillaloo, but I swear I'll not be compelled to stay here and listen to one of those silly and impossible stories of this insane cow-puncher."

At first some of the passengers thought that Bud and Ben were really angry at one another, but the wise ones soon saw that it was all bluff, as, of course, the broncho boys knew.

But it was very real to Dick Fosdick, who had yet many things to learn about the boys and their ways, and while the little chap was far too clever naturally to show his feelings, he sided with Bud, and thought that Ben was very unreasonable, especially as the boys, and some of the passengers, had flocked around Bud, who appeared not to notice them.

"I reckon, Dick, you'd like ter hear thet thar story erbout the time I lied down on ther Pecos in the summer o'—"

"Conductor," said Ben, detaining that official as he was passing through the car, "is there no way of stopping the noise this person is making? I cannot take my nap on account of his chatter."

Several persons who were not in the secret were for interfering in behalf of Bud and his story, which they wanted to hear, but were headed off by the conductor, who said:

"Sorry, but I cannot interfere with the gentleman. He does not seem to be annoying the other passengers. If you wish to take a nap you are at liberty to go up ahead in the smoking car."

At this Bud began to gloat.

"I hear they've put a cattle car up next ter ther injine fer sech sensitive people like you. Yer might enj'y a leetle siesta on ther straw."

Ben sank back into his seat, and began to snore gently.

"What about the story down on the Pecos, Bud?" said Dick.

"You'd like to hear it, eh? Then I'll tell it to you. Of course, the other folks may listen to it, but it is understood betwixt me an' you thet it's all yours, an' whatever goes inter their ears is jest ther leavin's. Is that a go?"

The boy nodded eagerly, even though he didn't understand the drift of Bud's remarks.

"What's the story about?" asked the boy.

"The goat, my boy. Perhaps you don't know it, but the goat is one of the noblest animals what walks. He is also one o' ther smartest, an' in former years used ter be able ter talk, but ez soon ez he got ter be so popular in secret societies ther gift o' speech was withdrawed from him, so thet he wouldn't be able ter give erway ther secret things what he saw an' heard at ther meetin's."

"But, Bud, are they really smart?" asked Dick.

"Smart ain't no name fer it. All yer got ter do to find out if they're smart is ter look at their whiskers. The smartest o' all animiles is man, an' don't he wear whiskers? An' I want ter ast yer what other animile hez whiskers exceptin' ther goat. Ther goat knew what he was about when he begin ter raise whiskers. He says ter hisself—"

"What bosh!" exclaimed Ben, snorting in his sleep.

"Aire you addressin' yer remarks ter me?" asked Bud, looking over the back of the seat at Bud. But the only answer was a gentle snore.

"What did he say?" asked Dick eagerly.

"'Why,' says he, 'if they won't let me talk they can't keep me from bein' ez near a man ez I kin go; by gravy, I'll raise whiskers like Deacon Smith,' who was a member o' ther lodge in which ther goat officiated; and, by jinks, he did, an' ther fashion wuz follered, an' they wear them ter this day.

"There ain't no question o' their smartness, an' their prominence. Ain't one o' ther signs o' the zodiac up in ther heavens named after ther goat— Capricornus is ther feller ter what I refer—an' them heathen chaps what wuz half man an' half goat? Didn't they come pretty near bein' ther whole thing?"

"But about the Pecos?" inquired Dick, who was not partial to preaching, but wanted to get at the heart of the story.

"Oh. yes. I wuz leadin' up ter it gradooal, fer what I'm goin' ter relate— if thet yap will choke off on thet moosical snore—"

"Here, wake up, you're snoring so loud we can't hear ourselves holler," said Kit, reaching over and shaking Ben.

"I can't keep awake while that fellow persists in yarning away like a fanning machine. It's so monotonous I can't keep awake," and Ben stretched and yawned.

"Let's get away from here and go to some other part of the car," whispered Dick.

"No, we'll just stay here an' spite him. He'll wake up after a while an' be glad to listen to ther story. So here goes!

"I was punchin' cow's down on the Pecos one summer fer ther Crazy B Ranch. We had eight punchers in ther bunch, a good chuck wagon, an' easy work, so I wuz pretty well suited, an' thet summer I gained twelve pounds, even if it wuz a hundred an' forty in ther shade, which we hed forgotten ter bring along with us."

"Forgotten to bring what?" asked the boy.

"Our shade. Yer see, down in thet country ther sun is so strong thet every one carries his own shade, fer there isn't a tree in ther whole country big enough ter cast a shadder o' any sort. Out on ther ranches, at certain seasons o' ther year, they serve out shade ter ther men jest ther same ez they do bacon an' saleratus ter ther outfit thet goes out herdin'."

Dick looked seriously at Bud for a moment, hardly knowing whether or not to doubt him, but Bud's face was as grave as a deacon's.

"I don't understand it, I'm sure," he said. "But where do they get the shade to give to the men?"

"That's easy enough. It's always gathered on dark nights, generally late in ther fall er in ther winter, so thet it'll be real cool."

"But where do they get it?"

"What—ther shade? Why, they just go out an' gather it off the ground in thin shapes, kinder longer than broad. It can be rolled up just like a blanket, an' carried behind ther saddle. It's gathered in ther cold months. Ye've heard o' ther 'cool shade.' Well, that's why they gather it late in the year. Summer shade is no good, because it's too warm."

"But what is it like?"

"Oh, it's black, an' I hear they strip it off close ter ther ground. We don't get no shade like it in this part o' ther country. Ther only place what hez it is ther West, whar it's needed most."

"But how about the Pecos?"

"Sho! I almost fergot it, didn't I, while teachin' yer something erbout ther way they do things in Arizony an' her sister-in-law, Noo Mexico? Now I'm off, shore.

"Ping-pong Martin wuz in ther outfit thet year. Mebbe yer knows him?" Bud looked at the small boy inquiringly, much to his embarrassment.

"No, sir, I never heard of him before."

"Well, no matter, but this Ping-pong cuss, he had a personal friend, a goat, what couldn't no more be shook than a sore thumb, and had follered Ping off ter ther wars, so to speak.

"Ping run off from home on ther quiet ter join our outfit, leavin' ther goat to home, locked up in ther barn. Ping thought he hed ther goat faded, but one day, when we wuz half asleep in our saddles, a feller over on ther other side come a-runnin' in.

"'What's ther matter?' sez I.

"Thar's a funny animile over here. He shore is ther devil, fer he wears horns, an' hez a face exactly like thet o' ole man Pillsbury. I ain't bettin' none it ain't him. But if it is Pillsbury, he better not go home lookin' like thet 'thout lettin' his wife know first.'

"Ping an' me rode over ter ther other side, an' thar stood a goat, lookin' so nice an' socierble.

"'Great hevings!' shouted Ping, makin' a rush fer ther goat, 'thet's my goat Ezra, ain't you?'"

"Did the goat understand him?"

"Did he understand him? Well, I should whisper sweetly. Why, thet goat jest jumped all over Ping, a-runnin' his whiskers inter his eyes, an' laughin', he wuz so glad ter see him. He'd traced Ping plumb ercross ther desert ter get ter us, an', o' course, we couldn't sic him home after that.

"We all got ter love Ezra fer his lovely ways; that is, all except 'Boney Bill' Henderson."

"Why? Didn't the goat like him?"

"Well, it wuz this way: Boney Bill had a habit o' beggin' ther grease from ther fryin' pan every night ter ile his boots. This made 'em good an' strong, ez well ez easy ter chew on. One night, Ezra bein' fond o' boots, finds 'em an' chews ther tops off'n 'em. They wuz ther only boots Bill hed, an' we wuz two hundred mile ter another pair, so Bill hed ter go through ther season barefoot, an' ther sun jest nacherly warped his feet out o' all shape.

"But thet wuzn't what I wuz goin' ter tell yer erbout. That fall ther Utes went on ther warpath, an' wuz headin' our way, an' I want ter tell yer we wuz some scared. We hed several brushes with ther Injuns, an' ther courier we sent ter ther fort fer help wuz killed an' scalped.

"Thar we wuz, in a little valley entirely surrounded by Injuns thirstin' fer our gore. How long we could hold out agin' 'em wuz ther problem. But whenever one o' 'em showed his head we took a pop at it, an' they returned ther compliment. We wuz prayin' fer ther comin' o' ther soldiers, which wuz ther only thing what could save us from a horrible death.

"Ther Injuns got next ter ther fact thet our ammunition wuz runnin' short, an' they wuz gittin' some gay; sorter takin' advantage o' us in a way. I could see thet they wuz gettin' ready ter make a rush down inter ther valley an' massacree us all, an' we prepared ter sell our lives dearly.

"One mornin' we missed Ezra, ther goat. I'll never fergit ther misery on ther face o' Ping-pong when he finds it out.

"'Bud,' he says ter me, 'I'm goin' out ter find Ezra, an' if them Injuns hez got him, I'm goin' ter bust ther whole tribe wide open.'

"I tried ter persuade him not ter go, but he will, so I goes with him. We sneaks up ther side o' ther hill, an' looks over ther ridge right down inter ther Injun village. The sight what met our gaze almost, but not quite, made me bust open with laughin'.

"Ther Injuns wuz all down on their hands an' knees, bowin' ter Ezra, who wuz walkin' eround on his hind legs, sashayin' sideways an' noddin' his head jest like a live bock-beer sign. Yer see, ther Injuns hed never seen a goat before, an' when Ezra walks onto them, waggin' his whiskers in a wise sort o' way, they thinks he's some kind o' a god, er somethin' like that. But when he got up on his hind legs an' begin ter sashay thet settled it. They wuz shore o' it then.

"We watched ther performance fer a while, then ther Injuns got up an' begin ter mosey. In an hour thar wuzn't a Injun within twenty mile. They jest hit ther high places fer home.

"Thet wuz ther way Ezra saved our party. After thet he could hev et every boot in ther outfit, an' thar wouldn't hev been a kick."

"What became of him?" asked Kit.

"Oh, he went back home with Ping an' raised a large family, an' they wuz talkin' o' runnin' him fer ther legislature an account o' his whiskers an' his smartness."

"He was a smart goat, wasn't he?" said Dick.

"You bet. Thet's why I said that some goats wuz jest ez smart ez lots o' collidge gradooates what I hev met."

CHAPTER XX
THE COUNTERFEIT BANK NOTE

When they arose in the morning the train was speeding over the prairie, and Dick could hardly be pulled away from the window long enough to go to breakfast with Stella and Mrs. Graham, so great was his delight at being in the "really and truly" wild West.

When they were all back in the car again, Ted, for the first time, noticed a large man, flashily dressed, who wore a flaming red necktie, and who evidently thought himself irresistible to the ladies.

He walked up and down the aisle on the slightest pretext, ogling every pretty woman in the car, and Ted was getting very tired of it, especially as once or twice he had the impertinence to stop and look into the stateroom in which Stella and Mrs. Graham were sitting.

"I'll take a fall out of that fellow if he keeps up that sort of thing much longer," said Ted, who was sitting beside Kit.

"I was thinking of the same thing," said Kit. "He makes me tired. I wonder what he is, anyway?"

"He has the make-up of a gambler or a saloon keeper," answered Ted. "He better keep away from me if he knows when he's well off."

At a town farther down the line a young lady entered the car, and took a seat directly in front of Kit, who was alone, Ted having gone to the front of the train to consult the conductor about a mistake that had been made in their tickets.

Presently the flashy man with the red necktie spied her and sauntered past her down the aisle. In a few moments he came back, twirling his black mustache, which evidently was dyed, and casting glances at the young lady.

Stopping in front of her, he said:

"Is this seat taken, lady?"

The young lady looked up, and answered coldly:

"No, sir; but there are plenty of other seats in the car which are unoccupied."

"This one looks good to me," said the fellow, with a smile which was supposed to be very fetching.

Without further excuse he plumped himself down in the seat beside her, and threw his arm familiarly over the back of it, at the same time hitching closer to her.

Then he tried to draw her into conversation, but she turned from him and looked out of the window.

But he persisted, and she showed that his attentions were annoying her.

Kit watched the proceedings, and was boiling with anger, but he did not feel that he had the right to interfere until the young lady showed by her manner that she desired assistance.

Presently the man said something to the young lady in a low voice that seemed to arouse her anger, for she rose hastily to her feet, her face burning.

"Let me pass!" she said.

"Don't leave me like this," said the fellow, blocking the way with his knees. "Sit down. We'll soon be good friends. You'll find me a good fellow."

"I insist, sir, that you allow me to pass," said the girl, growing pale, her voice rising a little.

Kit could stand it no longer. He reached over and tapped the fellow on the shoulder.

"Allow the lady to pass," he said quietly.

The hawk turned his head and sized Kit up. This did not take much time, for Kit was small and slender, his black eyes being the largest part of him, proportionately.

"What the deuce have you got to do with this?" he sneered, looking savagely at Kit.

"Just enough to make sure that you do it," said Kit, rising.

"Well, I don't allow no pups like you to interfere with me. You sit down an' let this gal an' me attend to our own business, er I'll bend you an' tie you into a knot an' throw you out of the window."

Kit did not reply, but he reached over and got the fellow by the coat collar and jerked him into the aisle, and, twisting him around, planted his toe between his coat tails with a force that sent him halfway down the length of the car.

"You're on the wrong train," said Kit. "The cattle train is on the other track."

The fellow soon regained his balance, and came rushing back like a charging bull.

"You little snipe!" he roared, "I'll kill you for that."

But as he got near Kit dodged into the space between the seats, and as the fellow rushed past, carried on by the momentum of his run, Kit swung at him with his right fist.

It caught the fellow back of the ear, and the force behind the blow, as well as the rate at which he had been coming, sent him headlong between two seats, where he lay crumpled up like a rag.

The commotion had attracted the attention of Bud and Ben, and they were by Kit's side in a moment.

"Need any help?" asked Bud.

"Not a bit," replied Kit. "I'm not very large, but no man of that sort can call me a pup."

The fellow lay where he fell, and Bud warned away several passengers who wanted to go to his assistance.

"He's all right," he said. "A crack like that never injured any one permanently, but sometimes it wakes them up ter ther foolishness of insulting a lady when ther broncho boys are around."

Kit lifted his hat to the young lady.

"Pardon me for making a disturbance," he said. "I don't think you'll be bothered again."

The young lady was profuse in her thanks, and resumed her seat.

Presently the fellow on the floor got up and sneaked into another car, without looking again at either Kit or the young lady.

"Hello, Kit! What was it all about?" asked Ted entering the car.

"Oh, I never could stand for red neckties, nohow," answered Kit apologetically.

When the train stopped for dinner they all trooped into the station dining room, and secured for themselves a long table, around which they sat like a big and happy family.

As Ted and Kit were walking along the platform toward the dining room Ted suddenly halted and stared at a man who was leaning against the wall of the station.

"By Jove, I believe it's him!" he muttered.

"Who's him?" asked Kit.

"The express robber, Checkers," answered Ted. "And yet I'm not sure. If it is him it's one of the best disguises I ever saw. Look at your friend of the red necktie hurrying up to him. By Jove, they're a good pair! I wish I could hear that fellow in the checked suit speak."

"That fellow will get caught up yet if he persists in wearing checked suits," said Kit. "It seems to be his badge, or a disease with him."

"I suppose that's why they call him Checkers," said Ted. "I wish I knew. I'd take a chance at arresting him."

At that moment the man in the checked suit looked up and caught Ted and Kit staring at him.

Hastily calling the attention of the man with the red necktie to them, he hurried around the corner, and the other followed.

Ted ran to the corner of the station, but all he could see of either was through a swirl of dust as the motor car in which they were riding flew up the street.

"By crickey! I'll bet anything that was Checkers," grumbled Ted. "I'm always too late to get to him. But next time I'll take a long chance with him."

The train pulled into Green River at eight o'clock that night, and they all went to the leading hotel, and Ted registered them as coming from the ranch.

During the evening the boys mingled with the crowd in the hotel lobby, talking cattle, and met many of the representative women of the section.

They were out after a bunch of stockers, and promised to be in the neighborhood for several days and to visit the ranches and look over the stock.

One of the men whom they met was introduced to them as Colonel Billings, ranch owner and speculator in cattle.

He was a middle-aged man of most pleasant features—benign, good-natured, and yet shrewd. He dressed well for a cowman, and from his pink, bald crown and gray chin whiskers down to his neat shoes, he looked the part of the prosperous business man.

"I have a lot of stock such as I think you boys need out at my ranch," he said to Ted, when he learned that they wanted to buy. "I'd like to have you bring your party out to the place and stay several days as my guests. You would then have plenty of time to look the stock over, and if you like them I'm sure we can strike a bargain."

Ted thanked him and promised to go out to look at the stock, but as for the invitation for the whole party to stop at the ranch, he would have to consult the wishes of the party. He rather liked the colonel, who was, apparently, bluff and sincere.

As Ted was on his way to the bank which had issued the bill which he had found in the haunted house, he stopped suddenly. He had just seen a young woman enter a store hurriedly, and look at him over her shoulder as she did so. She it was who had slipped the note of warning into his pocket in the Union Station, in St. Louis.

Evidently she was trying to avoid him. But why? He wanted to thank her for that kindly service, and, quite naturally, he had some curiosity to know who she was.

Without apparently hurrying he followed her into the store, and looked around for her. She was not in sight, and he walked up and down the aisles between the counters, but could not find her.

Then he observed that there was a back door to the store, which opened onto an arcade. She had escaped him through that, and Ted looked up and down the arcade. At the far end, where it opened out into the public square, a carriage stood, and a young lady was getting into it.

It was the young lady of the subtle perfume and the note.

In a moment she was gone.

He was not far from the bank, and giving the young woman no more thought, for he was sure he would see her again, for she seemed to be mixed up in his fortunes in some manner, he made his way to the financial institution and asked for the president.

"You will find Mr. Norcross in his private office at the end of the corridor," said the clerk.

At the door of the office Ted found a colored messenger, who stopped him and asked his business.

"Is Mr. Norcross in his office?" asked Ted.

"Yes, sah, but he is busy," answered the messenger.

"Well, take my card in to him, and tell him I would like to see him when he is at leisure."

The negro went away, and in a few moments returned to say that Mr. Norcross would be glad to see Mr. Strong presently.

While Ted waited he stood looking out of the window into the street. The door behind him opened, and he turned.

Walking rapidly down the corridor was the man with the pointed beard, whom he had seen in the Union Station in St. Louis give the signal to the girl who had slipped the note into his pocket.

Ted stared after him. The mystery of the note was getting thicker. But he would try to think it out later.

He found Mr. Norcross an elderly, but active man.

"What can I do for you, Mr. Strong," said the banker, referring to Ted's card.

"I come to you for information concerning a recent robbery and the murder of an express messenger in an express car in St. Louis," said Ted.

"In what capacity do you come?"

"As an officer of the government."

"Oh, ah, rather young for such work, aren't you?"

"Pardon, but that has nothing at all to do with it. I am a deputy United States marshal, and have received instructions to examine into certain matters regarding the recent robberies from express trains in this part of the country."

"I suppose you have your credentials as an officer."

"I think I can convince those who have the right to know that I am what I profess to be."

"Very well. I meant no offense, but there have been so many violent things done out here, that naturally a banker desires to at least know something of his callers. What can I do for you?"

"Did your bank make a shipment of currency to the East, last week?"

"Yes, sir, that is a well-known fact."

"What was the amount?"

"Forty thousand dollars. It was to meet some paper which was due in St. Louis."

"And it was stolen from the express car?"

"Yes. The express company has reimbursed us for it."

"What sort of currency was it?"

"Mostly of our own issue."

"Do you recognize this bill?"

Ted took from his pocket the counterfeit bill of the bank, and handed it to the president, who looked at it a moment and handed it back.

"Yes, that is one of the bills. The money sent was all in that series of numbers."

Ted picked the bill up, and put it in his pocket.

"Here, you mustn't take that," said the president. "That is the property of the bank. Give it to me. The express company will need it for evidence."

"Then I will keep it. It will be safer with me."

A suspicion had entered Ted's mind, which was strengthened by the conduct of the president, who was white-faced and trembling.

"From your examination of the bill, you are positive that it was one of those shipped to St. Louis?"

"I am not certain, of course, but as I said, it is within the series of numbers which we sent. Why do you ask?"

"Because it is a counterfeit."

The president sank down in his chair. He had suddenly become pale, and was trembling like a leaf.

"What will you take for that bill, young man? Name your own price," said Mr. Norcross.

"It is not for sale, and you have not money enough to buy it," replied Ted Strong.

CHAPTER XXI
A CRIME WITHIN A CRIME

"Well, friend, have you decided to come out to my ranch, and look my stock over?"

It was Colonel Billings, the genial ranchman, who addressed Ted, meeting him in the lobby of the hotel.

"Yes, I think I will," answered Ted. "When will it be convenient for you to be there?"

"I am going out to-morrow, and will be glad to see you and your friends."

"There are a good many of us," said Ted, laughing.

"The more the merrier. The house is large, and I could drop you all down into it, and the house would hardly know it."

"How do we get out there?"

"I see you have a couple of ladies with you, and I shall telephone over to my manager to send a carriage in for them, and horses for the use of you boys. How many horses and saddles will you need? There are plenty at the ranch."

"We will need eight horses. One of the ladies prefers to ride, and we'll need a gentle pony for the small boy, whose experience is limited."

"Sidesaddle for the lady?"

"No," said Ted, with a grin, "this young lady will not use one. She is a cowgirl, and rides a man's saddle."

"All right, my boy. The outfit will be here in the morning. By the way, I am going to have some other guests. I suppose you will not object."

"Certainly not."

"One of them is a young New Yorker, who has come West to invest in ranch property, and who has brought his sister with him. Charming people. The other is a rather uncouth person, but you will forgive his eccentricities, I am sure. To tell you the truth, he often grates on me, but I overlook it because he has lacked advantages. He made his money in the liquor business, in which he has been all his life. But he is a good fellow at heart, and is my partner in a way, having invested a large sum of money with me in cattle."

"I shall be very glad to meet them, although, I'm afraid I shall not be able to see much of them, as I shall be very busy."

"When you are under my roof, sir, you are as free as if you had been born there. I am glad you and your friends are coming. It does my old heart good to have young people around me. I will see you in the morning, and shall feel honored to escort you to my home."

With this they parted.

"Jolly old chap," said Ted to himself. "I know just how he feels about having a lot of people come to visit him. I like it myself."

Stella had been out for a ride with little Dick. She had secured a couple of ponies from the stable connected with the hotel, and had given Dick his first riding lesson.

Ted met them as they were dismounting in front of the hotel.

"Ted, that boy is going to be a second edition of you in the saddle," cried Stella enthusiastically. "I never saw such a seat for a kid. Why he takes to a horse like a young duck to water."

"That's good," said Ted. "Do you like to ride, Scrub, I mean Dick?"

The boy flushed at the name Scrub, but he recovered himself immediately.

"Yes, it's fine," he answered. "I like horses, and they seem to take to me. I'd like to ride a horse all the time."

"Well, you'll have all you want of it when you get out to Moon Valley," said Ted. "Would you like to go out again? If you do, go ahead. I guess we can trust you not to break your neck."

The boy smiled and nodded, and climbed into his saddle again, and was off.

"Ted, that boy is going to be a credit to us all," said Stella. "But he must have an education. Although he speaks well and doesn't use much slang, that is, for a boy, he knows absolutely nothing that he hasn't picked up. He must go to school some day, but not now, for he hardly knows his alphabet, and as for other branches of knowledge, why, he doesn't know they exist, and he is as full of superstition as a Cocopo squaw. Wherever he got his beliefs, I can't imagine."

"All right, Stella, he shall go to school. It doesn't really matter much, that he has never been to school before. He'll learn so fast that he'll make up for lost time, don't fear. That boy has a good head."

"I'm going to teach him myself until he is able to take his place in school with boys of his own age. He's just crazy to learn."

"His early education is up to you. I'm not afraid he will learn anything he shouldn't from you. Go at him slowly and sensibly. Don't try to stuff it all into him at once. Meanwhile, I'll teach him to ride, shoot, herd, rope, and all that, occasionally impressing upon him the cardinal principles of the broncho boys—truth, honesty, sincerity, courage, and kindness."

"He'll be a fine fellow some of these days, Ted, and a good-looking and good-tempered one."

"I think he will. Suppose we take a little walk, if you have nothing better to do. I want to get your opinion on some matters."

"The very thing. I saw a pretty little park on the bank of a river. We'll walk there."

"I have promised to go out to Colonel Billings' ranch to-morrow, and I took the liberty of accepting the invitation for you all, as there is nothing to do around here, and I have a hunch that something good will come of it."

"I'll be glad to go. You know how much I like the town. I wouldn't care if I never saw one again."

"It's all right, then. We'll start in the morning. I am more than anxious to go now, especially as Billings tells me he has invited several other people to be his guests."

"Who are they?"

"You remember the girl who slipped the note into my pocket in the St. Louis station, and the young fellow with the pointed beard. Well, I saw them both in town this morning. The girl ran away from me on the street, jumped into a carriage, and drove away."

"There's nothing about you to cause a girl to run." Stella looked up at Ted in a teasing way.

"That'll be all right," said he. "But a few minutes after I saw the fellow with the pointed beard coming out of the private office of Norcross, the president of the bank that was robbed of the forty thousand dollars. He went by me like a rocket, as if he were afraid of me."

"Sure it was he?"

"Positive. But the strange part of it was my interview with the banker. He acknowledged that the bank had been robbed of the money, and identified the bill dropped by Checkers in his flight, as one of the shipment, but when I announced that it was a counterfeit, he went all to pieces, and, after trying to bluff me into giving him the note, wanted to buy it, asking me to name my own price."

"What does that mean, I wonder?"

"It means, that this case of the robbery and the murder of the express messenger is not the simple thing I thought. There is a crime within a crime."

"What in the world do you mean?"

"Just this, Norcross, the banker, is mixed in the crime, and Heaven only knows how many more men quite as prominent as he. The express-robbing syndicate is a strong one, and hard to beat."

"But you'll beat it yet. I know you."

"Thank you for your faith and encouragement, Stella. But it's going to be a hard pull, and it will take all of us to do it."

"What do you think of it now?"

"My idea is, that the alleged forty thousand dollars was not real money at all, and that Norcross was trying to double-cross the very men he was standing in with."

"Still, I hardly understand."

"Well, Norcross agreed with the members of the syndicate to ship forty thousand dollars to St. Louis, which was to be stolen en route by the syndicate's own men. They would then have their forty thousand back, and the forty thousand which they could make the express company pay them. The original forty thousand would come back to Norcross, and he would get his share of the money which the express company would pay."

"That was easy."

"It would have been, but for the fact that Norcross insisted upon being insured for the use of his forty thousand in case anything else happened to it. In this way he got another large sum."

"I see. But from what you have found out so far, I don't quite understand how you figure it out."

"All I have to go by is my own way of deducing things. The forty thousand dollars which was to be stolen was supposed by the other members of the syndicate to be real money. It was for this that the syndicate insured Norcross. But, instead, he substituted counterfeits, if, indeed, most of the supposed money was not just blank paper."

"He is a real financier, eh?"

"Yes, but he didn't take into consideration that he had scoundrels just as shrewd as himself to deal with. For instance, I believe when the truth is known, it will be found out that the syndicate was going to beat Norcross. But that is mere supposition. The tug of war is coming soon. It will take place at the ranch of Colonel Billings."

"I thought you believed in him."

"I do. I have made a few inquiries about him. I wanted to find out what sort of a chap he was before taking you and your aunt out to his place. Every one speaks of him as one of the leading men in the county and State."

"Then why should he be drawn into this mess?"

"I think he has done it unconsciously. He has a partner who has invested money in Billings' cattle. Do you remember the fellow in the train whom Kit knocked down? The chap who insulted that pretty girl."

"Yes."

"From the description given me of one of his coming guests by the colonel, I believe the man with the red necktie is he."

"What? That horrid thing."

"I didn't tell you, but Kit and I saw him talking to a man at the station where we stopped for dinner, whom I am convinced was no other than Checkers himself."

"Whew! That looks suspicious."

"In addition to that, the colonel has invited a man and his sister to visit him while we are there. This man is a New Yorker; I don't know his name, but the colonel says he is out here to buy a ranch. Who do you suppose it is?"

"Haven't an idea."

"The girl who dropped the warning note into my pocket, and the young man with the pointed beard."

"Whew! again."

"Looks pretty complicated, doesn't it?"

"Worse than that. Ted, are you sure about this Colonel Billings?"

"One is sure of nothing in this world, but I have taken a fancy to Billings, and when I like a man he generally turns out all right, making allowances for minor faults and habits. Yes, I think I can trust Billings."

"But not his friends. Ted, do you want to know what I think?"

"Certainly."

"I feel that the invitation out there is a trap to catch you, and possibly keep you away from the town."

"Nonsense! Why should they want to keep me away from the town? There doesn't seem to be anything wrong in town that I could bother them in, except the Norcross incident, and if, as I suspect, he has duped his partners, he will say nothing to them about me."

"Suppose they want to get out there to do away with you."

"They wouldn't ask all of you out there with me in that case."

"That is where you are mistaken. They are too shrewd to excite your suspicions by inviting you alone. It will not be hard for them to get you away from the ranch to look at some cattle and then kill you. Ted, you are too dangerous to them to be let alone."

"Well, it can't be helped now, and being right in among them is a hope I did not expect to see realized so easily. But they will have no advantage over me, for none of the syndicate, I take it, know of the counterfeits as yet, except Norcross and the inevitable Checkers. But at that, I don't think they will resort to violence. We are too strong for them, at the ranch, at least I believe they will use diplomacy."

"Well, we can play at the game ourselves. There, perhaps, I can help you."

"You bet you can. But let us go down to the station and see if the red motor car, 118, has arrived yet."

When they reached the station, Ted went to the express agent and asked for the car.

"Yes," said the agent, "the car arrived this morning, Mr. Strong, and I delivered it according to your instructions. The charges are not paid yet. Your messenger said you would call later and settle for them, and, knowing you by reputation, I let it go."

Ted was staring at the agent.

"You delivered it according to my instructions?"

"Yes, sir."

"I didn't give any one an order for the car."

"Why, you must have forgotten it. Here it is. I happened to see one of your boys down here, and called him to one side and asked him if it was your signature, and he very promptly identified it."

"Let me see that order."

The agent produced an order written on the note paper of the hotel.

Ted stared at it incredulously.

"It looks like my writing, but I didn't write it. I'll swear to that. Look at this, Stella. Is that my hand?"

Stella looked at the paper studiously for a minute or two, then handed it back.

"A casual look at it would deceive me, but you did not write it. It lacks several of your individualisms, and has others that are not yours."

"That is right. This order is a forgery. I did not write it. The express-robber syndicate is getting bolder every minute. They'll come in and steal you some day," Ted said to the agent. "Notify your company that my car has been stolen, and that I want it restored to me."

"Great Scott!" was all the agent could say.

"What sort of looking chap was it that presented the order?" asked Ted.

"Well, he was an ordinary-looking chap. He had on a—"

"Checked suit?"

"Yes, sir. How did you know?"

"Checkers has come into his own at last," said Ted, turning to Stella.

CHAPTER XXII
TED IN THE TOILS

The following morning an impressive cavalcade set out for the ranch of Colonel Billings, led by the genial owner himself. Behind him came Ted and Stella, between whom rode little Dick.

Then came Mrs. Graham in a well-appointed carriage, and acting as her outriders and escorts were the boys. When they arrived at the ranch, after passing numerous herds of fine cattle on the way, they found one of the finest ranch houses in the West.

It was a great, white modern structure that could be seen for miles across the level prairie, which showed hardly a single rise or depression in all the miles they had ridden.

None of the guests whom the colonel had told Ted would be present accompanied the party. The colonel explained this by saying that other matters had detained them in town, and that he preferred to permit them to follow, rather than defer the pleasure of being their escort.

This was said with so much sincerity that Ted could not doubt him. Mrs. Graham and Stella were ensconced in a large apartment on the first floor, with large windows opening upon a wide veranda.

Both expressed themselves as delighted with their room, much to the gratification of their host. The broncho boys found quarters in the spacious second floor, which had as many rooms as the average hotel.

"Well, what do you think of Colonel Billings now?" Ted asked of Stella, when they met on the broad lawn in front of the ranch house after they had seen their rooms.

Stella simply shook her head.

"What do you mean by that?" asked Ted. "That you don't know, or that you don't care to say?"

"I can't tell you yet, Ted. I like him somehow for his genial ways, and yet something tells me to beware."

"Well, I'd sooner trust your intuition than my judgment. I'll keep an eye on him. And—yet, I feel the same as you in a way. But I hate to distrust any one."

"I know you do, Ted, and that is why you get fooled on some people sometimes."

"But not on all people all the time?"

"That's it."

"Then what does one's first impression amount to, anyway?"

"Not much, unless they can make good a good first impression."

"I'm not going to worry about him. The other fellows are the ones for that."

"That's what I think."

"I'm going to ride out over the range, and take a look at the cattle. Want to go along?"

"Of course I do."

They found their horses in the corral, and after telling Colonel Billings that they would be back for dinner, departed.

"When you go through the west gate into the big pasture, look out for a big Hereford bull in there," Colonel Billings called after them.

Ted nodded and waved his hand, and they were off. Colonel Billings certainly did have a splendid ranch. They rode for miles within the fences before they came to the west gate.

"Think we better go any farther?" asked Ted, when they had come this far.

"Yes. Let us go on," replied Stella. "We have plenty of time, and I would like to see just how big this ranch is."

"Don't forget the red bull," said Ted, as he closed the gate behind them.

"I've seen many a dangerous bull before," laughed Stella.

"If we find him and he takes after us, keep on the far side of me. I don't much fancy that pony you're on."

"I don't myself. I wish we had a bunch of Moon Valley ponies here to ride. I've never seen any that could come up to them."

They were following a trail that led directly into the west. It was a cattle trail, and Ted's practiced eye told him that it led to water. Several miles to the west he saw the plain became broken.

"There's water over there," he said.

"That's where we'll find the cattle," answered Stella. "Do you want to go that far and look at them?"

"I will if you think you can stand it."

Stella looked at him scornfully.

"I guess this beast will go the distance," she answered, giving the little gray a clip with her quirt, and galloping ahead of Ted, who was not slow to follow.

As they proceeded the ground became more and more broken.

"I believe there is a bit of 'bad land' over there," said Ted, pointing forward.

Still they saw no cattle, although Colonel Billings had told him that morning that his greatest herd, the one he wished the boys to examine with the view to purchase, lay in the big west pasture.

But all they could see so far was the broad stretch of green prairie and the low line of the rough land in the distance. Not a living thing was in sight.

The only movement was the flying shadows of the white clouds over the prairie, and the waving of the deep, rich grass when a vagrant breeze swept by.

But suddenly Ted pulled in his pony, and shaded his eyes with his hand, staring into the west.

"What is it?" asked Stella, reining in.

"I thought I saw something red shoot across the horizon to the west, where you see those gray rocks," answered Ted.

"A cow—or, perhaps, the dangerous red bull," laughed Stella.

"Nothing like that. It wasn't the right color. Did you ever see a scarlet cow?"

"Never did."

"Well, the thing I saw was scarlet, and it was not shaped like a cow."

He was still looking intently into the west.

"There it is again!" he exclaimed, unlimbering his field glasses.

After a moment of intense scrutiny, he raised the glasses suddenly to his eyes.

"By Jove!" he cried, "it's a motor car, and I believe it's 118."

"Impossible!" cried Stella.

"No, entirely possible," said Ted intensely. "Don't you see if it was this fellow Checkers who got the machine from the agent by false pretenses he would take it as far away from town as possible?"

"Yes, I see that."

"Then which direction would he take if, as I think, he is in league with the train-robbing syndicate, which we have persuaded ourselves to think made their headquarters at Green River, but in this direction? We have learned that others of those we believe to be in it are to be the guests of this ranch, and —"

"I see. He could not well bring the red car to the ranch house."

"That's it."

"Then where do you suppose he's going with it?"

"There's no better place to hide it than in those very 'bad lands,' if I am guessing right, at the rough land yonder."

"True. What are you going to do about it?"

"I'm going to find that red car and my friend, Checkers."

"Not alone, Ted. You're going to get the other boys to help you, aren't you?"

"Now is the accepted time. I'm going right away now. But it would be a good scheme for you to ride back to the ranch and tell Bud and the boys quietly what I am about, and have them come out in case I should need help."

"I hate to see you ride away alone, Ted. You can't tell what there is over there. Better let me go along."

"No, Stella, it would be no use. You know that I appreciate your courage and skill in every way, but this, probably, will be no work for girls."

Stella pouted at this. She did not like the idea of the long ride back to the ranch house alone.

She looked at Ted to see if he really was in earnest, and when she saw the look in his face she turned back with a wave of the hand and a "So long!" and started for the ranch house.

"Tell Bud to bring three or four of the boys out here with him," shouted Ted after her. "Thank you, Stella."

But she only nodded her head and pursued her way, and Ted, after looking after her for a moment, rode forward. He had not seen the red car for several minutes, it having disappeared behind a rocky butte.

Having a fair horse, he gave it the gad and struck into a gallop. Soon he entered upon the rough land, and from a rise saw a stream below and a herd of cattle beyond, where the prairie began again; the railroad, and a small red station house, with two or three low buildings about it.

He now understood that he had seen the red car on the far side of the ravine, through which the stream flowed, and went down to the stream, his horse sliding on its haunches amid a clatter of broken clay and pebbles.

He was soon across and clambered up the other wall of the ravine, and there in the clay found the impression of the tires of the red car.

"I'm all right now," he muttered to himself. "On the track of Checkers and the robbers' automobile. I wonder where it will end."

He had no difficulty in following the tracks of the automobile for a considerable distance, when the ravine ran out on that side and the bank of the stream flattened; and he rode along it, following the trail with ease.

Then the bank of the stream rose again, and the water flowed through a ravine, into which the red car had entered. It could not escape him, and Ted chuckled, and examined his revolver, loosening it well in its holster, for he had not forgotten the warning against Checkers given him by Chief Desmond.

The ravine grew deeper as he advanced, and soon it became tolerably dark at the bottom where the high walls shut out the light. Suddenly his horse stumbled, and, as Ted shot over its head, he heard the twang of a broken wire that had been stretched across the path.

He had fallen into a trap. As he struck the earth, he was stunned for a moment, then a heavy weight was upon him.

He twisted around and felt for his revolver, but it had fallen from his holster, and he felt his arms grasped and a thong passed around his wrists, and then around his ankles.

The weight was lifted from him and he rolled over on his back. Standing above him was the man whom he knew as Checkers.

"Well, my lad, you delivered yourself like a lamb to the slaughter," said Checkers, with a smile.

Ted could say nothing. He was too busy wondering how easily he had fallen into the toils.

"You went up against a tough proposition when yon tackled me," continued the man. "It would have been a good thing for you if you had never run across me. You know too much to be left alive. I shall see that you are properly taken care of."

Checkers issued a shrill whistle.

"Come," he said to Ted, "get to your feet."

Ted arose as three men came around an elbow of the wall of the ravine.

"Take care of this boy," said Checkers to them. "And if he escapes—"

He finished the sentence with a smile that made the men wince.

CHAPTER XXIII
STELLA IMITATES SANTA CLAUS

"Come on, fellow," said one of the men, jerking Ted along by hops.

"We'll attend to him all right, boss," said another.

"He'll get all that's coming to him," said the third, with a grin that was almost as diabolical as that of Checkers.

Around the elbow of the ravine wall, in a small cove was a log cabin with a lean-to shed, under which was sheltered the fatal red car which had lured him to captivity.

The cabin was backed up against the wall of the ravine, and was small and dirty as to interior. A fire burned in a big stone fireplace at one end, filling the room with a suffocating smudge.

The room was almost dark, but Ted, from the corner into which he had been flung, was soon able to make out that the men were cooking something over the glowing embers, at the same time taking swigs from a black bottle, and smoking reeking pipes of vile tobacco.

After the food was cooked they began to eat, but did not offer Ted any of it, all the while making jokes at his expense, and vaguely hinting at his fate.

Ted wished now that he had taken Stella's advice, and had not rushed in so rashly. Had he waited for Bud and two or three of the boys to come to his assistance, he could easily have caught the whole lot for their cabin was in a perfect pocket from which they could not have escaped.

Who were these rough fellows with whom Checkers would not associate, for Ted could hear his archenemy pacing up and down outside, and he had not forgotten how he had addressed these men?

Probably they were only ordinary villains who did the dirty work planned by the wiser heads of the syndicate. He wondered if the boys would be able to find him before they settled with him, as they had promised.

After the men had finished their meal the voice of the leader summoned them outside. Ted could hear commands being given in a low voice, and mumbles from the men.

It appeared from what Ted could gather from the tones of the voice, rather than from any words that he caught, that one of the men was protesting against what Checkers was ordering.

Suddenly there was a cry of agony.

"Don't do that, boss," said one of the men.

"Shut up, or you'll get a taste of the same knife," came the voice of Checkers in a tone of rage. "When I say a thing must be done it is as good as done. Now go ahead and do as I tell you."

"But, boss—"

"Go on, and do it. Are you a coward? You've done it before," Ted heard Checkers say. "I'm going away now, and if you can't show me what I want when I get back, well—you know."

In a moment Ted heard the chug of the motor car, then the grating of the tires on the earth as it started away.

"Remember what I said," the voice of Checkers came floating back.

"Say, Bill, this is a derned outrage," said one of the men outside. "I, fer one, am not in favor of standin' for it."

"Well, if yer don't, you'll get the same," said other man.

"I never see any one so handy with that bloomin' knife o' his."

"Look out you don't get a taste o' it, then."

"Is he dead, Bill?"

There was a shuffling of feet outside, and Ted knew that they were turning a body over.

"Yes, he's stone-dead."

"Pore Dick! He had his faults, but he was a good pal."

"He wuz, but too derned soft-hearted. He didn't want ter kill a feller in cold blood never."

"An' yet he wa'n't no coward. I never see ther time Dick w'd refuse ter fight if ther other feller had some show, an' he wa'n't squeamish about holdin' up a train er runnin' off a bunch o' cattle, but I always hear him say thet he didn't take no stock in plain, straight murder."

"That's so, but it's not murder, Tom, when yer kills ther feller what's yer enemy. Now, honor bright, is it?"

"I dunno. I was brought up ter fight, an' fight like ther devil hisself when it come ter fightin', but I reckon I'm too much o' a derned coward ter murder cold."

"Well, this is one o' ther times when it's got ter be did, an' I reckon we might as well be about it. Git ready."

"No, sir, I'm not goin' ter do it."

"Tom, yer a fool. Do yer know what'll happen when ther boss comes back an' finds out that it ain't been did?"

"I do."

"An' aire yer goin' ter resk it?"

"I be."

"Then ye're a bigger fool than I am. I'm goin' ter carry out orders. What's ther difference? A couple of good slashes an' it's all over."

"But think o' the death cry, Bill. I've heerd too many o' them already. I hears them when I sleep and they wake me up."

"Tom, yer talk ter me like a sick canary peeps. I always thought yer wuz a man."

"An' don't yer think so now, Bill?"

"Not from ther way yer talkin'."

"Well, if yer has any doubts erbout it I'll give yer a chanct ter prove it, any way yer like."

"Now, what's ther use o' talkin' that away, Tom? Dick's dead by ther hand o' ther boss. What's thar in it fer you or me if ther cub in thar dies er not? Be sensible."

"It ain't matterin' a chaw o' terbaccer ter me whether he dies er not, but he's got a right ter die in a natural way, so to speak."

"An' how is that, my Sunday-school friend?"

"In a fair fight, by gosh!"

"An' who's goin' ter give him a fair fight? I don't want none o' it."

"So that's ther way yer built, is it, Bill? I always thought yer was a game man."

"I reckon I be, but that's not in this question. Here's an enemy ter ther gang what lays bound in the cabin. Why should I resk my life in a fight with him er fer him. It's so derned easy fer a feller ter go in thar an' stick a knife inter him, an' then, yer see, it's all over with."

"Yer wrong, Bill."

"I'd sooner do that than have ther boss come back an' stick his knife inter me."

"Aire yer afraid ter fight ther boss?"

"He's ther only man I be afraid of."

There was a long silence following this, and Ted understood the terrible power of Checkers over his men, and Desmond's warning.

"Well, I'm tired o' chewin' erbout ther virtue o' killin' a man one way or another, an' I'm goin' ter foller orders. If you don't want ter jine in I reckon as how I'll have ter tell ther boss that yer flunked."

There was no response to this, and a few moments elapsed in which Ted listened hopefully for his champion's voice.

Suddenly something dropped in the fireplace, and Ted, straining his eyes in that direction, saw a tiny pair of tan riding boots come into view, followed by a tan skirt, and Stella dropped noiselessly into the room.

She held up a warning finger as she saw Ted in the corner.

"Sh, sh!" she whispered, as she felt for his bonds and cut them.

Ted was on his feet on the instant, and Stella pressed a revolver into his hand.

"I didn't go back to the ranch house, but followed you here. I saw the red car go out, and hid. Then I sneaked along until I heard those fellows quarreling. I was on the top of the bluff here, and guessed that you were inside the cabin, as I couldn't see you anywhere outside, so I just dropped in." As Stella whispered this she smiled, and Ted could only look his thanks.

The fellow named Tom, who had been opposed to killing Ted, had evidently been doing some hard thinking, and the threat of his mate to expose him to Checkers evidently convinced him that he would rather be alive than perish for a mere sentiment.

"All right, Bill," he said; "I don't like it, but we've got to share it."

"Sure," said the other. "It'll be blow and blow. We both strike together."

"Come on, then."

"Now," said Ted, putting Stella behind him and crouching in the darkness.

The two men entered the cabin noisily, knowing that they had nothing to fear from an unarmed boy bound hand and foot and lying in the corner with nothing to hope for.

As they approached the corner they were surprised to see a stalwart young form arise suddenly and a pair of revolvers gleam through the darkness as a voice rang out commandingly:

"Hands up!"

The hands of both went up very promptly.

"Drop those knives!"

A pair of knives clattered to the floor.

"Face about, both of you, and go out. The first to make a break gets a shot in the back."

At Ted's command both men obeyed. When they were outside in the sunlight, Ted looked them over. Both had revolvers in their holsters.

"Take their revolvers away from them, Stella," said Ted.

As the girl moved forward to comply with the request of Ted Strong, the men stared at her in amazement.

"Now, which of you is Tom?" asked Ted.

"I am," said one of them.

"You lie!" answered Ted. "I know you by your voice. You are not Tom:—you are Bill."

"Yes, I'm Tom," said the other fellow.

"That's right," said Ted.

"Now, see here, Tom, if I give you the chance will you dig out of this and escape? It won't be very long before you are caught, anyway, and you know what that means."

"You bet I will," said the fellow, who had protested against the murder of Ted.

"All right, I'll give you the chance. I'll take your friend in charge myself. You can take down your hands, Tom."

The fellow was in a state of wonderment as he did so.

"Who are you, anyway?" asked the fellow called Bill.

"I am Ted Strong."

"Then it's all up. We're done for," said the train robber, in a resigned voice.

CHAPTER XXIV
TED HOLDS A PROFITABLE BAG

Tom signaled to Ted to step aside, and, telling Stella to keep the other fellow covered with her revolver, Ted accompanied him.

"Thank yer fer turnin' me loose," said Tom. "I've been tryin' ter get away fer months, but couldn't. Here's a tip: They're goin' ter rob ther Overland Express t'-night right out yon at that little station yer can see from ther top o' ther rise. Ther loot is ter be hid near Bubbly Spring until things blow over, but ther gang will come here. Thar's my tip. Good-by. I'm off."

The fellow disappeared up the bank of the stream.

Ted bound the other upon the back of his pony, which he found not far from the scene of his own downfall, and conveyed him to Green River, where he placed him in jail, with instructions that he should be allowed to communicate with no one.

Then he and Stella returned to the Billings ranch house.

"Say nothing whatever about our adventure," said Ted, as he and Stella rode along discussing the matter. "I think there will be something doing there to-night."

When they got back to the ranch, Ted simply explained their absence by saying that they had ridden farther than they had at first intended.

Ted was introduced to the other guests, who had arrived in his absence. There was Mr. Norcross, the banker, who looked a little sheepish when Ted shook hands with him and acted as if he had never seen him before. The man with the black mustache and the red necktie was Mr. Dennis Corrigan, of Chicago, and neither he nor the boys appeared to have seen him before. The young man with the pointed beard was Mr. van Belder, of New York.

Colonel Billings was full of hospitable notions, and made the afternoon pass delightfully.

"They tell me there is very good shooting in the neighborhood at times," said Mr. Corrigan, as they all sat on the veranda in the afternoon.

"Excellent," said the colonel. "At this time of the year the snipe shooting is fine."

"What is the best time to shoot them?" asked Van Belder.

"I should say after dark," said the host, with an imperceptible wink at Mr. Corrigan.

"I don't see how you can shoot snipe after dark," said Ted.

"You don't exactly shoot them," explained Mr. Corrigan. "It's this way, and a fine game, and often practiced in South Chicago: The party goes out, and one holds the bag while the rest go along and drive the birds in, and the fellow who holds the bag catches them in it. It's lots easier than shooting them, and you get more birds."

"By Jove, that's a new experience to me!" said Ted. "I'd like to try it."

Mr. van Belder looked at him curiously, but drawled that he thought it very fine sport. So it was agreed that that night they should go on a snipe-bagging expedition.

The party was to be made up of Ted, who was eager to hold the bag for the snipe to run into; Mr. Corrigan, the colonel, Mr. van Belder, and a few others.

Most of the boys declined absolutely to go.

"Say, aire ye gittin' plumb dotty?" asked Bud, when he got Ted out of hearing. "Tell me, is it possible thet yer eyeteeth aire so far secreted up inter yer head thet yer don't know erbout baggin' snipe?"

But all the answer Bud got was a wink.

"Now, what hez ther hombre got up his sleeve, I wonder?" said Bud, as he wandered off.

Ted and Stella had an animated conversation a few minutes later out of the sight and hearing of the others. But Stella walked off, smiling. She knew.

It was just getting dark when the party left the ranch house.

Ted carried a large, empty sack over his shoulder. With the organizers of the party went Bud, Ben, Kit, Carl, and Clay.

The maddest person in the house that evening was Stella, because she couldn't go, too. But as she said good-by to the party from the steps of the ranch house she smiled comprehensively at Ted.

A walk of a half mile brought the party to the edge of a small creek.

"Now," said Mr. Corrigan, "here's where you wait with the bag while we go up to the creek and chase them down. You may have to wait a little while, and you must have patience."

"Don't worry about me," answered Ted; "I have plenty of that. I'll be here when the snipe come down, and if any of them get away, charge them to me."

After they had been gone some time Ted lit a match and looked at his watch. It was a quarter to nine.

The Overland Express was due in Green River at nine-twenty. The little red station of Polifax would foe passed by ten minutes after she left Green River.

While he was in Green River that afternoon Ted had been very careful to find the exact location of Bubbly Spring. He was more than two miles from it in his blind to wait for the snipe.

As soon as the crashing of the feet of the snipe drivers and the shouts and laughter had died away, Ted left his hiding place and darted through the dark woods and swampy ground for Bubbly Spring.

Long before he got there he heard the long screech of the whistle of the Overland Express announcing its approach at Green River, and a few minutes later its whistle that it was on its way. He had just reached Bubbly Spring and concealed himself in the bushes when the whistle gave a long shriek of danger.

The signal of the train robbers had been given at Polifax. The engineer had seen the red light and had whistled to the trainmen that danger was ahead, and that he was going to stop.

In a few moments Ted heard a few pops, and knew that the train robbers were firing their revolvers alongside of the train to prevent interference.

What if the train robbers should fail?

The train started up again, and Ted knew by that that nobody had been killed, and it added to his anxiety as to the success of the robbery. He wanted it to occur, for if he could secure the loot he could destroy the train robbers surely.

All he wanted now was tangible evidence. He lay back breathlessly in the bushes, waiting. Soon he heard the rapid hoofbeats of horses, then a crashing in the bushes.

These noises were approaching him rapidly. The crisis was at hand.

In a moment the moon burst through the clouds, illuminating the little valley through which the small stream from the spring flowed, and Ted crept into closer cover. Then into the glade galloped ten men.

Between two of them was swung a small, square thing, which was dropped at the foot of a cottonwood tree not a dozen feet from where Ted was concealed.

A man leaped from the back of a horse. He had a spade in his hand, and as he advanced Ted drew in his breath sharply.

It was Corrigan, the Chicago millionaire. Behind him was Norcross, the banker.

Ted looked vainly for Checkers. If he had been with the robbers at the holdup, he had not come here with them. Meanwhile, the dirt was flying, and a hole was being dug at the foot of the cotton wood.

After it was deep enough an iron box was dropped into it and covered with earth, and silently the men remounted and rode away.

Ted waited about fifteen minutes to be sure that none of them would return. Then he dug into the freshly laid earth and soon had exhumed the iron box. It was somewhat of a heavy load, but he packed it manfully, and in about half an hour carried it in his bag into the living room of the ranch house.

He was greeted with shouts of laughter from Corrigan and several of the others. But Stella looked at him anxiously, and he gave her a reassuring glance.

"Ha, ha!" laughed Corrigan. "What do you think of snipe hunting now?"

"It was a good joke," said the colonel, "but I'm sure you will take it good-naturedly."

"Yes," said Mr. Norcross, the banker. "It's quite a favorite amusement out here."

Only the New Yorker said nothing, but gave Ted a peculiar glance. Ted looked around at the group with a foolish smile.

"It was a good joke, gentlemen," said he, "and I have never been sore because I have been handed one."

Another burst of satisfied laughter greeted this from the big three—Corrigan, Norcross, and the colonel. But Stella and the boys looked glum that Ted was being made the butt of a joke.

Then Ted put his sack on the floor and opened it and lifted something out and placed it on the table. It was the iron box he had dug from the earth at Bubbly Spring, with the fresh earth still sticking to it.

Corrigan's face turned white. Norcross had to lean against the corner of the table to keep from falling.

Ted easily opened the lock of the box, and threw it open.

"You left me to hold the bag, did you?" he asked of the astounded conspirators. "Well, what do you think of these for snipe?"

The room was as quiet as a church.

"Gentlemen, you are all under arrest. Boys, get into your saddles. We are going to ride to the rendezvous of the gang of robbers which to-night robbed the Overland Express and stole the money I have here," and he lifted out package after package of stolen currency.

Stella was laughing and waving her hat.

"I knowed yer had somethin' up yer sleeve when yer consented ter go snipe huntin'! Yer ther limit," said Bud.

Only Mr. van Belder of all the conspirators was calm. He ripped a beard from his face, and there stood Darby O'Neill, the United States secret agent!

"Say, Ted, give me that counterfeit of the Green River National Bank. It is all I need to take Norcross away for a long term. I've been working on him for a long time, but you knocked the persimmon at last."

"You had me guessing," said Ted. "When I got that note that was slipped into my pocket in St. Louis I ought to have guessed that it was you, but you are so clever at disguise that you always fool me."

"But you've never fooled me yet," was the reply. "I've banked on you every time, and every time you've come back with the goods."

"But who was the young lady who slipped me the note?"

"My sister, who is a very clever girl detective, as you may know some day."

After the boys had made secure the three men at the head of the train robbers' syndicate, they went to the cabin in which Ted had so nearly lost his life, and secured the rest of the robbers.

Next morning at daylight they found the body of Checkers lying beside the fatal red car not far from the scene of the holdup. He had been killed by a stray shot fired by one of his own men.

Thus was the train robbers' syndicate wiped out through the acumen and courage of Ted Strong, and the loyal backing of his comrades.

The broncho boys decided that more stock was needed at the Moon Valley Ranch, and the entire outfit set out for No Man's Land, in northern Texas.

CHAPTER XXV
THE MAGPIE PONY

"Say, podner, might I be so free an' onquisitive ez ter inquire ez ter whar yer got thet thar palfrey yer ridin'?"

The speaker was a tall, gaunt old man with a tangled mass of grizzled whiskers, and the "podner" he addressed was Bud Morgan.

"Yer might," answered Bud, eying the questioner keenly.

"Well!"

"Why don't yer?"

"Oh, I see. Whar did yer git it?"

"I traded a Waterbury watch fer it, an' ther feller what made ther trade throwed in a pack o' cigareets."

"Oh!"

"Anything else ye'd like ter know?"

"Well, seein' ez yer so communicative, I'd like ter hev yer tell me how fur it's ter Yeller Fork."

"Betwixt grub."

"Come ergin."

"Ez fur ez yer kin ride betwixt 'arly breakfast an' dinner."

"Well, I'm obleegin' ter yer. I reckon we'll be hikin'."

"Who's ther kid?"

"Thet boy is my grandson. We come outer Missouri ter see what could be did in this yere new country, an' it's mighty hard sleddin'."

"What's ther trouble?"

"Well, stranger, so long ez yer kind ernuff ter inquire, I'll tell yer."

"I'm listenin'."

"I'm too old ter work at ther only thing what seems ter be out yere—cow-punchin'—an' ther kiddie is too young. Now, if 'twas farmin', we'd be in it."

"Thar ain't no more farmin' out yere than a rabbit, thet's shore. What might yer bizness be at home?"

"I'm a hoss trader."

"Thar ought ter be somethin' doin' out yere fer yer, then. All thar is in this country is hosses an' cattle."

"They ain't my kind o' hosses."

"Yer don't seem ter fancy cow ponies, eh?"

"I reckon they're all right in their way, podner, but they're a leetle too wild fer me to break, an' the kid's not strong enough."

"Askin' questions seems ter be fash'n'ble. Whar did yer git thet magpie hoss?"

Bud was looking over the old man's mount, a beautiful little black-and-white-spotted pony, as clean limbed as a racer, and with a round and compact body. It was a bizarre-looking little animal, with a long, black mane and tail, at the roots of which was a round, white spot. It was the sort of animal that would attract attention anywhere.

"Magpie! Podner, I riz her from a colt."

"She's shore a showy beast."

"She is some on ther picture, ain't she?" asked the old man, looking the pony over admiringly.

"She's all right, but—"

"But what, podner?" The old man looked at Bud with a frown.

"Well, I ain't none on knockin' another man's hoss, but I never see one o' them black-an'-white-spotted animiles what could do more than lope, an' out in this yere country hosses hez got ter run like a scared coyote ter be any good in ther cow business."

"Yer reckon this yere Magpie can't run?" asked the old man, bristling.

"I ain't said so."

"Well, yer alluded ter a magpie hoss as couldn't do nothin' but lope."

"I ain't never see none what could do much more."

"You ain't never see Magpie split ther wind, then."

"I ain't."

"Mebbe ye'd like ter."

"Mebbe I would."

"I reckon yer thinks ther cow what yer a-straddlin' of now kin run some."

"A leetle bit. But, yer see, when I got him he was a broken-down cow hoss what hed been ridden ter death an' fed on sand an' alkali water so long thet he wa'n't much good nohow."

"Jest picked him up wanderin'?"

"Not eggsactly. Yer see, it wuz this way: I was coming ercross Noo Mexico about a month back, when I runs foul o' a hombre what is all in. He hadn't et fer so long thet yer could see ther bumps made by his backbone through his shirt. I hed some grub in my war bag, an' I fed an' watered him. This yer nag wuz all in, too, an' he hed a long way ter go, so when ther feller ups an' perposes ter trade ponies I give him ther merry cachinnation."

"Ther what?"

"Ther laugh."

"Go ahead, podner, yer shore hez a splendid education."

"I see thet he'll never git ter whar he's goin' on ther nag, an' I thinks I'll do him a favor by sittin' him on a piece o' live hossmeat, an' I said I'd trade if he hed anythin' ter boot. Now, what do yer think he hed?"

"I ain't got a notion."

"A pack o' Mexican cigareets what burned like a bresh fire an' smelled like a wet dog under a stove."

"Haw, haw! An' yer traded?"

"I thought some fust, an' then I thinks what's ther odds? Thar's plenty o' hosses in camp, an' it'll probably save ther feller's life ter let him hev ther pony, what ain't none out o' ther common, so I says, 'It's a go, pard.' I clumb down an' we changed saddles, an' he handed over ther pack o' cigareets an' we went our ways."

"Yer shore is a kind-hearted man."

"I ain't, neither. I jest knows a hoss when I sees one."

"Yer don't call thet a hoss yer a-straddlin', I hope?"

"I shore do. He ain't much fer ter gaze on admirin', I agree, but he's a good little cayuse. I reckon, now, yer some proud o' thet magpie hoss."

"I be. It kin outrun anythin' this side o' ther State o' Newbrasky."

"P'r'aps yer lookin' fer a race ter see what ther best we've got in camp kin do, no?"

"Thar ain't nary time what I won't run a race if I think thar's ary merit in my hossflesh. How erbout ther animile what yer sits on so graceful?"

"Oh, I reckon he kin ride rings eround ther magpie hoss," said Bud, who was a trifle nettled at the old man's jeering tone.

"Yer certain got a lot o' confidence in a dead one."

"I reckernize ther fact that he ain't none pretty, but handsome is as handsome does. Hatrack is some shy on meat an' he's got a temper like a disappointed woman, ter say nothin' o' havin' had ther botts, ringbone, heaves, an' spavin', but he's a good nag, fer all thet, an' would be good-lookin' ernough if his wool wasn't wore off in so many places."

"Haw, haw! He ain't what ye'd call a show animile."

"He ain't, but, say, stranger, he *kin* run."

"What d'ye say ter a leetle brush betwixt Magpie an' yer Hatrack?"

"I'm ther gamest thing what ever yer see when it comes ter a hoss race."

"What'll we race fer?"

"Nag an' nag. If yer beats me, yer takes Hatrack, an' if he gits away with ther spotted pony, why, yer turns her over ter me. Is it a go?"

"If yer throw in a six-shooter fer odds."

"All right, pard, jest ter show yer thet I ain't no shorthorn, I'll go yer. I've got a shooter in my war-bag up ter camp what'll kick ther arm outer yer socket every time yer pulls ther trigger, but she'll send a bullet through a six-inch oak beam."

"Anything, so it's odds. I'll go yer. I reckon I could sell it fer a dollar er so."

"I reckon yer could," said Bud sarcastically. "I wuz offered ten dollars fer it by a hombre down ter Las Vegas a month ago. But he was a husky feller, an' wanted a strong shooter. He wanted ter go out huntin' fer a feller with it, an' I wouldn't let him hev it. Is it a go, shore enough?"

"It be."

"All right; come over ter ther camp an' stay overnight, an' fill yer pale American hides with ther best grub what ever wuz cooked on ther range. Our cook is an artist."

Bud led the way on his little, flea-bitten skeleton of a pony that snorted and reared, kicked, and showed the whites of its eyes when he woke it from the drooping position it had held while he was talking to the old man.

In half an hour they were in sight, from the hill they had topped, of a vast band of cattle grazing in a broad valley.

In a sheltered spot below the hill was a typical cow camp. A white-covered chuck wagon shone in the rays of the departing sun, and the smoke arose from the cook's fire, where he was baking biscuit in a Dutch oven, while the fragrant odors of frying bacon and steaming coffee filled the air.

"What have you found this time?" asked Ben Tremont, as Bud came into camp.

"This yere gent is a maverick from Missouri what I found wanderin' across the peerarie searchin' fer Yaller Fork, an' he hez bantered me ter a hoss race, I ast him ter come in an' stay overnight, an' eat, an' we'll run ther hosses in ther mornin'."

"What horses?"

"I'm goin' ter run Hatrack agin' thet magpie mare o' hisn, an' throw in a six-shooter with Hatrack if I lose."

"Say, are you going altogether dippy?" growled Ben. "Why, that little mare will run away from you as if Hatrack was tied to a post."

"Reckon so? Well, maybe I want to lose Hatrack, an' maybe all I want is ter capture thet magpie pony."

"Oh, what a lovely pony!"

Stella Fosdick had ridden into camp, and her exclamation of admiration for the magpie pony drew the attention of the boys to her.

"D'ye like thet thar pony?" asked Bud.

"I think it's beautiful," answered Stella enthusiastically.

"Then it's yours."

"What do you mean?"

"This old gent an' me is goin' ter hev a race in ther mornin', hoss fer hoss, an' when it's over ther magpie hoss is yours."

A peal of rippling laughter greeted this.

"See yere, gal, what is all this noise about?" asked Bud huffily. "If yer laughin' at ther idea o' Hatrack beatin' ther magpie hoss, don't yer do it, fer thet's showin' ignerance o' hossflesh, an' I thought yer wuz too well brought up at Moon Valley ter think thet pretty spots on a hoss hez anythin' ter do with his ability ter make a race er hold a cow."

"Forgive me, Bud, I didn't mean to laugh at Hatrack, but, really, he doesn't look as if he could run any faster than a lame dog."

"Oh, I reckon he'll git over ther ground fast ernough," said Bud, with a sly wink at the girl. "But he won't do it with me on his back. I'm a trifle heavy fer fast work. I'll hev ter git Kit ter pilot him, I reckon."

"I reckon you won't," said Stella. "If any one rides him it will be me. I'm a good many pounds lighter than Kit."

"All right, Stella. I wanted yer ter ride him, but I didn't like ter impose on good nature by askin' yer ter do it."

"Why, I'd love to ride the race. You ought to know me by this time."

"It's a go, an' if yer win, as win yer must, ther magpie hoss is yours."

"Oh, Bud, you don't mean it! Then I'll certainly ride to win."

So it was settled, and the old man and his grandson were accorded the hospitality of the camp.

After a hearty supper, while they were all sitting around the fire, and the old man was telling stories of his trip into the Southwest, for the broncho boys were now herding a big bunch of range cattle in what is known as No Man's Land, an arm of northern Texas lying west of Oklahoma, and claimed by both, the day watch rode into camp, and, stripping their saddles from their ponies, turned them loose. Then the boys threw themselves upon the ground to rest after several hours of constant riding.

One of the cowboys in the outfit, Sol Flatbush by name, stood staring at the old man and the boy.

He was scratching his forelock in a meditative sort of way, as if trying to remember something.

"What is it, Solly? I reckon what yer tryin' ter think of is that ye've forgot yer supper," said Bud.

"No, 'tain't that," said the cow-puncher, staring harder at the old man.

"Hear about ther race, Sol?" asked Ben.

"Now, don't yer expect me ter ask yer what race an' then spring thet ole gag about ther 'human race.' I won't stand fer it. I've got troubles enough. Thet buckskin pony o' mine hez hed ther very divil in him all day, an' I ain't feelin' none too amiable."

"This is on the square."

"Well, cut loose."

"Bud is going to race Hatrack against that magpie horse grazing out there, and throw in a six-shooter if the old gent wins."

Sol Flatbush turned and looked at the magpie pony, then at the old man. Suddenly a gleam of intelligence illuminated his face, and he grinned.

"Say, Bud, I wisht ye'd come over yere an' look at this buckskin's off hind foot, an' tell me what ye thinks o' it. He's been actin' powerful queer on it all day."

Bud rose lazily and followed Sol out of camp. The buckskin was grazing peacefully a few hundred yards away, and as they walked toward it Sol Flatbush said:

"Bud, d'ye know that ole maverick?"

"I shore don't. Never even ast him his name," answered Bud.

"Well, I do. That's ole 'Cap' Norris. He's a hoss sharp fer fair. He an' that boy don't do nothin' but ride the country with that magpie hoss, pickin' up races at cow camps an' ranches an' in towns. That hoss o' hisn is a 'ringer.' His real name is Idlewild, an' he's a perfessional race hoss. Boy, yer stung!"

CHAPTER XXVI
"VAMOSE!"

"Oh, I don't know," said Bud quietly, as Sol Flatbush made this announcement of the ability of Magpie, or Idlewild, as he was known elsewhere.

"But I do," urged Sol. "I see that hoss run at Ponca City on ther Fo'th o' July a year ago, an' he jest run away from ther best Indian racers what ther Osages could bring over, an' yer knows they kin go some."

"Sol, my son, don't git excited. Yer Uncle Bud knows what he's doin' when he's going inter this yere race. He ain't tellin' ther ole man, nor none o' you fellers, what thar is in thet Hatrack hoss."

"Got somethin' up yer sleeve?"

"I reckon I hev. If I was a bettin' man, I'd wager my share o' Moon Valley that Hatrack would win this yere race."

"Sho; yer don't say!"

"Ted seen him run. Ask him. Now, don't you worry none about me. I know a hoss when I see one standin' on its four legs. That magpie hoss is a good one, whether his name is Magpie or Idlewild. Ther name don't make him run no better. But Hatrack is some, too, an' I want that magpie pony for Stella. She ain't got no hoss of her own down yere, an' that spotted pony is jest ther sort o' showy hoss what a gal likes."

"Well, I ain't wantin' ter be buttin' in none," said Sol, in a crestfallen way.

"Yer ain't butted in none, Sol. I'm obliged ter yer fer givin' me ther tip erbout ther old sharp. When he fust braced me I sized him up fer a sharp, an' when he told me he was a hoss trader from Missouri I had a straight line on him."

They returned to camp, where the old man was still regaling the boys with anecdotes, having proved himself a most entertaining story-teller.

The boy sat close beside him listening, but never saying a word, except when he was addressed. He was small and slender, and evidently weighed much less than a hundred pounds.

His face was small and thin, and apparently youthful, but his eyes were old and shrewd, and there was a crafty look about his face at times when the old man brought out a point in a story. Evidently he had heard these stories many times before. When he smiled it was in a sly and furtive way.

Ted Strong had come in from riding around the herd, having inspected it before it was bedded down for the night. He had heard all about the proposed race, and smiled quietly as Ben joshed Bud about the loss of his pony Hatrack on the morrow.

He had looked the boy over carefully, and his impression was not pleasant.

"I tell yer what, boys," said the old man, when conversation began to lag. "S'posin' we put this race off until to-morrow afternoon, an' run it over at Snyder, across the line in Oklahomy?"

"What's ther occasion?" asked Bud.

"Jest ter give ther people over thar a chance ter see a real live race. Besides, I'm out o' money, an' I reckon we could have a reg'lar race, an' charge admission. That would enable me an' my grandson ter git back ter ole Missou' again. We ain't much use out here. What d'yer say?"

"I ain't no professional racer," said Bud slowly, "an' I ain't in this race fer what I kin make out o' it. Yer made yer brag about yer hoss an' slurred mine, an' I'm jest game enough ter lose him if he can't beat that calcimined hoss o' yours, but I don't go in fer bettin' er none o' thet sort o' thing."

"I ain't said nothin' about bettin'," said the old man, in an injured tone.

"I know yer ain't, an' I ain't accused yer o' it none. What I wuz goin' ter say wuz thet if yer hard up an' need ther money ter take yer home I'm ther first feller ter jump in ter help yer."

"We're all willing to help on a thing like that," said Ted.

"Then ye'll consent ter pull off ther race in Snyder?" asked the old man eagerly.

"I am, if ther other boys will consent ter it," said Bud.

"All right with me," said Ted, and the other boys voiced their assent.

It looked as if there was a good bit of fun in prospect.

"Thanks, boys," said the old man, with a catch in his voice, as if he was deeply touched. "Ye'll do a good turn fer me an' little Bill here. Bill, we'll git home fer Christmas yit."

"If you're going to make it a public race, you'll have to get over to Snyder early to make arrangements," said Ted.

"I'll leave before sunup in ther mornin', an' we'll have the race at three o'clock. Is that all satisfactory?"

This proved satisfactory to the boys, and, having agreed to be on hand in time with Hatrack, every one turned in.

When the boys turned out in the morning the blankets which the old man and the boy had occupied were empty and cold, showing that they had departed long before daylight.

"There's something fishy about that old chap," said Ben Tremont, as they were at breakfast.

"Of course, there is," said Ted. "He's an old horse sharp. Sol Flatbush knows him. He wants a race in town, thinking he can draw us into betting. He doesn't know that we never gamble, but he evidently believes that in the excitement of the moment he will be able to get some of our money."

"Well, he'll get fooled on that," said Ben.

"He'll git fooled in several other ways, too," grunted Bud.

After breakfast Bud went out and roped Hatrack, and after a tussle that lasted several strenuous minutes, brought him into camp. Hatrack certainly was a sorry-looking beast.

His long, dirty, yellowish-brown hair was rumpled and fluffed up. His ribs showed sharp, and his tail was full of burs, while his short and scraggy mane was missing in spots.

His flanks had been rubbed bare of hair where he had lain for many nights on the rocks and in the sands of the desert.

"Well, dog my cats, if he ain't ther orneriest-lookin' beast what ever toted a saddle," said Bud, looking him over, as Hatrack stood with drooping head and ears.

"Bud, he isn't worth making cat's meat out of," said Ben. "I guess you made that race to get rid of him. It's easier and more humane than shooting him or abandoning him to the prairie wolves."

"Reckon so?" asked Bud, looking at Ben out of the corner of a twinkling eye.

"Oh, dear me, but he's awfully ugly," said Stella, coming from the tent which she and her aunt, Mrs. Graham, occupied a short distance from the camp.

She was as spick and span as a new dollar, nattily dressed in a bifurcated riding skirt, from beneath which peeped a pair of high tan riding boots.

Her white Stetson had just the right curl of brim to be most becoming, and her wavy hair fell in profusion over her shoulders.

She was pulling on a pair of fringed gauntlets, and her braided quirt, with a silver knob for a handle, hung by its thong from her slender wrist.

"Now, see here, Stella, don't yer go ter feelin' knocky about yer mount, er yer won't hev no confidence in him, an' will lose. I want ter say ter yer right now that this hoss what looks like ther last rose o' summer, ther last run o' shad, an' ther breakin' up o' a hard winter in a last year's bird's nest, is all right, an' he can't lose this race. Ride him true, an' don't give him ther gad none. All yer got ter do is ter encourage him by a word now an' then, an' pilot him straight ter ther wire."

"All right, Bud. I was only joking," laughed Stella. "It isn't the prettiest horse that wins the race. I know that well, but, you see, like every girl, I like pretty things, and a horse might as well look good as run fast. It has always seemed to me that the two go together."

During the middle of the forenoon the broncho boys started for the town of Snyder to attend the race.

Bud led Hatrack, and a troublesome job he had of it, for the animated skeleton objected to being on the halter, as any self-respecting range horse would, and he pulled back and sideways and almost dragged Bud from his saddle several times.

"Ding bat yer," Bud would shout, "yer ornery, unsanctified, muley, harebrained, contaminated son o' a zebra, git down on yer feet an' foller. Ye'll git all that's comin' ter yer when ther race starts. Save yer sweat until then."

But Hatrack thought differently, and before they were halfway to Snyder it took all the efforts of Bud in the lead and Ben, Kit, and Clay Whipple in the rear, to keep him moving in a forward direction.

Only enough boys were left with the herd to keep it from scattering. Ted and Stella rode in the lead as they entered the town, which was crowded with a motley assemblage of cow-punchers, gamblers, and Indians in their gay blankets and with painted faces.

The Indians of the plains are keen on horse racing, and among the various tribes are to be found some of the fleetest horses in the West, many of them trained to all the tricks of racing. An Indian jockey is the shrewdest of his class, and is an adept at all the tricks of the trade.

"Hi! Look at the livin' skeleton!"

Bud swung around in his saddle and stared at a cow-puncher standing on the sidewalk in Snyder, as he rode into town dragging behind him the dejected Hatrack, who looked as if he had been living on two oats for dinner and a spear of grass for supper all his life.

He ambled along like a tired and footsore dog behind Bud, with his ears drooping and his toes kicking up the dust. He was a sad-looking animal, and the word having gone abroad that he was the horse that was to enter the race with Magpie, he was jeered from one end of the street to the other, as Bud led him to the corral at the edge of the town. Bud pretended to be angry at the joshing his steed received, but when he had turned his back upon the jokers he would wink gently to himself in a way that would have been puzzling to the supporters of the spotted horse.

Cap Norris had done his work well.

Every one in town knew of the coming race, and word had been sent to the ranches in the surrounding country, so that before noon the streets were crowded with people.

"Say, fellows," said Ted, when the boys met at the hotel for dinner, "this fellow Norris is sure a sharp. That talk about his wanting to get enough money to take him back home was a lie. He's a gambler, and is in league with a bunch of gamblers in this town."

"How do you know?" asked Ben.

"How do I know? Why, man alive, they're betting on Magpie all over town. The tip seems to have gotten out that Bud Morgan and the broncho boys have a surprise up their sleeves, and that they are going to ring in another horse than Hatrack."

"How is that?"

"They believe we're going to slip in another horse, a professional racing horse with a record."

"Let 'em think so. It won't be a professional race horse—at least, not in this country—that we will put in, but jest ole Hatrack, an' if he don't win the race by a city block I'll eat him, hoofs an' all."

"Put us next, Bud," said Ben.

"That's what," said Kit. "You've sure got a trick concealed somewhere. What is it?"

"No, I haven't," said Bud. "But if I wuz a bettin' man I know what hoss I'd back to win."

That was all the boys could get out of him on the subject, but they were convinced none the less that Bud had a secret concerning the horse, and that they would learn what it was in good time.

The race was to be held at the fair grounds, and was to be a dash of three hundred yards.

Cap Norris would not consent to a longer race, although Bud said he would run Hatrack any distance up to a quarter of a mile, but the innocent old man with the long whiskers objected to running his horse a long distance.

As the hour approached for the race, the grounds began to fill up. Several races between Indian ponies took place to keep the crowd amused until the big race of the day was to come off.

"They've been working us," said Ted, coming up to where Stella and the boys were standing beside Hatrack, which looked more sad and dejected than ever.

"In what way?" asked Bud.

"This race is a gambling game to get the money away from the innocents," answered Ted. "They've had men going among the people from the country and the cow-punchers, telling them that it is a put-up job on our part, and that we're sure to win. In that way they have got a lot of people to bet on Hatrack. I've a good mind to draw out of it altogether and spoil their game."

"For fear the innocents will lose their money?" asked Bud.

"Yes. I don't want to be a party to robbing those fellows."

"Don't you worry. If you want to punish Norris and his friends, don't interfere. Let it go on, I tell you. They'll be the worst-beaten lot o' crooks that ever robbed a town."

"All right, Bud, if you say so."

It was now time for the race of the day, and Bud and Norris marked off the course.

Ben was appointed judge, with a large man, apparently a stranger in the town, who was chosen by Norris, and the two selected a third.

The third man was a stranger to Ben, but he picked him out of the crowd, and the other judge accepted him.

As Stella climbed into the saddle, Hatrack gave two or three kittenish jumps, and the crowd yelled. It had not expected this added feature to the race, a girl jockey.

Shout after shout went up as she rode over the course slowly, Hatrack having settled down into his usual dejected manner. The cheers and some of the jeers that greeted him came from the men who had been induced to bet on him.

"Now, Stella," said Bud, as Stella rode back again, "when you start, shout 'Vamose!' in Hatrack's ear. That's the word he has always been sent away with. Stick tight, an' let him go. Don't forget the word 'Vamose!'"

CHAPTER XXVII
THE GREAT CHIQUITA

Hatrack and Magpie were now brought up to the starting point.

The boy who traveled with old man Norris was on the back of the latter horse, sitting in a regular jockey's saddle and stripped of all superfluous clothing.

He was the typical jockey now. He had put away all the appearance of youth, and was a crafty and sly man.

It was apparent that the whole outfit was in the racing business, and as the crowd looked at the discrepancy between the two horses, and observed that on the best-looking horse was a professional jockey, while on the crowbait was only a girl, something like a groan went up.

But some of them were game, and cheered Stella to the echo.

"You're all right!" shouted her supporters.

"Hurrah fer ther girl jockey," yelled the cow-punchers. "I got a month's wages that says she'll win the race."

But the other side had something to say, also. They made all sorts of fun of Hatrack, and roars of laughter went up as he ambled, stiff-legged, onto the course.

Clay Whipple was chosen to start the race, and stood beside the track with a red flag in his hand. The two horses were jockeyed back and forth for several minutes.

"Are you ready?" shouted Clay, as they came up.

"No!" shouted Stella.

"No!" answered the jockey.

Back again they went, and came up neck and neck, the riders nodding to Clay.

"Go!" cried Clay, bringing down the red flag with a swish through the air.

"Vamose!" Stella's clear young voice rang out.

Then an amazing thing happened. Hatrack seemed to be suddenly galvanized into life. He straightened out, and shot to the front with great, long horizontal leaps. His body seemed to be gliding close to the earth.

His head was between his legs, and he was running like a greyhound. Stella was bent low upon his neck, and every moment or two she would shout in Spanish, "Go it! Vamose!" or, "You're winning! Vamose!"

And winning Hatrack surely was. Now he was half a length ahead of the fleet Magpie, who was running the race of her life.

Behind her Stella could hear the crowd yelling like mad. The air fairly shook with the shouts of the multitude as the two horses shot forward. But it was a short race, and seemed to Stella to have ended almost as soon as it began.

As she flew past Bud, she got a fleeting glimpse of him jumping up and down in a very ecstasy of glee, and she knew that she had won, and began pulling in Hatrack. Looking over her shoulder, she saw that Magpie was already down to a walk a short distance from the wire, and that Cap Norris and the jockey were talking earnestly.

In a moment she had Hatrack turned, and was going back to where Bud was waiting for her.

"Bully for you, Stella," shouted Bud. "Yer rode a great race. Jest ez I wanted it run. Nobody couldn't hev done it better. I told yer ye'd win."

"That was too easy," laughed Stella. "I wish it had been four times as long."

"That makes it all the better."

"How much did I beat him?"

"A whole length."

"That ought to be enough."

"It was, but I'll bet a cooky they'll make a kick. These crooks always lay out to win, and won't race unless they can win. If they don't, they set up a cry of foul, or something of that sort."

"But they can't do that in this case, because I didn't foul him."

Stella became indignant at the very thought.

"Sure you didn't, but that won't keep those wolves from claiming some sort of a foul."

"You're not going to stand for it, are you?"

"Not in a blue moon. I've got the boys posted. Here comes Norris and his jockey back."

The old racing sharp walked up to Bud, leading Magpie.

"Well, Magpie's mine," said Bud, not giving the other a chance to speak first. "Sorry for your sake that you lost, Cap, but the fortunes of racing often turn unexpectedly, eh?"

"You haven't won," said the old man excitedly.

"Oh, I reckon we won, all right," answered Bud lazily, although there was an ugly gleam in his eye.

"No, sir, you didn't win fair. Thar wuz a foul at ther start. I see it, all right; I wasn't shore until I talked with my boy thar, an' he says as how ther young lady bumped him outer his stride jest ez they wuz gittin' off."

"Oh, no, you can't work me like that, Cap. They were five feet apart when the flag fell."

"I tell yer I see it with my own eyes. 'Twas a foul, an' I claim ther race, er it hez got ter be run over ag'in."

"Never, on yer life. The race goes to the young lady. But I'm not going to stand here and chew the thing over with you. It's up to the judges."

They all approached the judges' stand, where apparently a lively argument was in progress.

Ben and the big man who had been chosen by Norris were talking excitedly, and the other man was listening.

All about the stand an angry crowd of men was surging, all talking at once, so that nothing could be made out of the babel of shouts, except when some person with unusually good lungs made himself heard in a denunciation of one or the other riders.

Ted had joined the crowd, waiting for the arrival of Bud and Stella. Bud was walking by the side of Stella, whose face showed the disappointment she felt at not being declared at once the winner.

It was so evidently a job to steal the race from Hatrack that the leader of the broncho boys was both angry and disgusted.

"This is what you get for having anything to do with this mob of gamblers and thieves," he said to Kit, who was standing by his side.

"What's that you said, young feller?" said a man, edging up.

"I wasn't talking to you, my friend," answered Ted coolly.

"No, but you was talkin' at me," said the other.

"Why, are you a thief and a gambler?" asked Ted, with a lifting of his eyebrows that expressed a great deal that he did not say.

"I guess it's the other way around," answered the fellow, snarling.

"I don't see how you make that out."

"Well, I do. The gal bumped the rider o' Magpie."

"She did nothing of the sort. I stood beside the starter of the race, and I was nearer to the horses than you were, and if any one could see them I could. The horses were several feet apart when they started."

"Why, sure. You and your pals are interested in the bone heap that went in first through a foul."

"That will be about enough of that."

A bright red spot burned on each of Ted's cheeks, the danger signal of his wrath.

"Now, see here, young fellow, you can't throw any bluff into me," said the fellow, approaching Ted with one shoulder raised.

"You let him alone. He's all right, and has got as much right to talk as you have," said another man, elbowing his way up.

He was one of those who had bet on Hatrack, and Ted recognized him as the foreman of the Running Water horse ranch.

"Well, the gal stole the race fer these fellers, an' we ain't goin' ter stand fer it. They needn't think they kin bring any o' their gals in here to do their dirty work. They all look alike to us."

"See here," said Ted coolly, "let me give you a piece of advice. Leave the young lady out of it, or I'll give you something else to think about for a while."

"Rats fer you," said the fellow, snapping his fingers under Ted's nose.

He picked himself from the ground ten feet away, wiping his bleeding nose and wondering what had happened to him.

"Say, boy," said the foreman of the Running Water, "that was as pretty and clean a blow as ever I see. You can handle them mitts o' yours right handy."

A score of men had rushed up and surrounded Ted and Kit, all shouting and gesticulating at the same time.

Meantime, Ben was having his troubles in the judges' stand.

He had, of course, decided in favor of Hatrack, while the big man had declared for a foul and no decision, and the third judge stood wavering.

On the face of it the whole thing was a steal on the part of the gamblers, who had evidently decided beforehand that if the race went against them to claim a foul and bluff it through.

But they had argued without their host. They did not know what they were opposing when they ran against Ted Strong.

Ted was sorry that he had gone into the affair at all, but once in he was there to stick to the finish. The fellow whom he had knocked down had retired to the rear to attend to his broken nose, and to give his friends an opportunity to fight his battle.

The foreman of the Running Water had disappeared. He had foreseen trouble when the gamblers got together, and attempted to force the race through, and had gone to collect the cow-punchers and others who had been induced to bet on Hatrack.

Ted stood his ground patiently, waiting until a decision should be handed down by the judges before declaring himself.

Stella was sitting in her saddle on Hatrack a few feet away from the stand watching the proceedings, and listening to the arguments on both sides made by the angry men.

Bud and Kit stood on either side of her, to protect her from the remarks of the disgruntled gamblers.

Suddenly a man pushed his way through the throng, mounted on a Spanish mule.

He was a fine-looking man, dressed after the manner of the plainsman, and might have been either a cow-puncher in prosperity or a ranch owner.

As the crowd made way for him he caught sight of Bud, and stopped and stared for several moments without speaking.

Bud had not noticed him, but when he did look up he returned the stare, and his forehead was wrinkled in thought.

Somewhere in the back part of his head he carried a picture of this man, but under different circumstances.

Who could he be, and where had he been met, were the things that were puzzling Bud.

"Hello, pard, you don't seem to place me," said the man on the Spanish mule. "But I haven't forgotten you by a dern sight. Think hard."

"I've saw yer som'er's," said Bud thoughtfully, "but it wa'n't like this. You're som'er's in my picture gallery o' faces, but yer ain't ther same as when I saw yer last."

"Right ye are," said the man. "How's Chiquita getting along?"

"Ah, I've got yer now. How did yer come out? Middlin' well, ter jedge from ther mule yer ridin', an' yer ginral appearance o' prosperity."

"You bet I be," said the man, "an' if it hadn't been fer you I wouldn't have been nowhere. I've come a long ways ter hunt yer up, ter thank yer, an' to get better acquainted with yer."

"Well, ye've got me inter a heap o' trouble," said Bud, laughing.

"So I see, an' I'll help yer get out o' it. What seems ter be the trouble?"

"Well, old Chiquita, er Hatrack, ez ther boys in ther outfit calls him, won a race just now, an' ther gamblers won't stand by it. They sent out word that Hatrack was a sure winner, an'—"

"Same old thing. Chiquita fooled them all."

"I didn't know he could do it myself, but I remembered what you said about him, an' when an ole maverick come along an' banters me fer a race I jest took him up, an' this is how it come out. He took us fer a bunch o' gillies, an' used us to try to fleece the people."

"What's his name?" asked the man on the Spanish mule softly.

"Cap Norris."

"Oh, ole Pap Norris, eh? Calls hisself Cap now, does he?"

"That's what he does, an' he's a derned ole skin."

"None skinnier. But where is he? I should like to see him."

"He's sashayin' around here som'er's attendin' ter his dirty work. Lookin' after his grandson, little Willie, I reckon."

"What, is that thief still hangin' on to him?"

"Yes. I see you seem to know him."

"Know him! Well, I should gurgle I do know him. I thought every hoss man in the country knew him. Little Willie, the orphaned grandson, is almost old enough to be a grandfather himself. He's an outlawed jockey, an' he an' Pap go about the country skinning countrymen and cow-punchers with his fake races. He never won a square race in his life. I should say I did know him. Here he comes now. Watch me wake him up."

The old fellow was bustling up to the crowd.

"See here, young fellow, get ther gal offen that hoss, he's mine, er as good as mine in a moment. The jedges are goin' ter award ther race ter me on account o' ther foul," he shouted to Bud.

"I reckon ther hoss stays right with me," said Bud smoothly. "But I want ter tell yer thet yer better bring in that magpie hoss so's I kin git him quick. He ain't yours no more."

"Come, come! None o' yer foolishness with me," blustered the old man. "Git ther gal off before she's pulled off."

"You or any other man put your finger on thet young lady if yer dare," said Bud. "Jest try it once if yer think I'm bluffin', men."

"Hello, Pap," said the man on the Spanish mule. "Up ter yer ole tricks, I see."

The old man looked up at the man on the mule, then turned pale and slunk away without another word.

"Men," said the man on the mule, addressing the crowd, "you've been stung. This old bag o' bones is Chiquita, the best race horse ever produced in Mexico, an' I brought him over here, where I traded him for a plain cayuse an' gave something ter boot. If any o' you men know anything about hosses ye'll recognize ther great Chiquita, what made an' lost more money fer ther people o' Mexico than any one other thing. Pap didn't know it until he see me, then he suddenly remembered a little deal me an' him was in. I know this Magpie hoss well, an' it couldn't stand no more show of winnin' a race from Chiquita than a snail would. Take it from me that ye've been caught at yer own game, an' have been done."

At the name of Chiquita a groan went up from the gamblers.

"And who are you?" asked Bud.

"Come nearer, an' I'll tell you in your ear," was the reply.

Bud went close to him, and the man stooped in his saddle and whispered a word in his ear, at which the old cow-puncher looked startled, then burst into a fit of laughter.

CHAPTER XXVIII
TED'S GREAT VICTORY

"I tell you I'll never stand for it."

The voice of big Ben Tremont could be heard roaring above the noise made by the crowd around the judges' stand.

"It's a go. The race goes to Magpie on a foul."

The big man in the stand made this announcement in a voice of thunder.

"Bully for you, Shan Rhue!" yelled the gamblers, crowding to the stand in a body.

At the same moment Bud caught Hatrack by the bridle and led him out of the crowd, for he knew what was impending.

"I say it don't go," shouted Ben. "This man, who is in league with that old crook, Norris, declares a foul. I say there was no foul."

"How does the other judge go?" called a voice.

"He declines to give a voice in the matter," answered Ben.

"Throw the coyote down here, and we'll help him make up his mind," called the foreman of the Running Water. "If he's too much of a coward to decide for the right, we'll help him. Throw him over."

The foreman of the Running Water was a formidable-looking man.

He was tall and sinewy, with a seamed and scarred face, a map of many battles with the elements, the wild animals of mountain and plain, and with his fellow men.

He was heavily armed, and the town gamblers knew him for a bad fighter when he was aroused.

"Stick fer ther big show," he said to Ted, who was standing beside him. "I've got the boys bunched back there on the edge of the crowd. When it comes to a show-down we'll all be here. But it's no place fer wimmin an' children."

"I don't want to get into a fight if we can help it," said Ted.

"Yer ain't afraid o' these cattle, aire ye?" asked the foreman, looking at Ted curiously, but with a shade of disappointment in his eyes.

"Not for a minute," said Ted, throwing a straight glance into the other's eyes. "There's nothing to be afraid of, that I can see. But what's the use if we can get at it in some other way?"

"Well, I reckon yer right, bub," said the other slowly. "Some one is shore liable ter git hurt. But I'd sooner see ther whole crowd hurt than have this bunch o' thieves git away with their game."

"They won't do that. Never fear."

The crowd was now watching the men in the judges' stand.

Evidently Ben and Shan Rhue were wrestling in spirit with the third judge, who was still wavering. He knew that the right was with Ben, but he was afraid of the big bully Shan, and the gamblers, who were most in evidence.

He did not know that the cow-punchers and the townspeople who had bet on Hatrack were being organized on the outskirts of the crowd, and that Kit and Clay and the other broncho boys were with them to direct them to the attack when it might seem necessary to assert their rights.

Suddenly there was a roar from the crowd. Shan Rhue had struck Ben Tremont a staggering blow. They heard Ben let out a roar like a wounded bull, as he threw the great bulk of his body upon the man who had struck him.

Now they were wrestling, and the frail stand in which they were, fifteen feet above the ground, swayed with their struggle.

"Kill him!" shouted the gamblers.

"Throw him down here!"

"Let us finish him!"

"Stay with him, Shan!"

These and other cries and threats were shouted by the mob. But Ted Strong said nothing. He was watching the struggle intently and quietly.

He had no fear but that Ben would be able to hold his own. His great strength hardly matched that of Shan Rhue, who was a giant, and the most feared man in the Wichita Mountains. But Ben was more than his match in wrestling skill, and, moreover, he was younger and more supple for all his bulk, and his work on the football gridiron when in college had taught him tricks of the tackle of which the big bully did not dream.

He had a hold on the bully now, and was gradually forcing him backward toward the frail railing that inclosed the floor of the stand.

Ted saw his intention. It was to throw Shan Rhue against the railing, then spring away. Rhue evidently divined the same thing, for he struggled with all his force against it, striking Ben in the ribs and occasionally in the face.

But his blows were not very effective, as Ben had him caught so closely that his blows lost their power. Thus the struggle went on for a few moments. Then, when it was least expected, there was a crash of breaking wood.

A yell went up from the crowd as it surged back, and the gigantic body of Shan Rhue came hurtling through the railing, which went into splinters from the impact of his bulk.

Shan Rhue grasped at the air, as with a roar he went over. He turned a complete somersault as he descended and landed on his shoulders. For a moment he lay quivering, half stunned.

There was dead silence in the crowd and none dared go to his assistance. But presently the bully sat up and passed his hand over his eyes. With a roar of pain and rage he sprang to his feet and looked around.

The nearest person to him was the leader of the broncho boys, who stood on the edge of the crowd, alert and smiling. Ted knew that it meant fight now.

He was convinced that Ben was in the right, but right or wrong, Ben had started it, and it was now up to the broncho boys to see that their side did not get the worst of it.

Realizing that Ted was an enemy, Shan Rhue made a rush at him. Those beside Ted turned and ran. But Ted did not move. He only stood a little tenser.

It took but a moment for the bully to cross the distance that lay between him and Ted. His rush was like that of a bull, and as irresistible. But Ted did not propose to take the brunt of it. He knew several tricks better than that.

As Rhue was about to launch himself upon Ted, the latter stepped lightly aside. So sure was Rhue of landing on Ted and bearing him to the ground that he had leaped into the air, and, finding nothing to stop his progress, was overbalanced. A sweep of Ted's foot completed it, for the legs of the bully were swept from under him, and he went to the sod on his face with a crash that seemed to shake the earth.

Like an eagle upon its prey, Ted was on the back of the bully. The crowd shouted like mad, eager to go to the rescue of their champion. But Ted heard the voice of the foreman of Running Water high above the din.

"It's the boy's fight, an' any man that breaks through the line will get a ball from my forty-four plumb through him. Stand back, you cattle!"

"Let 'em go, fellers. Shan will kill him in a minute," shouted one of the gamblers.

Shan Rhue had been badly shaken up by the jolt that had been his when he struck the ground. For several moments he did not stir, and Ted thought he had been knocked out.

Many of the men in the crowd knew things about Shan Rhue which Ted did not.

Rhue was considered the strongest man in the Southwest at that time. He was barely forty years old, in the prime of his life, and a man who had never dissipated. But he was a thoroughly bad man for all that, and the number of men whom he had killed had been forgotten.

His feats of strength were the talk of barrooms and bunk houses. He had been seen many times to break horseshoes with his hands, and as for bending a bar of iron by striking the muscles of his forearm with it, that was one of his ordinary tricks.

But the thing of which he was proudest was his ability to buck a man off his back. In this feat he barred none, no matter how heavy. He would get on his hands and knees, place a surcingle around his body under his arms for his rider to hold on by, and then proceed to buck.

It would seem impossible for a man to stick to him under such circumstances, and no one had been found yet who could do so.

Thus it was that those of the crowd who had witnessed this feat sometimes in a fight, and more often in friendly contest, looked to see Ted sailing through the air, and then the finish, for Shan Rhue was a merciless enemy.

Ted was now straddling the prostrate bully, who was breathing heavily, his body heaving as his lungs tried to get back into commission.

Presently he was all right again, and, feeling a weight upon him, shook himself. This not having the effect of relieving him of his burden, he twisted his head around and saw Ted sitting on him.

With a growl like a wounded bear he slowly lifted himself to the height of his arms, then slowly rose to his knees.

"By golly, he's goin' ter buck him off," shouted one in the crowd.

"Look out fer some fun, lads," cried another.

"He'll kill ther kid sure," said a third.

In a moment Ted realized what was coming off. The hold he had on the back of Shan Rhue was none of the most secure at best, but he got a clutch on the fellow's shirt under the arm, just back of the armpits, and he felt that he had in his fingers great bunches of the bully's muscles.

By the merest chance he had secured the only hold by which he could hope to stick to the giant's back. Then the fun began. Shan Rhue plunged back and forth, sideways and up and down.

The movement was incessant. He reared and pitched, and, having cunning and intelligence, he was able to distinguish when Ted's seat was least secure and take advantage of it.

Ted had ridden many bucking bronchos, but Shan Rhue beat any of them in the surprises which he furnished. But Ted stuck grimly to him.

He knew that if the bully succeeded in throwing him off his life would not be worth a rushlight, for Shan was a rough fighter and would not hesitate to kick him brutally, if he did not shoot him to death before the boys could come to his assistance.

Thus the struggle went on for several minutes, Shan doing his utmost and Ted hanging on. But the big fellow was getting winded by his exertions.

He was not in the best condition, for all his tremendous power. He was going fast, and Ted was badly shaken up and out of breath, also. If Shan held out a few minutes longer Ted must be thrown, for his hold on the muscles under his antagonist's arms had begun to loosen, and he dared not let go for an instant to get a fresh grip.

It was close to the finish, and the crowd knew it.

"He's goin', Shan. A few more will finish him," shouted the gamblers.

"Stick to him, Ted. He's almost in," cried the boys.

Ted took heart at this, although his body was racked with pains, caused by the innumerable wrenchings to which it had been subjected.

Suddenly Shan Rhue was all in. His body flattened out upon the ground, and he lay there panting laboriously. Ted sprang to his feet gasping. Thus for a few minutes both remained, amid intense silence from the crowd.

Shan Rhue's body was heaving painfully. It was evident that he had never had before a struggle like this.

Little by little he recovered, but Ted's recovery was quicker than that of the man. His youth and strength were responsible for this.

But finally Shan Rhue was himself again, and suddenly he leaped to his feet and glared around. His eyes fell upon Ted, and he looked him up and down in a sort of amazement.

Had this stripling accomplished what older and stronger men had failed in?

Shan Rhue could hardly believe it, but it took some of the conceit out of him at that. However, his anger at Ted had not been in the least assuaged by the fact that the first honors had gone to this youth who now stood watching him with a smile on his lips, but with the light of battle in his eyes.

With a sneer Shan Rhue rushed at Ted. This time he would annihilate him.

But Ted was crouching, awaiting him. His muscles were like steel springs. His breath had come to him again, and he was ready to fight for his life, for it had come to that now. Suddenly there was a smack, sharp and clear in the silence that hung over the crowd.

Shan Rhue staggered back on his heels. The blow from Ted's fist had struck him fairly below the eye. Before he could recover Ted was upon him like a panther.

One, two, three, blows fell with a sharp, sickening sound upon the face and throat of the famous Shan Rhue, as he lurched backward, vainly trying to defend himself.

His body went to the earth with a crash, and he lay there moaning and quivering, beaten, discredited, and no more the hero, for he had been conquered by a boy.

CHAPTER XXIX
KIT MAKES A CAPTURE

Shan Rhue lay prostrate for a long time, but no one went to his assistance. As he fell the gamblers raised a shout, and made a motion to attack Ted.

But the foreman of Running Water sprang in front of them, and as if by magic the broncho boys and the cow-punchers and other supporters of Hatrack were by his side.

Ted had leaped to the fore and was standing shoulder to shoulder with the foreman of Running Water. He heard a ripple of laughter, and looked up to see Stella standing by his side.

"Bully for you, Ted," she said. "You did that fine."

Ted smiled back at her, then turned his eyes upon the surprised and angry gamblers. There was something there that demanded all his attention. The gamblers only needed a leader to make them a dangerous proposition.

But their leader was down and out by reason of a few neat and handy blows, and none other had the courage to come to the front. It was the psychological moment.

Ted Strong took advantage of it. Without a moment's hesitation, he stepped in front of the foreman of Running Water, who moved back to give him the place of vantage.

Ted had not even taken his six-shooter from its holster, but stood with his hands resting lightly on his hips, while his eyes roved inquiringly over the menacing crowd.

"Any of you gentlemen like to have some of the same sort of medicine?" he asked, nodding toward the prostrate Rhue.

There was no reply.

"Because if any of you would, I, or any of my friends, will be glad to accommodate you," he added.

An ominous growl came from some one back in the crowd.

"Would you like some of it?" asked Ted, turning suddenly in that direction.

He waited for several moments for an answer, but none came.

"Now, you fellows, I want to say that this incident is closed," said he firmly. "You are beaten every way from the jack, as you would say. You put up this race to skin innocent parties, and you thought to use my friends for your purposes, and have failed. The face was fairly won by our horse, and that goes. If any man doubts it, I will prove it to him by any means he wishes, from fists up to howitzers. You have made a lot of fools of yourselves by allowing an old crook like Norris to play in with you. I haven't a bit of sympathy for you. I'm glad you lost your money, and I'd feel gladder if you all went broke. This is the end of this adventure. Where's Norris? We want that magpie horse which we won."

The men dispersed after this speech, which closed with a ringing cheer from the broncho boys and the cow-punchers and other friends of Hatrack.

But Norris could not be found. He and the horse and the jockey had disappeared. Ted rounded the boys up, and all were present except Kit.

"Where's Kit?" he asked.

"Don't know," said Bud. "He was around here a few minutes ago. Reckon he's somewhere about."

The crowd having dispersed uptown, a search was made for Kit, but he could not be found.

"I wonder if some of that gang hasn't got square with us by some foul play on Kit," said Ted. "It would be like the coyotes. Kit was the smallest of the lot, and naturally the cowards would pick him."

"Kit's small, all right," said Stella stoutly, for she and Kit were great friends, and Stella was always one to stick up for those she liked. "If they pick Kit for his size, and think they have got an easy thing, they will find that they have gathered up a red-hot Chile pepper. He'll give them the hottest fight they ever had, as long as he lasts."

"Hurray fer you, Stella," exclaimed Bud. "You speak for fair. Kit's not much on size, but he's a whirlwind."

Shan Rhue was slowly getting on his feet. His broad, brutal face was badly discolored where Ted's fists had come in contact with it.

One of his eyes was bloodshot and rapidly taking on a green-and-purple hue, and his upper lip stuck out like an overhanging roof. As he looked around and saw that the broncho boys were alone, and that he had been left to recover as best he might by those whom he had called his friends and supporters, he growled deep in his chest.

"The skunks," he muttered, between his swollen lips. "They'd make me fight an' steal fer them, an' then leave me in the hole, would they? Well, I'll make them hump fer this."

Then he looked unsteadily at Ted out of his good eye, as if he was wondering how it all had happened. But while his glance was not as belligerent as it had been, still there was nothing but hatred in his expression.

Ted eyed him back fearlessly, but this time his hand rested upon the handle of his revolver, and Stella, by his side, was on the alert also. Shan Rhue was not one to be trusted, especially after he had met defeat. After staring for a moment he spoke.

"I reckon yer beat me fair, young feller," he said, "although I don't know yet how yer did it. But I want ter say ter yer now that this ain't the end, by no means."

"That's all right," said Ted easily. "You keep out of my way, and you will be all right."

"I go where I please, an' do what I please, an' ask ther right o' no man," retorted Shan Rhue truculently.

"All right, go where you please, but don't run afoul of me," said Ted sharply. "I don't want to have anything to do with such cattle as you, and I don't propose to. Keep off my trail if you know when you're well off. This is a friendly tip—take it or leave it."

"I don't want none o' yer tips," growled Shan Rhue. "Ye've beaten me, an' I hate yer. Look out fer me next time, that's all."

"Yes, that's all. Skidoo! You're not pretty to look at."

Ted turned his back upon the defeated bully, but Stella did not, and had Shan Rhue made a motion toward his gun there would have been one with a pearl handle and trimmed with silver in commission in an instant.

With a long, malignant look after Ted, the bully turned and hobbled slowly from the fair grounds.

"I'm going to start on the trail of Norris," said Ted. "Want to come along, Stella?"

"You bet I do," said the girl. "Wait till I catch my pony."

"Ben, you and Bud ride through the town and see if you can't get on to the movements of that old rip Norris, also, and look out for Kit. If we don't get Norris, and make him give up that magpie pony, our work has not been half done. As long as we have won out all around, we might as well have the fruits of our victory," said Ted.

"What'll we do to ther coyote?" asked Bud.

"Part his coat tails and give him a good, swift kick," answered Ted. "But don't get into any fights with these town gamblers. We can't afford anything of that sort, you know."

"All righty; but I'd shore like ter git a crack at some o' them mavericks," said Bud grudgingly.

"They're all licked in their minds already," said Ted. "Of course, they're sore at losing their money, and if a dozen or more of them were to tackle you, you'd have a hard time getting away with it. When the fight comes off, if ever it does, we all want to be in on it."

They parted, and Ted and Stella rode into the town.

"Say, friend, have you seen anything of that old skin Norris?" asked Ted, meeting one of the Running Water outfit on the street.

"Yep. I wuz jest goin' ter look yer up an' post yer," was the reply.

"Which way did he go, or is he still in town?"

"Jest after yer put ther finish onto Shan—an', say, that wuz a beaut, if any one should ask you—I see Norris an' ther jock makin' fer ther gate, leadin' ther magpie bronc. I thinks they're goin' ter put him in ther corral fer yer, an' didn't pay much 'tention ter him."

"Then he's up at the corral?"

"No, he ain't. He's foggin' along to'rds ther Wichita Mountains as fast as he kin go."

"How do you know?"

"I met one o' our outfit a bit ago, an' he was sore because yer let ther old feller git away with ther magpie, after yer won him fair. Yer see, he thinks ye flunked on collectin' ther pony."

"Not on your life. We don't do business that way."

"That's what I was thinkin', so I ast him whichever way ther ole man was headin'. He says inter ther east, tickity-brindle."

"Which road?"

"Right out ther east end o' ther main street."

"Thank you, pard."

"Yer almighty welcome. Good luck. If yer ketch up with ther coyote, bring him in an' let us have a good squint at him."

"Oh, I'll bring him in, all right, if I get him."

"So long!"

"So long! Come on, Stella, we'll have to kick dust if we're going to connect with that old party."

They dashed down the street, followed by an equal mingling of smiles and frowns. Smiles from the cow-punchers and townspeople whose champion he had been, and frowns from the gamblers.

But they saw neither, for they were intent upon their business. They made a mighty handsome couple as they dashed along, for they were well mounted and both were perfect riders.

Many a young girl walking along the street looked enviously after Stella, and wished she could ride as well and was as beautiful. And many a lad looked after his ideal of a hero of the West, dashing and brave Ted Strong, who had so lately vanquished the bully who had been feared of all men, and who could ride like a centaur, and shoot perfectly.

It did not take long for them to clear the town, and dash out onto the prairie road which led into the Wichita Mountains.

They did not spare their horses, for Ted knew that if Norris once succeeded in reaching the mountains it would be almost impossible to find him among the many fastnesses and deep and rough cañons which abound in those most picturesque hills and peaks.

While Ted knew the Wichita Mountains well, he was also aware that even the most expert scout did not know all about them, and that there were places in them that had never been explored, unless, perhaps, by renegade Indians and white outlaws, with which the mountains had at times been infested.

They had ridden an hour or more when Ted pulled in his pony.

"No use riding our ponies to death the first heat," he said to Stella, with a smile.

"My cayuse is good for another hour," said Stella; "I can tell by the way he's going under me."

"Yours would last because you're such a light and easy rider. You take weight off a pony. But I'm a good deal heavier, and I can feel this fellow tiring, although he'd go until he dropped in his tracks if I'd let him."

They walked their ponies over the springy sod beside the road, which was becoming fainter the farther they got from the town. In the distance they could see the mountains, a dark mass against the sky.

"Some one on the road," said Stella, pointing ahead.

"It is a little hazy. Dust, I guess," said Ted. "I think we better hit it up a bit. Perhaps it is Norris and his precious 'grandson,' and if it is we'll get to them before they get to the mountains."

They put their ponies, at a lope, and seemed to be catching up with the dust cloud rapidly. Soon they were able to distinguish two riders.

"By Jove, I believe we are on the right track," said Ted.

Stella's bright eyes had been watching the riders in front of them for some time.

"Ted, it's not Norris. There are two riders, one behind the other, and they are coming this way," she said.

Ted reined in his pony, and took a long look.

"You're right, Stella," he said. "But, perhaps, we can get some news of the fugitives from them."

Again they spurred forward.

"Ted, that's Kit, as sure as you live," cried Stella, "I'd know him anywhere."

In a few minutes they were within hailing distance, and Ted gave the long yell, which was answered, and in a few minutes they were reining in beside Kit. Behind him, securely bound to the back of Magpie, was old man Norris, who looked very crestfallen.

"Hello, Kit, you rascal, I see that you got him," said Ted.

"You bet, and a merry chase I had after him," answered Kit.

"Why, Kit, what's the matter with your arm?" cried Stella.

Kit's arm was hanging by his side, and his coat sleeve near his shoulder was stained with blood.

"Shot!" answered Kit laconically.

"Bad?" asked Stella anxiously.

"Not so very. Just touched the bone. But it has been bleeding like the deuce."

"Ted, take charge of the prisoner. Kit, get off that horse and let me see that wound."

Stella's commands were promptly obeyed, and Kit groaned slightly as Stella helped him off with his coat and cut away his sleeve. He had received a nasty flesh wound near the shoulder, made by a ball of large caliber, which had passed clear through.

As soon as she had washed the wound with water from Ted's canteen, and had bound it up, Kit felt much more comfortable.

"How did it happen?" asked Stella.

"I heard that the old man and the jockey had made a sneak from the grounds when Ted was having his fun with the big fellow, and I got my bronc and followed them. I came up with them a ways back, and made the old duffer halt, but the jock potted me and got away. That's all."

CHAPTER XXX
KIT'S TROUBLESOME PRISONER

"Kit, you're the most reckless boy I ever knew," said Stella, as he climbed into his saddle with some effort, for his arm was stiff and swollen, and it was all he could do to keep from groaning with every jump of his pony.

"What in the world made you start after them alone?" asked Ted.

"Well, you were busy with the big bully, and, although I felt certain that you would get the best of him in the end, I thought it wouldn't be good policy to take any of the boys with me, in case there should be a general fight. I know you would need all the fellows."

"Well, but, dog-gone you, you ought to have taken some one," said Ted. "How did you know but the old man and the jockey were not dangerous fellows? Men in their business are generally bad actors when it comes to a scrimmage."

"Oh, I thought I could handle them," laughed Kit. "And I could, too, only I got careless, and let that jockey get the drop on me. The old man knuckled under gracefully when I presented my card."

"Did you get the old man after you were shot?"

"Yes. You see, this was how it was: I got sight of them a short ways ahead of me. They were evidently saving their horses, for they were traveling slowly."

"Didn't they get next that they were being followed?"

"I don't think so. They saw only one rider, and I suppose they thought that if they were pursued at all it would be by several men, and they were confident that with their horses they could run away from anything we had except Hatrack."

"It's a wonder they didn't light out quick."

"I think they figured to save their horses until they were sure they were being followed."

"Then what happened?"

"I saw them look back at me several times, but they did not hit up their speed any."

"Were you fogging along pretty fast?"

"Not so very. You see, I didn't want them to think that I was on their trail. I went just fast enough to overtake them gradually. If they had got on to me they would have been out of sight before I could gather up my reins."

"Foxy Kit," said Stella.

"And they let you come right up with them?" asked Ted.

"Yep. I was right up on them before they got on to me."

"They recognized you, eh?"

"They did when I was about twenty feet away. Then I heard the old man holler, 'It's one o' them dern broncho boys.'"

"And then what?"

"Well, you see, I didn't have my gun out, and, as he says that, the jockey pulls and fires one shot, which landed in my arm. Then, before I can reach around and get my gun out with my left hand, he gets away. But the action was too quick for the old man, and he sat still until I had him covered, when I had sent a couple of balls after the jock to make him hit up the pace a bit."

"The old man was easy, eh?"

"Easiest kind. But he might have got away from me if he had the nerve."

"Well, Kit, you did a great stunt. I'm mighty glad you landed the old coot. But I don't know what to do with him now that we have him."

"Well, we better take him to town, anyway. He'd get lost if we turned him loose out here. Let his friends take care of him, when he gets there."

"All right; let's move on."

Not much was said as they made their way back to town. Old man Norris did not open his mouth, but looked dejected and sad, as if he was brooding over what would happen to him when he arrived at his destination. He was plainly uneasy, and probably wished they would turn him loose.

When they were within a mile of the town they saw a cloud of dust approaching them rapidly, and watched it curiously. It was a horseman, fogging along at a rapid pace.

Finally out of the dust emerged Bud Morgan, and as he came abreast of them he pulled his horse down on its haunches.

"Howdy?" he said.

"How?" answered the others.

"So yer got ther ole pelican, eh?" said Bud, with a grin.

"Kit did," said Ted.

"Bully for you, Kit," said Bud heartily. "I was in town, an' a feller from over to Running Water told me you and Stella had come out this way, an' I follered. What's the matter with your arm, Kit?"

"Got a shot through it."

"Sho! Did that old pirate give it to you?"

"No, the jockey, and then he flew."

"I've got a good mind to go after him, an' bring him in."

"Wouldn't do any good. At the rate he was going when I sent a message after him, he's clear into the suburbs of Chicago by this time."

They were soon on the outskirts of the town, and as they entered the main street they saw a crowd of men coming toward them.

"Here comes a reception committee," said Ted. "Wonder who they are, and what they want."

"By Jove, there's that big fellow Shan Rhue," exclaimed Kit. "I wonder what he's after."

"I thought he had enough o' our kind o' medicine not to want ter tackle us so soon again," said Bud.

"I don't like the looks of that gang," said Ted.

"Neither do I," said Stella. "I've a hunch that they mean mischief."

"In what way?" asked Ted.

"Well, I can't exactly define the feeling I have, but somehow I think they don't want *us*."

"Eh? Whom do they want?"

For reply Stella made a motion toward Norris. Ted looked at her thoughtfully for a moment, then comprehended.

"I see," he said seriously. "Well, they won't get him."

"Bud, where are the other boys?" asked Stella.

"Uptown som'er's. Why?" said Bud.

"They ought to be here," said the girl seriously. "I think we'll be needing them soon."

"I tumble, an' I'll jest fog on ahead an' gather them up."

"Yes," said Ted. "and while you're about it see if you can't find that foreman of the Running Water Ranch, and have him round up his boys or a few good fellows who will back us up if it comes to trouble. I don't know what his name is, do you?"

"Yes, his name is Andy Bowles, an' he's as good as three ordinary men."

"Then fly. There's no telling what's coming off."

Bud gave his pony the rowels, and in a moment was out of sight in a cloud of dust. Ted and the others rode steadily forward, the two parties approaching nearer every moment.

The party headed by Shan Rhue had taken to the middle of the road, and soon they had come together, and both halted. For a moment nothing was said.

Ted was in advance, holding the reins of the pony on which Norris was tied hand and foot, Stella was on one side of Norris, and Kit on the other.

"Well?" said Ted inquiringly, as they came face to face.

He looked directly at Shan Rhue as he said it, then allowed his eyes to wander over the crowd. In it he saw some of the toughest characters in that part of the country.

They were men who bore the reputation of being cattle rustlers on provocation, and who had been suspected of horse stealing and other crimes.

"We want that man," said Shan Rhue shortly and roughly.

"Is that so?" said Ted, with feigned surprise.

"Yes, that's so," was the surly reply.

"Then why didn't you go out and get him?"

"We left that to you," said Shan, with a nasty laugh.

"Then you'll still leave him to me."

"Well, we want him, and that's all there is to it."

"What do you want with him?"

"We'll show you when we get him."

"It's a cinch you won't get him until you do show me."

"Now, I don't want to have any trouble with you, young feller, but—"

"I shouldn't think you would."

At this retort a snicker went up in the crowd, and Shan turned upon his followers with a brow like a thundercloud. But he said nothing, as the snicker subsided as soon as it began.

"And I don't want any of your lip, either. Give us the old man peaceable, an' you can go."

"Say, that's real good of you. But I want to tell you one thing, Shan Rhue, before you lose any more breath in conversation, you don't get him unless you tell me what you propose doing with him, and perhaps not then. It's up to me to say who gets him, or what is done with him. You seem to forget that he's my prisoner, not yours."

"Well, I'll tell you what we're going to do with him," said the bully, with a blustering air. "We're goin' to hang him as high as that telegraph pole out thar."

"Bet you anything you've got you don't," said Ted, with a pleasant smile.

There was a murmur of anger in the crowd.

"Don't let them get me," wailed old Norris.

"Dry up!" said Stella sternly. "Don't you see he's trying to save you."

"Why do you want to hang this old man?" asked Ted.

"Because he whipsawed us all. He's the only one who got any money out of that race. We gave him five hundred dollars to pull it off. He was broke, and couldn't have bet a cent on it, anyway. That's why. He said his horse would win in a walk, and every one of us went broke on it."

"Good! I'm glad to hear it," said Ted heartily. "You ought to have lost. But I'll tell you one thing, the old man really thought his horse would win. He didn't know that Bud's horse was the old Mexican racer, Chiquita; neither did any of us except Bud, who kept the matter to himself, and there you are. The old man is a professional skin, I'm free to confess, but he was out to skin us, not you. You've got nothing against him. You were beaten by gambler's luck, and now you're not game to stand by it. But there is one sure thing, you'll not get old Norris from me until you kill me. That's a cinch."

"You're a game kid, all right," said Shan Rhue, "but you're committing suicide with that kind o' talk. I didn't lose so much myself, an' I ain't got nothin' agin' the ole man; it's you I'm after—"

"Why didn't you come alone if you wanted me? Was it necessary for you to bring a whole posse with you?"

"Now, the less I hear of that kind o' talk, the easier it will be for you. Hand over the old gaffer, an' go your way peaceful. You'll get that much chance."

"Thank you for nothing. I stay by the old man."

Farther up the street Ted saw a commotion out of which evolved a party of men moving in his direction. He had no doubt it was Bud and Andy Bowles, the foreman of the Running Water Ranch.

"For the last time, give up that man!" commanded Shan Rhue.

"No."

"Then we'll take him."

Kit had cut the old man's bonds, and thrust a revolver into his hand.

"Fight for your life," he said.

With a roar the mob was upon them. Revolvers were drawn, and as they rushed forward the dauntless three surrounded Norris—three against fifty.

"Halt!" cried Ted. "The first man to lay a hand on any of us is a dead one."

"Go on an' take him. I'll attend to the kid," shouted Shan Rhue.

"Get him!" "String him up!" "Lynch the old thief!"

These were the cries with which the mob advanced.

Out of the mob came several shots. Ted heard a cry of pain behind him, and turned to see Stella reel in her saddle, pale to the lips, with her hand pressing her head, Then she fell.

With a cry of horror and rage, Ted turned toward her, but just then he felt himself seized and dragged from his saddle. Something struck him on the back of the head, and all became black.

But as he was going off into unconsciousness he heard a shout. It was the old Moon Valley yell, and he knew that Norris would be safe.

Bud was coming with reënforcements. Ted had dropped to the road under the feet of the terrified ponies, and it was a miracle that he was not trampled to death.

All about him the fight was going on.

Bud and Andy Bowles, and about twenty men whom they had hastily got together, had come to the rescue, and the gamblers' gang was soon on the run. They had not been able to get near Norris, for Kit had fought them off with his one good arm until, finding themselves attacked in the rear, the would-be lynchers ran for their lives.

The fight was swift and decisive, and several men lay in the dust when it was over, for Andy Bowles and Bud and Ben had fought like tigers.

When Ted recovered consciousness again he found himself lying in the road beside Shan Rhue, who had been knocked senseless by a blow from the butt of Bud's pistol.

Ted staggered to his feet.

"Where's Stella?" he cried.

The other boys looked around. Just before the fight began they had seen her, Kit, and the old man, but now she was gone.

"Stella was wounded," cried Ted. "Where is she? Scatter, men, and find her. She cannot be far away. If anything has happened to her, some one will suffer."

CHAPTER XXXI
STELLA A CAPTIVE

We will leave Ted and the broncho boys, to follow the misadventures of Stella.

After securing Magpie, which was taken back to the cow camp by Kit, who, much against his inclinations, was compelled to go into retirement until his arm healed, Ted released old man Norris, who secured a pony and rode rapidly out of town.

When Stella fell from the back of her pony to the road she became insensible. A ball from the weapon of one of Shan Rhue's gang had clipped a lock of hair from her forehead, creasing the skull. By a miracle her life was saved, for the merest fraction of an inch lay between her and death.

During the hurly-burly of the fight, and as Ted was grasped in the powerful arms of Shan Rhue, one of the gang rushed up to her as she lay in the dust and picked her up.

He was a powerful man, and carried Stella's light body as if she had been a child. That he was not seen by some member of the Running Water outfit was due to the fact that they were too busily engaged in fighting to pay attention to anything else.

When Stella regained her senses she was conscious of a racking headache, and, placing her hand to her forehead, brought it away wet and sticky. It was quite dark, and she groaned feebly. The pain was excruciating, and the motion of her body made her deathly sick.

She felt around her, and her hand came in contact with a cold, hard, yet yielding substance. Then she heard the rumble of wheels, and knew that she was in a vehicle of some sort. The motion of the couch on which she was lying was such that she came to the conclusion that she was in one of those old stagecoaches hung on leather springs, which were so much in use in the West before the advent of the railroads.

As her mind grew clearer she tried to remember all that had occurred. Suddenly it flashed upon her. The capture of old Norris, the attempt of Shan

Rhue and his gang to take him away to lynch him, and the beginning of the fight. How it had been finished she did not know.

Neither did she know whether or not she was in the care of her friends or in the custody of her enemies. Probably the latter, for if Ted and the boys were taking her somewhere, surely she would have more attention, and the blood would have been washed from the wound on her forehead.

The curtains of the stage were down, and she did not know whether it was day or night.

Outside she heard the voices of men.

"Hurry up them mules, Bill," a man's voice came to her gruffly.

"Can't get any more out o' them. We've come nigh twenty mile on the run. I tell you, the mules is 'most all in," said a man, evidently the driver of the stage.

"Well, we ain't got much farther to go," said the other. "But we got to get there before moondown, er we'll be up against it."

"What time is the bunch goin' to be at the lone tree?"

"Ten o'clock."

"Then we've got just about an hour, eh?"

"Just about. But we're a long ways off yet. Git all y'u can out o' them mules. Kill 'em if y'u have to get them there on time."

"They're doin' all they can. Y'u don't want me to kill them before we get there, do y'u?" asked the driver crossly.

"No, but if y'u miss the bunch y'u know what will happen. Shan ain't much on the sweet temper since the kid bumped him so hard, an' he don't like y'u too well, nohow. I'm just givin' y'u a friendly tip."

"Keep it. I ain't so stuck on Shan myself as I used to be."

"Only don't let him know it. We ain't none of us in love with him, an' yet we come up an' eat out o' his hand when he calls us, just like a lot o' hound dogs."

The conversation told Stella the truth she had dreaded. She had been captured by Shan Rhue's ruffians, and she knew that she was in a precarious predicament, for she could hope for no mercy from Ted's merciless and beaten enemy.

She would be used to punish Ted, and she sighed at the thought of what grief her disappearance would cause her aunt and the boys.

Suddenly the curtain on the window was drawn aside. It was bright moonlight without, and in it she saw the villainous face of a man looking in upon her.

Her eyes met his, and she uttered an exclamation.

"Hello!" he exclaimed, in surprise. "Come to, have y'u?"

Stella made no reply.

"Thought fer a while that y'u'd slipped over the Great Divide," the fellow continued.

"No fault of yours that I didn't," said Stella weakly, for the pain and nausea to which she was being subjected had taken all her strength.

"I ain't had nothin' to do with it, lady. I'm just guidin' the outfit. I don't know y'u, er how y'u got hurt. Feelin' better?"

"I would be much better if I could get out and walk. The motion of this carriage makes me deathly sick."

"Can't let y'u do that, lady. We're in too much of a hurry to stop now."

"But you might let me have a drink of water. I am dying of thirst."

"I reckon I can do that."

The flap over the stage window dropped, and in a moment she heard hushed voices outside. Then a canteen was thrust through the window.

"Take all y'u want, lady, an' drink hearty," said her guide.

Stella wet her handkerchief and bathed her throbbing forehead, then took a deep draft, and felt much refreshed.

"Here's your canteen," she said.

Again the flap was thrust aside, and the ugly face looked in upon her with a leer.

"Where are we, and where are we going?" asked Stella.

"We're in the Wich—"

"Hey, Jack, stow that," cried the driver.

"But it won't do no harm—"

"You know what the orders is," said the other significantly.

"Sorry I can't tell y'u, lady. Orders is orders."

"Oh, well, I don't suppose it would do me any good to know where I am, anyway, but you might as well tell me what you are going to do with me. It would relieve my anxiety, and make me feel better."

"There ain't no harm comin' to y'u, lady, while I am with y'u," said the fellow, with a hateful leer that made Stella shudder.

"Thank you," she said faintly, as with a sigh she laid her head back again with her wet handkerchief on her brow.

So the stage rumbled on for almost an hour, with Stella the prey of sickness and pain. She doubted if she could have walked even if she had been permitted to leave the stage.

But as she lay there she thought, and from the scraps of conversation she had heard, and from what her guide was about to tell her when he was interrupted by the driver, she knew that she had been captured and abducted during the fight by Shan Rhue's men, and that she was in the Wichita Mountains.

That much, at least, she knew, but what caused her much anxiety was that she did not know the result of the fight.

She came to the conclusion that the broncho boys and their friends must have lost in the encounter, else she would not be in her present predicament.

But what of poor old Norris, for in spite of his rascality she was sorry that he had fallen into the hands of the ruthless Shan Rhue.

"Keep off to the left," shouted the guide. "We're almost there. Down into that coulee y'u go. There ain't another crossin' this side o' three mile, an' we ain't got time to go so far out o' our way."

"Say, we're liable to turn over down there. Better get the gal out, an' let her walk down. I can get safe up the other side."

"All right. Stop 'er."

The stage stopped, and the cessation of the swaying, swinging motion was a blessed relief to the tortured girl.

"Come on out," said the guide, as he threw the door open. "We'll have to ask you to walk to the bottom o' this coulee, if y'u don't want to be scrambled about on the bottom o' the coach."

Stella was glad to get out, but when her feet were on the ground she swayed and staggered like a drunken person from sheer sickness and weakness.

Beside her was her guide on his horse, and she was compelled to lean against it for a moment until she recovered herself.

The stage had gone lumbering and swaying down the bank of the coulee, and before it reached the bottom it turned on its side.

The driver leaped in safety to the ground, and the guide went scrambling down the bank to his assistance.

The mules were plunging and kicking, and threatened to break their harness to pieces.

Stella was mutely thankful that she had not been in the stage when it went over, as she sat down on a rock to rest and watch the efforts of the swearing and angry men to right the stage.

Once she thought of trying to escape while the men were engrossed in their work, and she arose eagerly.

But when she got to her feet she realized the impossibility of such a thing, for she almost fell. Then she sank down again, and resigned herself to her fate.

But soon the stage was put back on its wheels again, and the guide called to her to come down.

This was a slow and painful operation, during which the driver swore impatiently at the delay. But she accomplished it, and crawled into the stage and sank down on the pallet which had been made for her with the seat cushions.

Now they were off again, faster than before, and with correspondingly more discomfort to Stella. Oh, if the journey would only end, she thought.

"Here we are," she heard the guide's voice in a shout.

The stage stopped, and Stella heard a rush of feet.

"Got her?" some one demanded gruffly.

"Yep, but she's all in," replied the guide. "Her forehead was creased by a bullet, an' the trip has about finished her."

"Can't help that. Get her out. We've got to be moving. The soldiers are out to-night."

"What's the matter?"

"Injuns.".

"Uprisin'?"

"Not yet, but the agent over to Fort Sill has a tip that they are putting on paint."

"What's the trouble?"

"Somethin' about beef issue. The last cows issued to the Injuns were no good, an' the Injuns made a kick, an' the agent told them to go to the deuce. Old Flatnose an' his son Moonface, the Apache chiefs, have always been bad actors, an' now they are tryin' to scare up a muss."

"Reckon they'll do it?"

"The commandant at Fort Sill seems to think they will, for he's got two companies out on the scout."

"The boys better look out, then. The Injuns don't like the gang over at the Hole in the Wall none too good."

"We stand all right with Flatnose and his son, an' it's their band that's actin' bad."

"Well, y'u better get a move on y'u. The moon will be down in an hour."

"Get the gal out, then, an' we'll be movin'."

"All right," said the guide, poking his head into the coach. "Here's where you get out. Boss said to treat her well," he continued, turning to the man with whom he had been talking.

"Oh, we'll do that, all right," was the reply.

Stella scrambled painfully out of the coach. All about her were mounted men, both whites and Indians. There were a score or more of them.

"Can you ride?" asked one of them of Stella.

"Yes," she replied, "if you don't go too fast. I'm sick and weak."

"We'll do the best we can," said the man shortly.

Then he called back to his followers:

"Jake, bring up that spare hoss."

In a moment, and with a staggering weakness, Stella climbed into the saddle. With a man on each side of her, she took up the march again.

Through dark defiles in the black mountains the cavalcade made its way, Stella clinging to the saddle, and often in danger of falling off. Presently they came into a glade, or park, which was surrounded by towering mountain walls. For half an hour they traversed this, then came to the end, and before them yawned an opening in the wall less than ten feet wide.

They entered this, and after traversing it a short distance Stella found herself in a circular chamber in the mountains with the starry sky for a roof.

Several fires were burning in the chamber, around which Indians and white men were sprawling, playing cards, talking, or silently smoking.

In one corner was a corral, in which many horses were confined.

"You can get down now," said the leader of the party that had conducted her to the place. "There is a shelter for you over there."

He pointed to a small tent on the farther side of the chamber.

"You will be perfectly safe here. You do not seem well. I will send you assistance."

"Where am I?" asked Stella.

"You are a prisoner in the Hole in the Wall," was the reply.

"Then Heaven help me," said Stella, sobbing.

CHAPTER XXXII
A HOLE IN THE HERD

The herd of cattle which Ted and the broncho boys were herding in No Man's Land he had branded Circle S, named after Stella.

There were more than two thousand head of them, which Ted was feeding on the rich range grasses of the Southwest to drive to the Moon Valley Ranch to winter, for it was well known to cowmen that a Southern or Southwestern beef animal will do better for a winter on the Northern range.

After Stella's disappearance Ted and the boys searched every nook and cranny of the town of Snyder, but were unable to get the slightest trace of her. Dividing into bands, they scoured the country roundabout, being assisted by the cow-punchers and the ranchers in the neighborhood.

But Stella had disappeared as if the earth had opened and swallowed her. With all his ingenuity, backed by the strong desire he had to find her, Ted was making no headway, and he hardly slept or ate during the long days and nights, but was in the saddle almost continuously.

Naturally, he suspected Shan Rhue of knowing something about Stella's absence, if, indeed, he was not actually responsible for it.

But he could not fasten anything on the man whom he had come to regard as his greatest enemy, and whom he knew hated him. Whenever he sought Shan Rhue, he was always to be found at his haunts.

Tired of the inaction, Ted met Shan Rhue on the street one day, and resolved to have it out with him.

"Shan Rhue, I want to speak with you," said Ted, stopping him.

"Well, what is it you want?" asked Shan Rhue.

"I want you to tell me where Stella is," said Ted.

Shan Rhue stared at him in apparent amazement.

"How should I know where she is?" asked Shan Rhue, with a wicked twinkling in his eye.

"I don't know," answered Ted; "but I think you do know."

"So I supposed, from the way in which you have had me followed. I suppose you miss her a good deal."

"Her aunt, Mrs. Graham, is distraught with grief and anxiety. Surely you have no fight on her, or on Miss Fosdick, either, that you should keep them apart."

"No. I have no fight with a woman. But why should I know where the young lady is?"

"There are several reasons why you should have had her taken away. But I think the principal reason is that you think you can get square with me by doing so."

"There might be something in that. Mind me, I am not confessing that I took her away, or that I know who did take her away, or where she is. You have seen me in town every day since the little trouble we had over that old thief Norris, haven't you?"

"Yes, but that tells me nothing. It might not be necessary for you to leave this town to have her hidden somewhere."

"But you and your friends searched the town from one end to the other, and you did not find her."

"True, but for all that I am satisfied that you know where she is. Suppose we call it off, and that you tell me where she is."

"If I knew, I would not tell you," said Shan Rhue, his voice intense with hatred.

"What do you mean? Are you such a coward that you will punish a woman for your spite against a man? I did not think that of you. I believe Stella Fosdick was carried off by you, of your men, acting under your instructions."

Shan Rhue's only reply was a sneering laugh.

"If I discover that what I say is true," said Ted, in a low voice so full of purpose that it was in itself a warning, "you will be the sorriest man in all this country. I will make you suffer by it even as you have caused suffering to others."

"So you have suffered, eh? That is good! Now I am a little better satisfied. But my debt to you is not yet paid. There are other things in store for you."

"What do you mean, you dog? By Heaven, I know now that you did cause her abduction, and I shall find her. You cannot keep me away from the place in which you have hidden her. I shall find her if she is at the end of the earth. When I do find her, if anything has harmed her, you, Shan Rhue, gambler, thief, and murderer, shall pay for it, and pay heavier than for any amusement you have had in all your miserable lying, thieving career."

As the epithets addressed to Shan Rhue left Ted's lips, the bully sprang back, and made a motion to draw his six-shooter.

But before he had his hand on his hip his eyes were looking into the bore of Ted's forty-four. Instead of drawing a gun, therefore, he pulled out his handkerchief and wiped his dry lips.

Shan Rhue feared Ted Strong.

"Remember," said Ted, before turning away, "I know that you have spirited Stella Fosdick away. But I shall find her, and when I am sure of it you better leave the country before I reach the place where you are, for as sure as I am standing here I will make my previous experience with you so tame that you will be glad to crawl in the dust on your face to be forgiven."

"Ha, ha!" laughed Shan Rhue. "So it hurts as bad as that, eh? Good!"

He went away laughing, and it was all Ted could do to control himself, and keep from leaping upon him and punching him. Instead, he jumped into his saddle and rode Sultan like the wind out to the cow camp.

For several days he had paid no attention to the herd, leaving it under the general direction of Bud, while he stayed in town trying to hear some news of Stella, or was riding all over the country with one or another of the boys, searching for her.

As he rode into camp with disappointment and dejection written on his face, he was met by Mrs. Graham, who had grown pale and wan with anxiety.

"Any news of her?" she asked Ted.

"None, but I haven't given up hope by any means. Don't worry so, Mrs. Graham. I think I am on the track at last, and that we shall soon have her with us again."

But Mrs. Graham only walked away with the tears coursing down her cheeks. The herd was grazing to the west of the camp, and Ted rode out to it, and to where Bud was sitting quietly in his saddle watching it.

There was an air of dejection about Bud, also. Indeed, every fellow in the outfit was secretly worrying and grieving for Stella.

"Say, Ted," said Bud, as Ted rode up, "I think thar's somethin' wrong with ther dogies."

Cow-punchers call the small Southwestern cattle "dogies."

"What do you mean?" asked Ted. "I was looking them over this morning. Rode through the bunch. They seemed to be all right then."

"Oh, they're eatin' well, an' aire as likely a lot o' beef ez ever I see," replied Bud.

"Well, what then?"

"Thar ain't so many o' them ez there wuz, er my eye hez gone back on me."

"Any of them get away?"

"I figger it so."

"What have you found out?"

"Some one is liftin' our cattle. That's what I mean."

"Great Scott! What makes you think so?"

"Ted, ther herd has shrunk."

"You judge by the eye, I suppose."

"Yes. That is the only way I have o' judgin'. We hev never had a count o' them since we drove them onto this range."

"How many do you think we are shy?"

"My eye tells me erbout five hundred."

"Great guns! How could five hundred head get away from us? And right under our noses, too."

"Easy enough. You must remember that since Stella has been gone we've paid no more attention to the herd than if we didn't own them."

"That's true. As for myself, I confess that I've given them no attention. And I've kept you fellows so busy that we've left the cattle to take care of themselves, almost."

"Well, it's time we woke up ter ther situation, er soon we won't hev no more cattle than a rabbit."

"That's so. We'll run a count of them in the morning."

"It's shore got me puzzled. I can't think whar they could hev gone."

"Strayed, possibly."

"P'r'aps. Ever hear o' there bein' any rustlers in this part o' ther country?"

"No, I never have. But there are some pretty bad citizens in this section, who, if they never have rustled cattle, certainly are capable of it."

"Alludin' to who?"

"Well, there's Shan Rhue and his gang, for instance."

"They're pretty bad actors, fer shore. But I ain't positive thet they're ther kind what would rustle. They're jest plain town thieves an' gamblers. They ain't cow-punchers. It gen'rally is fellers what has been in ther cow business at some time er another what rustles stock."

"Oh, it doesn't take much of a man to steal cattle. A thieving gambler could do it as well as another."

"But our brand and ear crop? They shore couldn't get away from them."

"They're not so hard, Bud. A good man could run our stock out of this part of the country and alter the brand without any trouble."

"Shore, ther brand is not so hard to alter."

"Let's ride back to camp and look at the brand book, and see if any one has a similar brand to ours, or one that they could alter without trouble. But, remember, I'm not going to give myself any uneasiness in the matter, and I think we will find the herd all there. I can't see how so many cattle as you think could get away from us."

"I do."

"In what manner could they?"

"Well, yer see, thar ain't ary o' us fellers been ridin' herd at night since Stella was taken away."

"Yes; go on."

"Ther fellers what hev been guardin' ther herd at night we picked up around here when we drove ther herd up from ther South."

"True. They were all local cow-punchers. I realize that we have made a mistake. One of us ought to have had charge of every night watch since we have been on this range."

"Shore. It's a cinch they wouldn't attempt to run 'em off in ther daytime."

"That's the idea. It would be as easy as shooting fish in a rain barrel for a crooked night foreman to drift a few cattle away from the herd in the dark, to be picked up by fellows waiting on the outside, and driven into the hills until the brands and marks could be changed."

They were at the camp now, and Ted got out the brand book and turned its leaves over in an attempt to find a brand similar to their own, the Circle S, which was a circle with the letter S in the center.

In every Western State or Territory in which cattle-raising is a business the law makes it imperative that every ranchman who uses the open range shall select a brand for his cattle which is registered. This brand is his own, and every head of cattle found with his brand on it belongs to him.

On the open range the cattle get mixed more or less, and in the spring there is a general round-up of the cattle, after the calves have been born and are following their mothers.

The cow-punchers go into the vast herds and drive out the calves. Of course, the mother follows the calf, lowing piteously for it.

When the cow is out with the calf, it can be plainly seen to whom she belongs by the brand on her. Her owner, or his men or representatives, promptly throw her and the calf into their own herd, and later put their brand on the calf.

Calves which are motherless and are unbranded are known as mavericks, and belong to whoever finds them. The cowman who finds a maverick promptly puts his own brand on it and it belongs to him.

The safety of the system is in choosing a brand that cannot be easily altered, and which will not be easily confounded with the brand of another.

When the boys had chosen the brand Circle S for this herd in honor of Stella, they had spoken of this, and Bud had remarked that it would be easily altered by making an eight of the S, but they had found no Circle 8 in the brand book, and took the chance, especially as Stella now insisted upon having no other brand for the herd than Circle S, her "own brand," as she called it.

Ted and Bud could find no brand in the Texas or Oklahoma brand books at all like theirs, and dismissed the matter from their minds.

The next morning early all hands turned out for a count of the herd. The herd was split, and the broncho boys took turns at the count, as the bunches of cattle were split and driven slowly past them on the point.

From the books, there should be two thousand three hundred cattle, or thereabouts, in the herd. A few cattle more or less would not have been surprising, for a great herd of cattle will, like a magnet, draw to it all the individual strays in the country roundabout.

It was well in the afternoon before the count was finished, and the boys rode into camp to count up and compare with the books. Ted totaled the figures, while the boys hung eagerly over him to learn the result.

"Well, what d'yer make it?" asked Bud, as Ted, with an expression of perplexity on his face, looked up from his work.

"The count is seventeen hundred and fifty," answered Ted slowly.

"Gee! And that's how many shy?"

"Five hundred and fifty. Bud, you have a good eye."

"Orter hev. I've been runnin' my eye over herds fer many a year. So, we've been done out o' more'n five hundred head, eh? Well, Stella comes fust, an' then ther man what thinks he kin rustle cattle from the broncho boys had better take a runnin' jump outer this man's country."

CHAPTER XXXIII
LITTLE DICK IN TROUBLE

Little Dick Fosdick had been forgotten by Ted and the broncho boys in their anxiety over the absence of Stella.

They had seen him around the camp, but as it was impossible for him to accompany them on their hard rides, he had been left to his own devices.

He spent his days riding with one of the cowboys on the herd, and grieving in his own way for Stella.

He was a sensible little chap, and seldom complained at his loneliness. His life alone had made him patient, and he took it out in thinking.

He was now well able to take care of himself, although Stella insisted in "mothering" him when she was in camp.

Little Dick, as most of the boys called him, felt himself quite a man, for he could now catch his own pony and saddle it whenever he wanted to ride, and no one paid any attention to him as he came and went.

Ted had bought for him a little, wiry bay cayuse, and both he and Stella had taught him to ride, and Dick could now throw a rope with reasonable accuracy and speed.

Ted had given him a small revolver, and they had had great fun learning to shoot at a target, which was usually a bleached skull of a cow that had died long since on the prairie, and its bones picked clean by the coyotes.

Dick's revolver was only of thirty-two caliber, as befitted his strength, but the youngster had a good eye and the steady nerves of youth, and he soon got so that he could hit the skull with reasonable accuracy.

"Putting the shot through the eye" was one of the jokes of these shooting tournaments, in which Stella, and sometimes Bud, joined.

One day when they were shooting at a skull target, Bud missed — probably intentionally, for Bud was a crack shot.

Dick jumped up and down in glee, for he had just knocked a chip of bone from the skull himself.

"Bud missed! Bud missed!" he shouted, in glee. "Bud, you're an old tenderfoot. Couldn't hit a skull as big as the head of a barrel a hundred feet away."

"Didn't miss, neither," said Bud, in a tone of mock anger. "There's where you're fooled. That is what I call a good shot. See that left eye hole? Well, I aimed at that, and the bullet went through it. Ha! That's where the joke is on you." He grinned, and winked at Stella.

A few minutes later Dick shot and missed the skull.

"Yah!" shouted Bud. "Goody! You missed. You shoot like a hayseed. Couldn't hit a skull as big as the head of a barrel."

"That's where you're left," said the boy. "See that right eye hole? That's what I aimed at."

The laugh was on Bud.

"All right, kiddie," he laughed. "You're on. We'd be in a dickens of a fix if that ole cow hadn't left two eye holes when she died."

So it was that Dick had made great progress in the rudiments of a cow-puncher's life, and it exactly suited him, but, in the meanwhile, Stella was teaching him to read, and telling him the story of the rise and grandeur of his own country, and of the lands that lay beyond the seas.

So it was that Dick was unconsciously getting a better education than if he had gone to school, for he had a mind for the absorption of all sorts of knowledge like a sponge, and once a thing was told him he never forgot it.

The morning of the count he had started onto the range with the other boys, but as there would be great confusion, and perhaps danger of a stampede, Ted sent him back to camp.

"Run on back, Dick," Ted said kindly. "I'm afraid that pony of yours isn't quick enough to get out of the way if these dogies should take it into their heads to act ugly."

Dick never thought of rebelling when Ted spoke, for he knew that Ted was boss, and that he knew what was good for him.

"All right, Ted," he said. "Would it be any harm if I took a ride away from the camp?"

"Of course not, Dick," answered Ted kindly. He felt a little sore at himself for sending the boy away, but he knew that it was for the best. There would be plenty of time and many occasions for Dick to run into danger when he grew up.

Dick went back to camp, which was deserted save for Bill McCall, the cook, who was asleep under the chuck wagon, and Mrs. Graham, who was lying down in her tent.

Dick buckled on his belt and holster, and, mounting his pony Spraddle, set out for a long ride across the prairie.

In the boot of his saddle rested his little Remington, a present from Stella. He was going to look for an antelope, and he thought how proud Ted would be if he brought one back with him.

He knew how hard it was to get close enough to an antelope to shoot it, but he had just enough gameness to think that he could get one if he came within range of it.

Anyhow, there were coyotes and jack rabbits.

He rode across the prairie at a smart gallop, occasionally changing his course to chase a jack rabbit, which generally disappeared over a rise in the ground like a streak of gray dust, and was seen no more.

At noon he stopped for a few minutes to eat the biscuit and piece of bacon which he had taken from the rear of the chuck wagon before setting forth. He found a spring not far away, and, having given Spraddle a good, deep drink, and filling his small canteen, which was tied to the cantle of his saddle, he set forth again.

It was about two o'clock when he came in sight of the first real game of the day. On the top of the rise ahead of him he saw an animal about the size of a dog. As he rode toward it, it raised its head and gave a long, low, mournful howl.

"Coyote," exclaimed Dick to himself breathlessly. "I'll get that fellow, and take him back to camp. Won't Ted be surprised when he sees it?"

He took his Remington out of the boot, slipped in the necessary cartridges to fill the magazine, and rode forward slowly and cautiously.

The coyote watched him sharply, occasionally raising its head to utter its mournful cry. When Dick thought he had got within shooting distance, he stopped Spraddle, took a good, long aim at the coyote, and fired.

The ball kicked up the dust several feet in advance of the coyote, which, with another howl, this time one of derision, as it seemed to Dick, turned and trotted away.

"That was a bum shot," muttered Dick. "I'm glad Ted or Stella did not see it. Better luck next time."

The coyote ran a short distance, then stopped and looked over its shoulder to see if Dick was following, and, seeing that he was, took up its lope again.

It had got some distance from Dick, when, on the top of another rise, it stopped again, and Dick heard once more its luring cry.

It seemed to be an invitation to follow him. Dick had not paid any attention to the direction in which he was going, and had kept no track of time.

That he was following game, and that he intended to get it if it took all day, was all he thought of. Soon the coyote stopped again, and looked at Dick in a tantalizing sort of way, and again Dick approached it cautiously.

When he thought he was within range, he raised his Remington, and, taking a long, deliberate aim, fired. Again he missed. But he had the satisfaction of seeing that the ball had struck the earth several feet nearer the coyote than the first.

The coyote realized it, too, for he did not wait for another invitation, but started on his way in a hurry, with Dick riding pell-mell after him.

Dick for the first time realized that the day was going when he noticed the long shadow cast by himself and the pony on the prairie sod. He had not the slightest idea how far he had come, and there crept into his mind a sort of dread.

He pulled Spraddle down to a walk, and looked about him. Behind him there was no trace of the cow camp, nothing but the everlasting rise and fall of the prairie.

But ahead was the ragged line of the blue mountains. These he knew to be the Wichita Mountains, for, although he had never seen them before, he had heard the boys talking about them in camp.

Then he saw the coyote on a hill a little ways ahead, looking at him in the most aggravating way. The coyote's lips were curled back from his teeth in a contemptuous sort of a smile, it seemed to Dick, and as he started forward again the coyote threw up its head and actually laughed at him.

That settled it with Dick. No coyote that ever trotted the plains could laugh at him, but as this thought came to him he felt the dread of being lost on the prairie, or even having to stay alone in this waste all night.

Dick had heard the boys talk of the danger of being alone at night, for there were wolves and other animals that would daunt a man, to say nothing of a small boy.

He thought he would follow the coyote only long enough to get another shot at him, and then retrace his way back to the camp. By putting Spraddle through his paces he ought to be able to reach it before dark.

So he set forth again in the wake of the coyote, which was becoming more and more aggravating every minute. Suddenly the coyote disappeared altogether. It had done this before when it had gone down into the trough between two of the great, rolling swales of the prairie, but always it had come into sight again in a few minutes.

This time, however, it did not, and Dick wondered why.

In a few minutes he understood why, for he found himself at the edge of a coulee which had been washed deep by the storms of many winters.

Dick looked up and down the coulee for the wolf, and saw a form, gray and lithe, slinking among the bowlders with which it was filled. Dick forced Spraddle down the steep bank of the coulee, and was soon at the bottom.

Hastily he set after the coyote, but suddenly stopped, for a man stepped from behind a shoulder of rock and clay and caught his bridle.

Spraddle stopped so quickly that Dick was almost unseated. But he soon recovered himself, and stared in amazement at the man who had thus stopped him.

He was an Indian.

Dick had often seen Indians in the towns through which the broncho boys had passed, and occasionally they had come into the camps they had established on the drive of the herd up from Texas.

But this was the first time Dick had ever come in contact with an Indian when he was alone. For a moment his heart stopped beating, for he was afraid.

"How?" grunted the Indian.

It was all Dick could do to reply with a feeble, quavering "How?"

Many times around the camp fire, with the boys all about, when Bud was telling one of his tales of Indians, Dick had thought what he would do if he ever came in contact with a real, live, sure-enough redskin, and always he had thought how brave he would be. But now that he had actually met one, he felt his nerve ooze away.

However, the Indian was not aware of it, for Dick had a way of keeping his feelings to himself, and he seldom showed whether he was surprised or angry, although he never hesitated to let his friends know his pleasure at their kindness, or gratitude for what they did for him.

He was looking at the Indian steadily, taking stock of him, and this is what he saw: A broad, dirty face, in which burned two small, narrow eyes. The cheek bones were prominent, and on each one was a spot of red paint. The long, black, coarse hair was braided with pieces of otter fur, and covered with an old cavalry cap, in which was stuck a crow's wing feather, and around his neck hung a small, round pocket mirror attached to a red string, by way of ornament.

The Indian wore a dirty cotton shirt and a pair of brown overalls, and his feet were covered with green moccasins, decorated with small tubes of tin, which jingled every time he took a step.

A belt and holster hung at his hip, and the handle of a Colt forty-four was within easy reach.

"White papoose where go?" asked the Indian, showing a row of sharpened teeth.

"Hunt coyote," replied Dick, in a voice that trembled.

"Heap fool. No catch coyote," said the Indian, reaching over and lifting Dick's Remington from the saddle.

He sighted it, turned it around in his hand, and then coolly slung it over his shoulder.

"Here, give that to me," said Dick sturdily. With this act of theft all his courage came back to him. No dirty Indian should have the rifle Stella had given him.

But the Indian only grinned.

"Me heap brave," said the Indian. "Me Pokopokowo."

He looked at Dick as if he expected the boy to be deeply impressed.

"I don't care who you are. I want my rifle," cried Dick.

"Papoose heap fool. Get off pony." The Indian was scowling now, and looked very ferocious, and once more Dick's courage oozed. The Indian did not seem to be a bit frightened.

As Dick was slow in descending from the saddle, the Indian grasped him by the arm and jerked him to the ground.

Dick was as angry as he ever got, but was sensible enough to know that he could not fight the Indian, and that all he could do was to escape as rapidly as possible.

He turned and ran up the coulee.

But he had not gone far when he was overtaken, and knocked flat with a cuff on the side of the head. As he rose slowly with his head ringing, Pokopokowo grasped him by the shoulder, and bound his hands behind him.

In a moment he was back at the pony's side, and was thrown upon its back, but not in the saddle. This was occupied by the Indian, who directed it down the coulee, and in the direction of the mountains.

Dick Fosdick was a prisoner.

CHAPTER XXXIV
A MESSAGE FROM STELLA

Dick had some difficulty in keeping his seat on the pony's back, for he could not hold on to the cantle of the saddle, and Spraddle wabbled dreadfully, as he stumbled among the bowlders in the coulee.

But before long they were out on the prairie again, and Dick observed that they were headed toward the mountains.

They had several miles to go to reach the mountains, and it was just getting dusk when they entered upon a broad and beautiful valley, which, as it ran east and west, was flooded with the light from the setting sun.

Here the Indian turned in the saddle and looked at Dick with a malevolent smile.

"Turn white boy loose," he grunted.

Dick twisted around, and the Indian untied the cord that bound his wrists.

"White boy try to run away, I kill um," said the Indian, showing his teeth in a horrible look of ferocity that chilled Dick to the bone.

"All right," he said; "I'll not try to run away again."

"Kill um if do," growled the Indian, hissing, at the pony, which is the Indian way of making a pony go forward, and means the same as a white man's "Get up!"

Dick was dreadfully hungry, but he said nothing, clinging to the cantle of the saddle with both hands, for the pony was now loping.

They had gone up the valley for several miles, when suddenly the Indian turned aside down a dark and narrow defile, still at a lope.

Even Dick realized the danger of this, for the floor of the defile was covered with large, loose stones, over which Spraddle was continually stumbling, for he had come a long way and was tired, besides the added weight of the Indian was more than he was accustomed to carry.

It had grown very dark, and Dick could not see the pony's ears when he twisted around to look past the Indian.

He knew that it was to be a moonlight night, but the moon was not up yet, and would not be for an hour or more. In fact, it was doubtful if the light of the moon would penetrate to the bottom of the defile until it was high in the heavens, so deep was the defile and so steep its walls.

Dick had given up wondering and worrying, and had forced himself to be content with his situation, as he knew that he could not better it any.

Suddenly he became aware that the Indian was asleep, for he was drooping in the saddle, and was breathing deeply and steadily.

Now, thought Dick, was the time to escape, if any. He tried to slip from the pony's back, but in an instant the Indian was awake, and, reaching around, grasped Dick's wrist, twisting it until the boy gave a sharp cry of pain.

The Indian slipped from the back of the pony, and again bound Dick's wrists behind him, and with a grunt climbed into the saddle and urged Spraddle on, slapping him across the face with the end of the rein.

"Don't you do that," cried Dick, who never abused Spraddle himself, and couldn't stand it to see any one else, particularly a dirty Indian, beat his pet.

"White boy shut up, or Pokopokowo beat him plenty," growled the Indian.

"If you dare beat me, Ted Strong will fix you when he gets you," said Dick hotly.

But the Indian only laughed, and continued to beat poor Spraddle over the face, to the pain and anger of Dick, who, however, realized that he was absolutely helpless.

But Pokopokowo was soon to be paid for his cruelty, and by poor Spraddle himself.

Spraddle, stung by the blows, was stumbling along at a good pace over the bowlders that lay in his way, with the Indian urging him faster all the time.

Suddenly there was a great heave. Spraddle went down, almost turning a somersault, as his tired feet struck a larger bowlder than he had encountered before.

The Indian, who was dozing again, shot over his head as if from a catapult, and Dick went sprawling forward over the saddle onto the neck of the pony.

Fortunately, the pony righted itself in time to save Dick from a hard fall, and he stayed on Spraddle's back, talking to him gently.

At the sound of Dick's voice the pony became quiet, and Dick half sprawled, half fell to the ground. The boy was in a pretty bad fix, for the Indian had tied his hands securely. He thought of ways by which he might cut the cord, but it seemed hopeless. He had heard somewhere of bound men releasing themselves by wearing their bonds asunder against the rough edge of a rock, and determined to try it for himself.

If he could only get his hands free, he might escape yet. Backing up to the wall of the cañon, he felt with his hands for a rock, and soon knew that he was against one. As he sawed his hands back and forth, he was listening for some sound from the Indian, but heard none.

Could it be that the fall had killed Pokopokowo?

To his joy, he felt the cord part, and his hands were free. At that moment there came a flood of light into the defile, for the moon had risen overhead.

Lying on the floor of the defile, lay the Indian, with a deep gash across his forehead, where it had struck a sharp rock. His ugly face was covered with blood, making it additionally hideous.

By the side of the Indian lay Dick's precious rifle, and he stooped to pick it up. As he did so, something glistened beside it, and Dick picked it up.

It was the little, round mirror that the Indian had worn around his neck. Dick pocketed it for proof of his adventure when he should again reach camp, and, picking up his rifle, climbed upon Spraddle's back, turned him around, and drove down the defile.

When he reached the open valley it was as bright as day, and under his coaxing and kind words the tired little pony, relieved of the Indian's weight, picked up his feet and set forth at a brisk pace into the west, in which direction Dick knew the cow camp lay.

It was almost daylight when Bill McCall, the cook, roused from his blankets to begin the preparations for breakfast. He leaped to his feet and listened.

Not far away he heard the sound of the pony's footsteps approaching. Bill was an old cow-puncher, and he knew instantly that the pony was tired, and that he was under saddle, and also that the saddle was occupied.

The footsteps came nearer, and just as they were close to the camp daylight came on with a rush, as it does on the plains, and Bill gave a great shout of joy which brought every puncher in camp scrambling out of his blankets, for there rode in a very tired little boy on a very tired little, pony.

The boy was pale and tired from hunger and his long hours in the saddle, and it was all the pony could do to stagger in.

"It's little Dick," shouted Bud. "Well, jumpin' sand hills, whar you-all been all night? Takin' a leetle pleasure pasear?"

"Oh, Bud, I'm so tired and hungry," said Dick, as Bud lifted him from the saddle.

"Here you, Bill, git busy in a hurry. This kid ain't hed nothin' ter eat in a week. He's 'most starved. Bile yer coffee double-quick, an' git up a mess o' bacon an' flapjacks pretty dern pronto, if yer don't want me ter git inter yer wool."

Bud was rubbing the cold and chafed wrists of the boy beside the fire, which one of the boys had replenished. The boys surrounded little Dick with many inquiries, but Bud shooed them away.

"Don't yer answer a bloomin' question until yer gits yer system packed with cooky's best grub. I reckon, now, yer could eat erbout eighteen o' them twelve-inch flapjacks what Bill makes, an' drink somethin' like a gallon o' ther fust coffee what comes out o' ther pot."

Little Dick smiled, as he watched with glistening eyes the rapid movements of Bill McCall as he hustled over his fire, the air redolent with the odors of coffee and bacon and griddle cakes, so that his mouth fairly watered.

When Bill shouted breakfast, Ted and Bud sat Dick down and loaded his plate with good things, which he caused to disappear in a hurry.

But after a while he was stuffed like a Christmas turkey, and put his tin plate away with a sigh, and absolutely cleaned.

"Now," said Ted, when he saw this good sign, "where have you been all day and all night? We've been scared about you. Thought we had lost you, too."

Dick went ahead with his story from the very beginning, and told of the downfall of Pokopokowo, and his escape, and of his all-night ride into the west, to accidentally stumble, at daylight, into camp.

The boys listened in amazement to this record of courage on the part of its youngest member, and some seemed to doubt the Indian part of it.

"Sho, yer dreamin', kid," said Sol Flatbush, the cow-puncher. "Thar ain't no Injuns like that in this yere part o' ther country. Why, an Injun wouldn't dare carry off a kid like that."

"You don't believe it, eh?" exclaimed Dick hotly.

"I believe yer," said Bud soothingly, for the boy was very nervous from being up all night and his hard ride, which would have taxed the energies of a grown man. "Don't yer mind what thet ole pelican says. He ain't got no more sense than a last year's bird's nest, nohow."

"The Indian had this around his neck," said Dick, "and when he fell it came loose from his neck, and I picked it up, for I thought some one might think I wasn't telling the truth. Now, I'm tired, and I can't keep my eyes open."

His head began to nod, and his eyes closed.

Bud picked him up and carried him to a pair of blankets which had been spread on the shady side of Mrs. Graham's tent, and laid him down and left him dead to the world.

Dick had placed the little, round looking-glass in Ted's hand.

As he took it, Ted uttered an exclamation.

"By Jove," he exclaimed, "I believe this is the little glass Stella used to carry in her pocket. Why, what is this?"

Ted was holding the little mirror up to the sky, apparently in an endeavor to look through it.

"What is it?" asked Bud, approaching the fire.

"Dick has brought back Stella's little pocket mirror," said Ted. "I'd know it anywhere. But the back has been torn off it."

"Tooken off ther neck o' an Injun?" said Bud, dropping his usual jolly manner. "I thought yer said thar wa'n't no bad Injuns eround yere, Sol Flatbush. What d'yer make o' that?"

Sol Flatbush got a little pale.

"Thar ain't none," he said. "All ther Injuns on the reservation is peaceable. They knows they couldn't do no monkey business with all them sojers at Fort Sill."

"Yet here's a kid run off with by an Injun, and he brings back a pocket mirror what belonged to Stella Fosdick. Sol Flatbush, ye've got ter give a better defense o' ther Injuns than that."

"What hev I got ter do with ther Injuns?" asked Flatbush defiantly.

"Search me. But ye've made a wrong diagnosis, an' I don't like yer brand o' talk none. I think myself thet yer too friendly ter ther redskins."

"What d'ye mean?" cried Flatbush, springing to his feet.

"I mean thet I don't trust yer none. I think ye're a skunk, an' I don't like ter see yer face eround this yere camp. How much do this outfit owe yer?"

"Three months' wage," answered the cow-puncher sourly.

Bud went down into his leather pouch and extracted a roll of bills, and skinned off several.

"Thar it is. Skidoo! An' don't try ter mingle with this outfit none hereafter. Thar'll be a new foreman o' ther night herd what ain't got so many friends in this yere locality."

"What d'yer mean by that?" Flatbush's hand sprang to his side.

But Bud was quicker, and in the flash of an eye had the muzzle of his six-shooter under the nose of the night foreman, who shrank from it.

"I mean thet yer a crook, an' I'll give yer jest three minutes ter rope yer hoss an' git."

Flatbush turned and hurried to the remuda, caught and saddled his horse, and rode out of camp.

"I've had my eye on that maverick fer quite some time," said Bud, turning to the boys after he had watched Flatbush fade into the distance. "I've suspected him o' turnin' off our cattle every night. I haven't caught him at it, or thar wouldn't've been no necessity o' chasin' him out. He'd've gone feet foremost."

"What do you think of it, Bud?" asked Ted, handing the little mirror over to the golden-haired puncher.

Bud took it in his hand, and looked at it a long time.

"It shore is Stella's," he said. "I reckernize it by this leetle dent on ther side o' it."

He was holding it in the palm of his hand, looking down at it intently.

"Hello, what's this?" Bud held the mirror against the sleeve of his blue shirt.

"Pipin' pelicans," he muttered, "if thar ain't some kind o' a pitcher on it."

Ted went to his side and looked at the mirror.

"I believe you're right," he said. "Let me look at it."

"What do you make of it?" asked Bud.

All the boys crowded around, watching Ted eagerly.

"This is evidently intended for the picture of a stone wall," said Ted, "and that wavy line behind it is meant for mountains."

"What's that?" asked Bud, pointing to the picture.

"I guess it is meant for a hole in the stone wall," said Ted.

"Wow!" said Bud. "That's as easy as livin' on a farm. Don't yer see? It is a message from the Hole in the Wall."

"By Jove, you're right. The Hole in the Wall in the Wichita Mountains."

"What is that right below it?"

"It looks like a star. It is a star."

"It is Stella's signature," said Ben. "Stella is the Latin for star. Don't you see, she has sent this message out from the Hole in the Wall, where she is a prisoner? It's as plain as day to me."

"You're right," shouted Ted. "Into your saddles, boys; we're off to the Hole in the Wall at once."

CHAPTER XXXV
"HOLE IN THE WALL"

"Kit, you will stay and take care of the herd," said Ted, just before the boys galloped off.

"All right, but I'd mighty well like to go with you," said Kit, who, although he was eager to be in the fight that he knew would come off if Ted found that Shan Rhue had anything to do with the abduction of Stella, was not one to get disgruntled.

Ted would have been well pleased to have Kit with him, but Kit's arm was not yet well enough to risk in a possible rough-and-tumble adventure.

"Say, Ted," Kit called after the leader of the broncho boys.

"What?" asked Ted, riding back.

"Don't you think you better take Stella's pony, Magpie, along with you? She'll have to have something to ride coming back."

He did not say "if you find her," for he knew that if she was anywhere in the Wichita Mountains Ted would find her.

"Glad you spoke of it," said Ted.

It did not take long to rope the magpie pony and throw Stella's saddle on it.

Now they were off into the northeast, where the Wichita Mountains lay. None of them knew just where the Hole in the Wall was, but Ted felt confident of finding it if there was such a place.

They rode so hard, only stopping at noon to water the ponies, that early in the afternoon they entered the mountains.

As they were going up the valley they saw the flying figure of a man on horseback coming toward them.

As he approached, they saw that he was a cavalryman.

"Hello, what's up?" said Bud. "I never see a sojer goin' so fast, except there was somethin' doin'."

A few minutes later the soldier rode up to them.

He proved to be a sergeant of cavalry.

"Where are you going?" he asked, pulling his horse to its haunches.

"What's that ter you?" asked Bud jovially.

"Just this: The Indians are threatening to rise, perhaps to-night, perhaps not until to-morrow. But when they do, this will be no place for white men."

"Where is the place called the Hole in the Wall?" asked Ted.

"Do you want to go there, or do you want to avoid it?" asked the sergeant.

"We want to go there as soon as we can."

"I'd advise you to keep away until the troops get there and clean things up."

"Why?"

"That is where the dissatisfied Indians are camped. I do not know it officially, but I understand that Flatnose and Moonface, the two chiefs, are there now, and that the orders from Washington are to send us in to drive them out."

"When is this to take place?"

"The Indians have made no open declaration of war as yet, but it is looked for at any time."

"How will it be announced?"

"By the signal fires on the hills. A detachment of our men picked up early this morning a wounded Indian, named Pokopokowo. He was wounded, and was taken to the post surgeon to be cared for. He has just confessed that it is the intention of the Indians to rise and kill all the white settlers they can lay their hands on. I am on my way to send out the alarm."

"And you say the Indians are camped at the Hole in the Wall?"

"Yes, the detachment sent out early this morning were on a scouting expedition when they picked up Pokopokowo."

"Where is this Hole in the Wall, and how do you get there?"

"You are bound to go there? I would advise you not to."

"We must go. A young lady belonging to our party has been captured and taken there. We did not know there were any Indians there, but only white outlaws."

"That is different. I suppose you must go. But why don't you wait and go in with the troops? The Hole in the Wall is the rendezvous for all the white outlaws in this part of the country, and they are believed to be in league with the Indians, and will use the uprising of the Indians as a cover under which to run off all the stock in the country."

"There is no use of our waiting for the troops when the young lady is in there, we don't know under what indignities. The troops put off attacking the Indians as long as they can for the sake of policy. We are all deputy United States marshals, and we get quicker action. Tell us where the Hole in the Wall is, and we will go in and get our own. The troops can do what they please later."

"Weil, pardner, you talk straight, and you feel about the young lady as I would if she was a friend of mine. But they are a bad bunch in there."

"I appreciate your warning, but it will not stop us."

"All right; go ahead, and good luck to you. About a mile farther on you will come to a narrow defile leading to the north, cutting the range. That leads into a broad valley, at the west end of which is the place called the Hole in the Wall. It is practically impregnable. It is entered by a narrow passage which one man could hold against an army. It can be approached at night by riding down the valley, dismounting, and crawling over the mountain until you are above the Hole in the Wall, when every man can be wiped out by a few rifles."

"Thanks, sergeant. We will take to the hills."

With mutual good wishes, they parted, and the boys were soon riding in single file up the defile.

In the valley they secreted themselves and their horses, while Ted and Bud went forward to reconnoiter. It was rapidly growing dark in the mountains as Ted and Bud crawled along the mountain paths toward the end of the valley.

Suddenly Ted placed his hand on Bud's arm.

"Some one right ahead of us," he whispered.

"Sentinel, I reckon," answered Bud.

Ted nodded: "You stay here. I'm going forward. I'll be back soon."

Ted glided away into the gloom. Presently Bud heard a muffled cry. Then all was still again.

He waited a few minutes, and was about to go forward, when he heard a slight rustle beside him, and there stood Ted.

"It was a guard," he said. "I jumped him, and gagged him, but he gave me a pretty good fight. I've rolled him away where his pals won't find him. I guess we can go on now, but we must go slowly and quietly. I don't know how many more of them are about."

"Get a line on where the hole is?"

"Yes, we're on the right track. It is ahead of us."

On they went, and, having proceeded about half a mile, they suddenly became aware of the neighing of horses and the voices of men, which seemed to come from beneath them, and it was not long before they saw a glare of light against the rocks not far ahead.

They went more cautiously now, crawling forward on their hands and knees. Ted, in advance, soon threw up his hand and lay flat on the rocks, and Bud crawled to his side.

They found themselves looking down into a circular little valley, in reality a hole in the wall of the mountain.

Several camp fires were burning here and there, and about fifty Indians and white men were lounging about.

Near the rear wall was a small tent, before which sat a fat old squaw.

As Ted was looking, the flap of the tent was pushed aside, and Ted clutched Bud's arm, for Stella had come forth, and stood looking up at the sky.

"By Jove, if we could only attract her attention," muttered Ted.

"It would help her a lot if she knew we were so close to her," said Bud.

The glare from the fires flaring upward fell full upon their faces, and they knew that if she looked in their direction she would not fail to see them.

They saw her cast her eyes all around the sky, and in their direction. Ted dared not make a noise, but he nodded his head several times so that she would know who it was, should she chance to see him.

Evidently she did not, for she turned away, and again her eyes swung around in the circle with her back to them.

"I've a mind to throw somethin' down at her, and attract her attention ter us," said Bud.

"And have every one of those cutthroats get on to us. Don't you do it," said Ted.

In a moment Stella looked up again, and this time they saw her start, then stare fixedly at them. Ted nodded his head again, and this time she made a gesture that told them that she had seen them, and knew that they were there.

"Duck yer head quick," said Bud, rapidly getting out of sight himself.

"What's the matter?" asked Ted.

"I saw Shan Rhue walking toward Stella."

"But she saw us, just before she ducked into her tent. Now it's up to us to get her out of there."

"You bet. But it will be a big job to get in there."

"I've got a plan that ought to work out."

"What is it?"

"You go back and get the boys. Put Ben and Clay down in the valley to hold the entrance to the Hole in the Wall. Bring the rest up here. Hurry! I'll stay here on guard. If any man attempts to touch Stella, I'll pot him from here. Bring your lariat with you."

Bud hurried away as he was bid, and in the course of half an hour, during which Ted, looking over the edge of the Hole, saw the men preparing to retire for the night, he returned with seven of the boys.

"Now, fellows," said Ted, "I'm going down into the hole to send Stella up on the rope."

"Jeering jackals!" exclaimed Bud. "Don't you ever do that. It means sure death ter you, an' p'r'aps ter Stella, too."

"No, I don't think so. At any rate, I'm going to take a chance. It will be up to you fellows to keep the bunch down there busy while I'm at work. Three of you will stay on this side of the hole, and four on the other. If you do your firing right, you will keep those fellows jumping from side to side so fast that they won't have any time for me."

"I see yer scheme, but I wouldn't like ter undertake it myself."

"Did you bring the rope?"

"Here it is," said Bud, unwinding it from around his waist.

Ted took it from him while the boys distributed themselves in their firing positions as he had directed.

Ted looped the rope under his arms. "You'll lower me down, Bud," he said. "Maybe I'll come up hand over hand if I can, and you will pull away when I give the rope two jerks."

He took another look over the edge. All the men were rolled up in their blankets asleep, except an old Indian who sat crouched over the fire.

Ted carefully lowered himself over the edge for the descent.

Down he went slowly and quietly, and soon his feet touched the ground just back of Stella's tent.

"Hiss-t!" He gave a low, sibilant warning of his presence, and in a moment the corner of the tent moved aside, and he saw Stella's bright eyes looking into his. He motioned her to come out, and the flap was gently lowered again.

In a few moments, which seemed hours, the flap was raised again, and Stella crawled forth.

"Oh, Ted," she whispered, pressing his hand. He held up a warning finger as he rapidly tied the rope beneath her arms.

"Bud will pull you up. Good luck," he whispered.

"Are you going to stay down here?" she whispered back.

"Yes, I must. Hurry!" He gave the rope two jerks, and it at once began to tighten, and Stella's feet left the ground as she slowly ascended skyward.

Ted, concealed against the wall back of the tent, saw her go up and up. She was more than halfway to the top when an old Indian woman crawled out of the tent, and, casting her eyes aloft, saw Stella.

A sudden scream rang through the hole. It was the Indian's warning. The rope began to go faster, and before the sleepy men in the hole had been able to sit up and rub their eyes, Ted saw Stella reach the top and disappear over its edge.

But the old Indian woman had run among the men crying out something in her native tongue. Evidently she was telling of the escape of Stella, for in an instant all sleep vanished and the place was full of men running about or staring up at the edge of the wall over which Stella had gone.

Then Shan Rhue came forth, swearing horribly. He caught the old squaw by the arm and threw her down.

"So you let the white squaw go, did you?" he asked. "And how much was you paid for it?" But the poor old wretch only shrank closer to the ground and moaned her protests that she had nothing to do with the escape of the white squaw.

Shan Rhue strode toward the tent, behind which Ted was crouching with his hand on his revolver.

Shan Rhue threw open the front of the tent and looked within. Then he straightened up, and caught a glimpse of Ted, whom he did not at first recognize in the gloom.

He reached in his powerful right arm to pull the intruder out, and looked into the muzzle of Ted's six-shooter, behind which he now saw Ted's smiling face.

At that he straightened up with a loud laugh that filled the Hole in the Wall and reverberated from side to side.

"Well, of all the luck," he shouted. "This has worked out just as I expected. I knew that if I got ther gal in yere that you'd be after her, an' here you are. Well, my bucko, you remember what I said about getting even with you. Now is the time. You've come to the end."

"Oh, I don't know," said Ted coolly. "I'm a long ways from a dead one yet. Be careful what you do. This six-shooter of mine is mighty sensitive on the trigger."

He heard a soft, swishing noise behind him, and knew that Bud was lowering the rope again. As he thrust his gun forward into the face of Shan Rhue, the bully backed away a few feet.

At that moment the rope swung down in front of his face, and, hastily putting his revolver into his pocket, Ted grasped it and went sailing up into the air hand over hand, assisted by Bud and Carl, who were pulling on the rope for all they were worth.

CHAPTER XXXVI
THE ALTERED BRAND

As Ted went up into the air, Shan Rhue shouted a command, and the white men in the Hole in the Wall ran to him.

"That boy must not get to the top," he shouted. "I want him."

"What will we do?" asked one of them.

"Here, Sol Flatbush, you are the best shot of us all. See if you can't bring him down. But don't shoot him. I need him for other things. Shoot the rope in two."

This was easier said than done, for the rope was so high that it was almost out of the light cast by the fires.

Flatbush was, indeed, a splendid shot, and he fired twice at the rope with his revolver, but missed each time on account of the uncertain light and the swaying motion of the rope.

"Give me my rifle," he called, and one of the men fetched it for him.

Ted was within fifteen feet of the top when Flatbush, leaning against the opposite wall, took deliberate aim and fired.

At the second shot Ted, who was aware that some one was trying to cut the rope, felt it vibrate suddenly beneath his hand.

Before the last thread was severed he reached up and began to climb, hand over hand. In a few seconds he was at the top, and the boys were helping him over the edge.

For a moment or two he could say nothing; he could only listen to the yells of rage and disappointment below. Now he was surrounded by his friends, and Stella was free. Away on a mountain peak a light flared up.

"What does that mean?" asked Stella, pointing to it.

"It is the signal that the Indians have gone on the warpath," said Ted. "The sergeant was right. It is up to us now to do stunts."

"In what way?" asked Stella.

"We must keep those Indians and renegades confined in the Hole in the Wall. If we can keep them there until the arrival of the troops we can end the uprising without shedding a drop of blood. See, there is another fire!"

Ted pointed to a blaze upon another peak, and this was followed by others until there was a ring of fires on the crests of the mountains for miles around.

"It is up to us to do a good thing here," he said. "Bud, take two or three of the boys and go to Ben's assistance. Hold the mouth to the entrance to the hole at all hazards. From what the sergeant said I have no doubt but the troops will be here at least by daylight. We will keep them busy down there from this place."

Bud hurried away with two of the boys, and Ted and the others composed themselves to await developments. In the meantime, Stella told Ted the details of her capture. Since she had been a prisoner she had been well treated, so far as most of the men were concerned, although Shan Rhue had insisted on seeing her every day, and had told her that he was going to take her away to the North and make her marry him. She had defied him, and had scorned him so scathingly that he had put many petty persecutions on her, and had deprived her of her liberty for revenge.

"How did you happen to find me?" asked Stella, after she told all that had happened to her.

"Little Dick was captured by an Indian, and while he was being brought here the pony Spraddle stumbled and threw him. A small looking-glass which was slung around his neck fell off, and Dick picked it up and brought it to camp."

"The Indian was Pokopokowo," said Stella.

"That was his name."

"I tried in every way to get a message out to you, but it seemed impossible. Then I hit upon the mirror, ripped the back off it, and made my cryptogram on it with a pin. I let Pokopokowo see it, and when he saw that there was a picture on it, and I told him it was good medicine, he wanted it. Of course, I let him take it, hoping that it would be taken outside, and that you would chance to see it, and so learn where I was."

"It was a very clever idea, and I doubt but for the mirror we should have been able to get here in time. It was little Dick who saved you."

"Yes, little Dick and big Ted. Ted, you are wonderful!"

Below, in the hole, there were signs of activity. Men were rushing here and there, saddling horses, packing mules, filling their cartridge belts, and getting ready for some sort of action.

"They have seen the war fires on the hills," said Ted, "and are getting ready for their raid upon the settlers. Evidently they do not know that the gate to the outside is guarded, and they think that we are gone, having succeeded in getting you."

Having finished their preparations for departure, an old Indian rode forth on a pony decorated with eagle feathers.

"That is old Flatnose, the head chief," said Ted.

Flatnose was painted for war, and as he rode toward the passage from the Hole in the Wall he swung his rifle above his head and shouted a guttural command, at which a war whoop, shrill and terrifying, went up from the Indians, followed by a hoarse shout from the white renegades.

"Now, we'll see some fun," whispered Ted to Stella, who was lying on the crest of the hole beside him, watching the proceedings below. "I guess Bud has got there by this time, and is ready to protect the opening out to the valley."

Only a few minutes had passed before there came to their ears a volley of rifle shots, followed by yells of fear, and the whites and Indians came rushing back into the hole, scrambling and falling over one another in confusion.

"I thought so," chuckled Ted. "They are trapped and they know it. They can defend the hole against all comers by that passage, but it didn't seem to occur to them that they might be made prisoners by the same means."

The inmates of the hole were in the confusion of terror, but at last Flatnose and his son, Moonface, succeeded in pacifying them, and a consultation was under way.

"Where is Shan Rhue?" asked Stella. "I haven't seen him for some time."

"That's so," answered Ted. "I don't see him." He scanned the hole carefully, but Shan Rhue was not there.

"Is there any secret passage by which he might escape?" asked Ted.

"Do you see that little shelter of canvas over against the wall?" said Stella.

Ted nodded.

"I believe there is a way out there known only to Shan Rhue. That is where he slept," she continued.

"Then he has escaped by it. Sol Flatbush is not in evidence, either. I'll bet a cooky they've skipped."

It was getting light in the east, and the Indians rode once more into the passage, firing their rifles. Then they charged.

But soon they came rushing back; the boys at the entrance had again repulsed them.

From far away came the soft but clear call of a bugle.

"The troops!" cried Ted, springing to his feet. "The cavalry is coming from Fort Sill. This thing will soon be over now."

He and Stella went to the edge of the cliff overlooking the valley, and far away saw a dark mass, in the midst of which they caught the flash of the rising sun on polished swords and carbines, and a gleam of color from the flag that fluttered in the fresh morning breeze.

The Indians in the hole had heard the bugle also, and now there was confusion indescribable. On came the troops, and Ted and Stella went down to meet them.

Captain Hendry was in command, and it did not take him long to get in possession of the facts.

"So you've got them bottled up, eh?" he said to Ted.

"Yes; all you have to do is to make them surrender," answered Ted.

"Which I don't think will be such an easy thing."

"I don't think you'll have any trouble about it. Come with me, and bring a firing squad of your men."

The captain gave the order, and followed Ted to where he could look down into the hole.

Then the captain laughed. "You have done better than I expected," he said.

Raising his voice, Captain Hendry shouted:

"Flatnose, you know me. This is Captain Hendry. I have got you in that hole like a rat in a trap. If you are wise, you will throw down your arms and surrender. I have my men here with me, and if you do not surrender, we will have to shoot you to death one by one. Will you surrender?"

The old chief looked up and saw the captain leaning over the edge above. For several minutes he stared upward, then he threw his rifle to the ground and gave a hoarse command, and his followers threw their arms upon that of their leader.

One of the troopers ran down into the valley with a command, while those above lay flat on the edge with their carbines in a ring pointed at the throng below.

In a few minutes the bugle sounded again, and the troops were seen marching into the hole. The war was at an end without a fatal shot having been fired.

As Captain Hendry marched away with his prisoners, he thanked Ted for the great service which he had done the government by holding the Indians and renegades until the arrival of the troops.

"Well, that's over," said Ted, as the last of them faded out of sight at the end of the valley. "But *our* work is just begun. We've got to find those five hundred head of stolen Circle S cattle."

"I suggest that we take a look behind that shelter of Shan Rhue's, and see if there is a passage leading from it," said Stella.

"Good idea," said Ted, and they climbed down into the valley and entered the Hole in the Wall, where the other boys were waiting for them.

Ted went at once to the shelter, which was only a piece of canvas which had been at one time a wagon cover, and tore it away.

There was revealed a hole in the rock wall, and beside it a small mound of earth.

Evidently the hole had been known to the white desperadoes who had used the hole as a hiding place for many years, and that it had been their habit to conceal it by means of a stopper of earth. This Shan and Sol had removed, and had made their escape while the Indians and renegades were preparing for their raid on the settlements.

Ted at once showed it to the other boys, and it was decided to follow the passage and find out what was at the other end.

The hole was so small that Ted was compelled to enter it on his hands and knees. Bud followed him, and then came Stella. Ben remained with Carl to guard the entrance in case any of the white renegades should return.

A short distance in, the passage, or tunnel, became larger, and soon opened out into a natural cave, so that they were able to assume an upright position.

Ted lighted his pocket electric searchlight and led the way. They walked for some distance when they saw a gleam of light ahead, and a few minutes later walked out of the cave into another valley, larger than that which they had just left.

"Great Scott! Look at that," said Ted, pointing to where a large herd of cattle was grazing.

"What?" asked Stella, who could see nothing unusual in a bunch of cattle grazing in the valley.

"I believe they're ours."

Ted strode toward the cattle, which seemed to become uneasy at seeing a man on foot, which range cattle will not tolerate.

"Don't go any closer, Ted," said Stella. "Wait until Bud goes back after the horses."

"I just want to get a glimpse of the brand. By Jove, here's our lost Circle S brand, I believe. But look at it. It has been altered."

"How?"

"See those two perpendicular lines drawn through the S, making the brand Circle Dollar-mark. That's a most ingenious thing. It has been done with a running iron. The fellow who stole our cattle has just changed it by running a curved hot iron through the S."

"Yer shore right," said Bud. "That Circle Dollar brand hez been registered somewhere. It's up to us ter find out who registered it, an' we've got ther thief. I'll skip out fer ther hosses an' ther boys. I reckon we kin git in here by ridin' across ther backbone o' ther hills."

"All right, get back as soon as you can, and we'll wait for you in the cave."

Bud and the boys were back within half an hour, having found a pass into the valley through the hills which inclosed it.

"It's as plain as the face of the sun to me," said Ted, when they were mounted and were riding toward the cattle. "Shan Rhue would have had those cattle over the border in a day or two, had he not been so unwise as to have abducted Stella. It's up to us now to get that bunch back to the herd."

It did not take the boys long to get the bunch together, and Ted and Stella rode out to the front of it to point it down the valley, while the other boys started back to the rear to drive up.

Suddenly they heard yells in the rear, accompanied by pistol shots and the cracking of quirts. In an instant the herd was up with distended eyeballs and lifted tails. The poison of fear was in them.

Looking back, Ted saw several men riding toward the herd at a terrific pace. At the head of the band rode Shan Rhue and Sol Flatbush.

Then a remarkable thing happened: Every man of them produced a red blanket. They dashed among the cattle waving the blankets in the faces of the now terrified cattle.

"Look out for trouble," shouted Ted, for he saw at once the intention of Shan Rhue. It was to stampede the herd.

The effort was immediately successful, for the terrified animals, with a deafening roar that expressed abject fear, started forward on a gallop, with a front as resistless as the prow of a battleship.

Stella was on the side of the herd opposite Ted.

She heard his warning cry, and then looked back at the herd. If she stayed where she was, there was no escape from death, for by her side was the sheer wall of the valley. There was only one way to safety, to ride across to the side of Ted.

She gave one look, then started.

Stella rode quartering the path of the stampede, and would have made it in safety had it not been for a prairie-dog hole, into which her pony's foot went. Magpie went down. The thundering host of frantic cattle was upon her when she felt herself caught in mid-air.

The thought of death was still ringing in her head, and everything swam before her eyes.

"You're all right! Stick close!" It was the reassuring voice of Ted, who, at the imminent risk of his own life, had ridden out and plucked her from the jaws of death.

Behind them, as Sultan, straining every nerve and muscle to carry them to safety, galloped ahead of the cattle, the boys rode into the ruck, beating the brutes with their quirts in an endeavor to stop them.

But they went a mile before they began to slow down, and Ted was able to deflect the course of Sultan, who was beginning to tire from the double burden and the terrific pace.

But at last the steers calmed down, and permitted themselves to be driven quietly to where the rest of the herd were grazing.

As soon as Ted had restored the stolen cattle, he and Bud started back into the valley in search of Shan Rhue and Sol Flatbush, but, although they searched everywhere, the renegades could not be found.

In the cave through which they had come from the Hole in the Wall they found a running branding iron, and fastened to the wall the following notice:

"To TED STRONG AND OTHERS: You win this time, but there will be others, and I am a lucky man in the end. You can't beat me.

"S. R."

Later they discovered that Shan Rhue had recently registere 1 in Colorado the Circle Dollar brand, and evidently it was his purpose to steal nearly all of the Circle S herd.

But although he escaped with his lieutenant, Sol Flatbush, the men of his band, who had been captured by the soldiers, were convicted and sent to prison for long terms, after they had confessed that Shan Rhue's organization had made a business of rustling cattle all through the Southwest for many years.

Ted received several letters from the authorities in Washington commending his services in averting an uprising of the Indians, and the capture of the white renegades, but while this was gratifying, he felt disappointed that Shan Rhue and Sol Flatbush were not in prison, also. However, Ted believed in the motto, "I bide my time," and he felt in his bones that some time in the future his path and that of the bully, Shan Rhue, would cross again.